Portugal
A Traveller's History

Portugal
A Traveller's History

Harold Livermore

THE BOYDELL PRESS

First published 2004
The Boydell Press, Woodbridge

ISBN 1 84383 063 9

The Boydell Press is an imprint of Boydell & Brewer Ltd
PO Box 9, Woodbridge, Suffolk IP12 3DF, UK
and of Boydell & Brewer Inc.
668 Mt. Hope Avenue, Rochester, NY 14620, USA
website: www.boydellandbrewer.com

A CIP catalogue record for this book is available
from the British Library
Library of Congress Cataloging-in-Publication Data

Livermore, H. V., 1914-
Portugal: a traveller's history/Harold Livermore.
p. cm.
Includes bibliographical references and index.
ISBN 1-84383-063-9 (pbk. : alk. paper)
1. Portugal–Description and travel. 2. Portugal–Civilization. 3. Livermore, H. V., 1914–Travel. I. Title.

DP526.5.L583 2004
946.9–dc22

2004010337

This publication is printed on acid-free paper

Printed in Great Britain by
Antony Rowe Ltd, Chippenham, Wiltshire

Contents

Illustrations

All illustrations have been kindly provided by ECIP and Turismo de Lisboa. The names of the photographers are indicated when available.

Foreword

When I was invited to write this book some years ago, circumstances prevented me from accepting. I feared that arthritis would stop my travels. I first visited Portugal in May 1936 as a graduate working in Spain, but the outbreak of civil war obliged me to come home. Cambridge then kindly made an award, intended for study in Spain, available in Portugal. My wife and I went to Coimbra, and I was made headmaster of the English school near Lisbon. We returned to England in November 1942, and my earliest history of Portugal appeared in 1947; this will explain why my interest was originally historical. I see Portugal and the Portuguese as they emerge from their past. If I qualify as a tourist, it is because I have returned almost every year for one or more visits.

I am indebted to many friends – some of them not known to me by name. But they include the late Susan Lowndes, who with her husband Luiz Marques founded the *Anglo-Portuguese News*. She knew Portugal well and published her *Selective Traveller* in 1949. Dr Paul Lowndes Marques has given me valuable help with the illustrations, selected by him with the help of Dr George Winius, and I am glad to record my thanks for the kindness of the Portuguese tourist authorities. I must also mention Dr Carlos Estorninho of Lisbon and Figueira da Foz, as well as Dr A J Miranda of Santo Tirso and his family, who have afforded me hospitality and driven me round the Minho. On the one occasion, Dr Winius both drove and pushed me round the Alentejo and Algarve. I had not thought it feasible to visit Portugal in a wheel-chair until TAP, the Portuguese airline, and George and Grace made it possible. In London, Mr António de Figueiredo has helped on many occasions and lent me books I did not possess, and Mrs Andrea White has undertaken the formidable task of making sense of my script. None of these is to blame for such errors as I may have made.

I have inserted one or two poems, which strike a nostalgic note: *Saudade*, the yearning for people and places no longer present, is often thought to be characteristic of Portugal.

The author and publishers would like to record their gratitude to the Calouste Gulbenkian Foundation for assistance with the publication costs of this book.

I

Introduction

Portugal is a land, its people, and their language. It is not one of the larger European states, comprising about a fifth of the Iberian Peninsula. Its population is about ten million, comparable with those of Scotland, Wales and Northern Ireland combined, Norway and Sweden combined, Belgium, or Greece. Yet its language is more widely spoken than French, German, or any other European tongue, except English and Spanish. This is due largely to the vastness and growth of Brazil, which exceeds in population any state of Europe, even Britain and France combined. Portuguese has also been implanted in a large part of Africa south of the Sahara, and exists in places in Asia as far as Macau in China, and in Timor in Oceania. Its most remarkable feature has been its capacity to expand and endure. Both Portuguese and Castilian were once the provincial Latin of the late Roman army spoken only in small areas.

Though the language is as Latin as Italian and much more so than French, the word Portugal – like Castile – would have meant nothing to an ancient Roman. He would have heard of the Further Province or of Lusitania, but the political divisions of antiquity were effaced by the Muslim expansion into Europe of AD 711. Portugal emerged, as did the other states of the Peninsula, from the Christian Reconquest. The name is first used in the ninth century, when it applied to the area of Oporto. Portugal reached its present limits in about 1250, since when its frontiers have scarcely altered.

The expansion of Europe began when the Portuguese conquered the North African port of Ceuta in 1415. Soon after, Portuguese navigators annexed the Atlantic Isles of the Madeiras and the Azores. Both groups had been uninhabited since the formation of the world, and are therefore properly Portuguese. A distinction is made between 'continental Portugal' and the 'adjacent isles'. Madeira is 600 miles south of Lisbon and the Azores 800 miles to its west. In the fifteenth century, when Vasco de Gama took two years to find the sea-route to India and to return, and in 1519 when Fernão de Magalhães (Magellan) set out on the first circumnavigation of the globe, these distances did not seem enormous. Nowadays, the islands are reached from Lisbon by air in two or three hours.

Continental Portugal measures about 350 miles from north to south. The width in the north is about 140 miles, and at the level of Lisbon only 70 miles. It comprises 34,254 square miles, and the islands add a further 1,236 square miles. There are only two frontiers, the ocean and Spain. In 1940 nearly two-thirds of the population lived in the coastal half of the country, and only a third in the interior. Lisbon and Oporto – the port – are at the estuaries of the two great rivers, the Tagus and the Douro, which rise far away to the east in Spain: neither is navigable beyond the frontier. The third largest city is now the port of Madeira, Funchal. The continental coastline was formerly dotted with ports and fisheries, many of which have become holiday resorts. In the nineteenth century, the great ocean sea-routes to South America, Africa and the Orient converged on the Portuguese ports, confirming the predominance of Lisbon and Oporto. Most visitors arrived by sea, and even travel between Lisbon and Oporto was by packet-boat. Oswald Crawfurd, for many years British consul in Oporto and the author of three books on Portugal, advised visitors to disembark at Vigo in Spain and purchase a horse for their travels in Portugal. It is hardly surprising that many Portuguese saw their country, if not as an island, at least as an enclave of Europe, parted from the rest by the Iberian plateau, the *meseta*.

This semi-insular situation was broken down by the railway age, which arrived in Portugal only after 1856. The Spanish network was financed by an enterprising polit- ician and capitalist, Don José de Salamanca y Livermoore, and thirty years later Lisbon was linked to Paris by rail, bringing the journey down to 34.5 hours. The extraordinary Rossio station that is one of the curiosities of Lisbon was opened in 1890. The trains plunged straight into a long tunnel to emerge at Campolide in the suburbs. Even in 1950 tearful relations used to attend the departures, for all the world as if their loved ones were leaving on some lengthy voyage. The Sud-Express from Paris-Austerlitz crosses into Portugal at the neat little station of Vilar Formoso, and divides at Pampilhosa, one section going to Lisbon and the other to Oporto. The Spanish habit used to be to travel everywhere overnight and very slowly, thus avoiding the heat of the day. My first visit to Portugal was from Salamanca in 1936: the train left in the evening and followed the course of the Douro, stopping with clanking and shouting everywhere it could. I arrived in Oporto, sleepless and weary, in the early hours. This line no longer operates but there are lines to Lisbon from Madrid, and to Oporto from Galicia.

By road, the route from London or Paris to Lisbon requires several days; more for those who are not in a hurry and less if there is more than one to drive. The route taken through France can be varied, and is shortened by putting the car on the train overnight from Boulogne to Biarritz. Driving through south-western France is easy enough, but the Basque hills, though not high, cannot be crossed in haste.

The great age of navigation has given way, at least for passengers, to aircraft. The main airport is at the Portela de Sacavém, only four miles from the centre of Lisbon. It is in the style of 2000, lavishly faced with white marble and well-lit, less con- fusing than Heathrow, though with a similar tendency to become a bazaar. At Oporto, the airport of Pedras Rubras is a dozen miles to the north of the city, to which it is con- nected by taxi or bus. Second place has now been taken by Faro, the capital of the tourist region of the Algarve, which receives a large number of holiday flights. The international airports serve the coastal cities and ports which have always predom- inated. Access to the towns of the interior was co-ordinated by the Highways Board set up in 1926, and in the last quarter of the twentieth century a system of motorways, with their attendant clover-leaves, by-passes and toll-booths, covered the whole coun- try in outline.

Although geographers are apt to call Portugal Mediterranean for their own reasons, it comes nowhere near the inland sea of the Romans, and is entirely Atlantic, with a coastline of over 500 miles consisting of sandy beaches broken by rocky outcrops and cliffs, and the estuaries of its rivers. Its climate is benign, in contrast with the extremes of heat and cold suffered by the high *meseta* of Spain. Throughout its length, Portugal is tempered by its proximity to the sea. Only its land frontier in the north is mountainous where the *meseta* breaks up into mountain ranges (se*rras*) intersected by numerous rivers. The highest land in Portugal is the Serra da Estrêla in the centre, which reaches 6,540 feet, half as high again as Ben Nevis, and which is sufficiently snow-bound in winter to provide for skiers. South of the Tagus, Portugal is much lower, and there are places in the Alentejo where there is 'no shade but what comes from the sky'. The rise in popularity of southern Portugal is relatively recent and springs from the attraction of its climate and beaches for visitors and settlers. It is sep-arated from the Alentejo by a range of low hills that constitute an amphitheatre to catch the summer sun, while its coast is sheltered from the breakers of the open Atlantic. However, the daily rate of sunshine throughout the year is no different from that of Estoril on the Lisbon coast or from the Alentejo, though the summer heat is more intense in the flatter Alentejo. At the level of Lisbon, the heat is tempered by a north wind, the *nortada*, which blows in the late afternoon to freshen the air. There is usually no rain in July or August: it falls in the autumn or winter. Snow is almost never seen in Lisbon, and snowball fights are unknown to Lisbon children until they see them on television. The sky supplies as many temperate days and blue skies as mortals have a right to expect.

North of Lisbon the sea-coast is cooler than the interior, and the climate is more affected by the mountains. In summer, the Portuguese flock to Figueira da Foz and smaller resorts of central Portugal. Those of Oporto frequent places south of the city where the Atlantic rollers break on sands and dunes. The resorts of the Minho, reached from Viana do Castelo, provide a quieter alternative. Coimbra, a little inland from Figueira, can be very hot in summer since the air in the narrow valley of the Mondego traps the sunshine. The same phenomenon occurs in the valley of the Douro, where it serves to ripen the grapes on the terraced slopes. At Oporto, the sum-mer temperatures are not much below those of Lisbon, though the daily ration of sun is less. Oporto is wetter than Lisbon, and the winter is misty: the result is a much greener countryside. Beyond the Minho, in Spanish Galicia, the rainfall is high, and the Minho is one of the few Peninsular rivers that do not dry up in the summer. However, it and the other rivers have been harnessed for hydroelectric or irrigational purposes and do not reflect the immediate rainfall. Coimbra on the Mondego was a port in medieval times, until 1960 a dry river-bed in summer, and has now a full river. The winter brings a fine warm rain, *chuva miuda*, that damps without drenching. The country-people of the Minho take an umbrella with them to the fields and plant it in the corner in case of a shower while they work: it replaces the ancient cloak of reeds.

The Portuguese mountains have no permanent snow, but are covered in the win-ter. Late falls occur in Braga, but Bragança is probably the only Portuguese city that sells postcards of itself under snow. Guarda, on the central frontier, is the highest city in Portugal, at 3,500 feet: it stands on a mountain nearly four miles from its station, and is almost as high as Ávila on the Castilian *meseta*. Like other places in the interior, it is exposed to the gales which gather force on that *meseta*. According to a saying, Spain sends no good wind and no good marriage, the allusion being to royal matches that have in the past compromised Portuguese independence. Where the frontier is not defined by the rivers Minho, Douro, Tagus and Guadiana, it is often a rock-strewn waste. The only 'international' river that does not form part of the frontier is the Lima, Limia in Spanish, which flows through the mountainous nature-reserve of the Peneda-Gerez national park. Guarda itself stands back some thirty miles from the border, and the nearest thing to a frontier city is Elvas in the Alentejo, once important as a fortress preventing access to the plains and to Lisbon.

The natural assets of Portugal are the sun, which is present a great deal of the time, the ocean, which is always there, and the landscape, which given its compact space is extremely varied. It has been said that Portugal has no single ingredient not to be found in other parts of the Iberian Peninsula. It may be equally said that no other parts possess such a variety of scenery, nor so high a proportion of coastline. For Byron, Sintra was a 'glorious Eden' and many others have heaped it with justifiable admiration. To the romantic Portuguese, their country is a 'garden planted by the sea'. These favoured spots are relatively restricted. Much of the north and centre is mountain-side which is highly picturesque but reluctant to yield a livelihood. It was used mainly for grazing, and whole villages subsisted by shepherding and clipping wool. The hillside soil was too thin for anything but pines, which were the main source of timber for shipbuilding and furniture. There is no lack of granite, from which the cottages of central Beira were made. Much of Portugal was better suited for silviculture than for other forms of farming. The slopes are still covered with heather, gorse and the northern oak, which have their southern limit here. The chestnut, which flourishes in the north, is confined to clumps on higher ground south of the Tagus. The vine and the olive were introduced by the Romans from the south and have spread everywhere. South of the Tagus the evergreen oaks, including the classical ilex, replace the northern oak. The cork-oak or *sobreiro* grows in groves or separately and is cultivated in the Alentejo and centre, Portugal being the largest producer of cork. The heather is replaced by the pink flowers of the cistus. In the Alentejo there are patches of sandy waste where only scrub grows: these are *charnecas*, a word applied to wastelands in other places, but more properly to the patches of uncultivable soil in the Alentejo. The interior and southern part of the province is an extensive wheat-belt, and was once Roman *latifundia*, or large estates with a few owners and a landless peasantry. The fertile Algarve is distinguished by the plants introduced in Muslim times; the almond, fig, orange and lemon, though the orange has adapted itself also to the north. The profusion of growth in Portugal arises partly from the acclimatisation of exotic plants introduced from Africa, America and the Orient. The banana grows in Madeira, and the pineapple and tea in the Azores. Other plants have made the transition to the mainland, including the most beautiful of Brazilian flowering trees, the jacaranda, which flourishes in the streets of Lisbon, but has not yet adapted itself to Oporto. The European fruits, apples, pears and plums, are grown almost everywhere, as are the medlar and quince, or *marmelo*, which makes a rich sweet named *marmelada*, a word misapplied by the English to the orange.

Although large stretches of yellowing wheat are a characteristic sight of the Alentejo, the crops north of the Tagus were rather barley and rye, which make brown bread, now eaten chiefly at festival times. City-dwellers have for long favoured wheaten bread, which is certainly more adaptable for culinary purposes. The 'wheat campaigns' of the first part of the twentieth century were successful, but only by putting into use marginal land and applying artificial fertiliser, so that the additional production was costly. In the nineteenth century, the staple diet was enlarged by the cultivation of the Andean potato and American maize (*milho grosso*). In the twentieth century, the remedy was to cultivate the estuaries of the rivers Mondego and Sado as rice-paddies. The area under vines has also greatly increased. The hills to the north of Lisbon provided wine for the capital. The cultivation of the Douro valley began in earnest in the seventeenth century. To these are added the valley of the Dão in Viseu, neighbouring Bairrada, southern Trás-os-Montes, the Minho with its 'green wine', the Ribatejo, and parts of the Alentejo and Setúbal, with muscatel, not to mention the famous wines of Madeira. One modern addition to the Portuguese landscape is the Australian eucalyptus, which provides material for the plastics industry. It is much faster-growing than the pillar pine, which was chosen for its straightness and readiness to multiply. This pine is also dark and gloomy, while the eucalyptus introduces a brighter colour. However, the pine produces resin and is also valued in the furniture industry.

Portugal has always had an overwhelmingly rural population. As late as 1930, half the Portuguese were dependent on agriculture. Since then, farming itself has been mechanised, and there has been much movement towards the cities. By 1980 Lisbon had reached 800,000, while its hinterland could count two million. But there has been no wholesale flight from the countryside. Many of those who went as guest-workers to other parts of Europe returned home each summer and built themselves houses in the style they had seen in the countries where they worked. Portuguese emigrants are perhaps always countrymen at heart. The eminent historian Jaime Cortesão, when in exile in Brazil, had as barber a Sr Castro who had emigrated to Rio de Janeiro at sixteen, married there, and had a son who was a lawyer and a daughter who was a teacher: he had done well and was content. Yet his subject of conversation was always the village of Fonte Arcada, its characters, its ham, its rye-bread, its festivities, its pilgrimages, or *romarias*. One day, Dr Cortesão asked him if he had thought of going back. The barber, thinking that perhaps his range of conversation was being questioned, replied: 'But one always thinks of the place where one was born and bred.'

Portugal has no large industrial zone. It has drab corners, but nowhere so polluted that birds prefer not to nest there. It no longer possesses the gold and other metals that attracted the Phoenicians and Romans, whose slag-heaps exist in Trás-os-Montes. The English company that mined copper at São Domingos east of Mértola closed down in 1965 and the village is deserted. In Beira, wolfram was discovered in 1907, and during the war of 1940 there was a wave of prosperity caused by pre-emptive buying of the metal for hardening steel. More recently, Portugal has become a successful exporter of marble from Estremós. Its whiteness was prized by the Romans, and not far away there are veins of pink and green. Portugal has a little coal, but what is produced suffices only to feed one electric generating plant.

We may well ask who are these Portuguese who inhabit a small territory and set out to discover the world. One may as well ask who the English are. The English have no written constitution and leave it to the law to decide. The Portuguese have a Constitution of 1974 – the sixth or seventh since 1820 – and it says that Portuguese citizens are all those who are so considered by law and international usage. After this explanation, it goes on to declare Portugal as 'the territory so historically defined in Europe and the archipelagos of Madeira and the Azores'. This passes the responsibility on to history. The Portuguese are the sons and daughters of other Portuguese most of whom were born in Portugal and speak Portuguese. It is not absolutely necessary to be born in Portugal or to speak Portuguese, but this certainly helps. The Portuguese are conscious of the existence of their ancestry: for more than eight centuries they have been administered in and have spoken a provincial form of Latin distinct from that of their neighbours. Latin was the language of the church until the tenth century and was the only form of record until the eleventh, when the colloquial form was written. It is preserved in poems of the twelfth: the orthography of prose was fixed only later. The contribution of Arabic was reduced to place-names, almost all south of the Douro, and a few proper names with a vestigial vocabulary for dress, household-goods, plants and administrative terms. Many of these words are still alive; in 1950 Portugal was still governed by edicts or *alvarás*, but it is curious to note that the Constitution of 1974 contains scarcely a single word of Arabic derivation. There are no linguistic minorities, such as the Basques in Spain, and very little trace of pre-Roman languages. Portuguese was once one with Galician, but the Galician of Galicia, part of Spain, has gradually been reduced to a dialect, particularly since the imposition of Castilian on local government in about 1400. Portugal remains closer to Galicia than to other parts of Spain: the daily stream of passengers on foot by the bridges across the Minho is absent at other frontier points.

The only appreciable addition to the population since the days of Afonso I has been the immigration of Jews on their expulsion from Spain in 1492. Since they were required to purchase residence-permits, those who sought refuge in Portugal were in easy circumstances and literate: they married into the Portuguese governing classes and exercised an influence out of proportion to their numbers. The gipsies (*ciganos*) are first recorded in about 1500, and remain a small minority. There has been a small flow of Portuguese returning from Brazil, Goa and the Far East with their families and dependants. In the nineteenth century the returned immigrant who had made his fortune in Brazil was a familiar figure, especially in the north. More recently, the abandonment of Angola in 1974 brought a flood of *retornados*. Since then, many Africans, especially from Cape Verde, have come to Lisbon to work. The development of tourist centres and apartment blocks in the Algarve has given an international cast to the southern province.

The Portuguese attained fame in the fifteenth and sixteenth centuries as explorers of the oceans, and this part of their history is not forgotten. Lisbon and Oporto were trading-places in medieval times, and the discoverers set out from the Algarve and from Lisbon. It was the arrival of crusaders from the north that ensured the conquest of Lisbon in 1147, and the Atlantic Alliance with England guaranteed the independence and survival of the house of Avis in the fourteenth century. Brazil was discovered in 1500, and it was to Brazil that the royal family withdrew in 1807 to avoid capture by Napoleon's invaders. It was from Lisbon and Oporto that Wellington liberated the Iberian Peninsula, and in 1814 the news of Napoleon's fall was carried to the royal family in Rio de Janeiro by a small fishing-boat from Olhão in the Algarve. Lisbon now repairs tankers and other vessels in dockyards at Barreiro on the South Bank. A new port has been added at Sines, the birthplace of Vasco da Gama, which now surpasses Lisbon in sheer weight of the cargo it handles owing to the concentration of petroleum imports and processing. In the nineteenth century the smaller ports were chiefly fisheries. The Azores hunted the whale and, with the aid of Quaker capital, manned the whale-fishery of New Bedford in New England, which served to light the streets of North America. Viana do Castelo sent its ships to North America. The Portuguese are, after the Danes and Spaniards, the leading fish-eaters in Europe, and used to send an annual fleet to the Grand Banks of Newfoundland for cod, which, salted and cured, made *bacalhau*, the 'faithful friend'. Since 1970 the imposition of territorial waters in Canada – no great consumer of fish – has closed this trade, and the 'faithful friend' is not quite the friend it was: it is imported and relatively expensive. The main catch is now the sardine, a young pilchard, which is brought in at Peniche, canned and consumed everywhere. There are over 30,000 Portuguese who depend on fishing for their living. For many it used to be a seasonal occupation, and men would go to the coast to practise it, living in wooden huts or *barracas.* Since about 1960 many former fisheries have become tourist resorts, and the huts have been replaced by houses. The little place known as Palheiros da Mira or 'Mira Huts' has become Praia de Mira, Mira Beach. In the Algarve the traditional fish was the tunny, which migrates annually between the Atlantic and the Mediterranean. The fishermen now go in for the less heroic pursuit of shellfish and are outnumbered by tourists, but continue to be photographed mending their nets by their brightly coloured boats. Lagos and Portimão, from which the discoverers sailed to the Islands and West Africa, are now havens for large numbers of pleasure craft, as are the docks of western Lisbon.

Portugal is a unitary state. It consists of half a dozen regions or provinces with a degree of historical reality, though they have been replaced by political divisions adopted in the nineteenth century, and by subdivisions created in the twentieth. The Minho, Entre Douro e Minho (between the rivers Minho and Douro), the district which was the cradle of the county and kingdom of Portugal, is a coastal plain, the most thickly populated part of rural Portugal, the origin of many emigrants. Trás-os-Montes 'behind the mountains' is higher, drier, more sparsely peopled and inclined towards the neighbouring *meseta*. The Beiras, the 'Side', is the whole of central Portugal from the Douro to the Tagus, centred on Coimbra, once a port on the Mondego. Estremadura is the district of Lisbon. The Alentejo (beyond the Tagus) is the extensive plains south of the river. Finally comes the small but well populated Algarve, which has no long river and no large city, but half a dozen maritime towns.

These historical regions are very diverse, ranging from the small and crowded Minho to the large and thinly occupied plains of the Alentejo. In the nineteenth century, in an attempt to establish equitable political divisions, Portugal was divided into districts; these were eighteen in number, each named after its chief town, with one more for the Madeiras and three for the Azores. But there was still a great disparity in the size of the district capitals, some of which are quite small. The *distritos* continue, but the former provinces have been rearranged on grounds of economic affinity. Lisbon has been extended southward to include Setúbal, so that Estremadura embraces the whole coast from Peniche to Sines. The Alentejo has been divided into 'upper', governed from Évora, and 'lower', from Beja. The middle valley of the Tagus is the Ribatejo, with Santarém as its capital. Beira has been divided into three: Litoral or coastal, with its capital at Coimbra; Beira Alta, with the mountain-range of the Estrela, administered from Viseu; and Beira Baixa, the interior with its seat at Castelo Branco. In the north, Oporto has been separated from the Alto Minho, and the middle valley of the Douro has become the Riba-Douro and Alto Douro, taking Vila Real from Trás-os-Montes.

All this may sound confusing. It is. When I consulted my oldest friend and contemporary, meaning to enquire about the legal implications, he asked the hotel
porter, who referred to the manager and sought the opinion of the page. Each produced a different list of what was a *distrito* and in which province. The result amused
everyone. I had unwittingly invented a new game. The differences are generational.
One can be in Lisbon for a long time without realising one is in Estremadura, which
has nothing to do with the Spanish province of Extremadura, except that they are
both considerably 'beyond the Douro'.

In Portugal, human settlements are carefully graded. There is no doubt that Lisbon
and Oporto are great cities. What is not a city is a *vila* or town. I have been informed,
though I would not like to be quoted on this, that in 1970 there were nineteen cities
and at the end of the century, seventy-five – a growth only exceeded by that of universities in Britain. Braga, the religious capital of Portugal is the centre of its *distrito*
and Guimarães, also a city, is subordinate to it: they share the university of the Minho.
To be a *vila* is to have a charter, and this confers the right to services. The districts are
divided into *concelhos* (councils), and these are divided into *freguesias* or parishes.
A place with no recognised centre is a *lugar* or *aldeia*, a hamlet. The classification as a
concelho confers dignity, and the town-hall was usually a building of importance
referred to as a 'palace', the *paço* or *paços do concelho*. It was not the seat of a nobleman,
but rather the place at which taxes were collected. The parish is both a religious and
an administrative unit since the church was the meeting-place where elections were
held. The two senses of parish co-exist, and the interests of the parishioners are
expressed by a *junta* or board. In medieval towns the place where justice was done was
marked by a stone pillar, adorned with a crown or coat of arms, often of considerable
artistic merit and mounted on steps. Many date from the reign of King Manuel I
(1495–1521). As in England, offences were punished from the pillory, but whereas in
English to pillory is to brand with disgrace, in Portugal the possession of a *pelourinho*
is a sign of ancient prestige.

2

Portugal in History

Portugal was a monarchy for eight centuries, and has been a republic since 1910. As every Portuguese schoolchild knows, its first king was Afonso Henriques, who was born in about 1109 and lived until 1185. He replaced his mother Queen Teresa in 1128, seized Santarém from the Muslims and took Lisbon after a long siege in 1147, thus carrying the frontier from the Mondego to the Tagus and beyond. He used the title of king from 1139 or 1140. Our pupil may or may not have been told that King Afonso I defeated five Muslim kings in the battle of Ourique and that his victory was assured by the aid of St James, or Santiago, mounted on a white charger. The great historian Alexandre Herculano (1811–77) found no contemporary evidence for the apostolic intervention, but concluded that the Portuguese state owed its existence to the strong arms of Afonso Henriques and the barons of the Douro valley who had brought him up. The conquest of Lisbon was achieved with the aid of several thousand crusaders who put in at Oporto on their way to Palestine. Many were Anglo-Normans from southern and eastern England. Expansion, first in the Iberian Peninsula and then in the overseas Discoveries, is a main theme of Portuguese history, in which the Ancient Alliance played its part. All Portuguese know this and are often surprised that many English visitors do not.

The notion of a Portugal suddenly springing into existence at the behest of Afonso Henriques is almost as extravagant as the visitation of St James. Our intelligent child knows that there was a county of Portugal long before it became a kingdom, that it was governed from the castle of Guimarães, where Afonso was born, and that his parents were Count Henry, a Burgundian, and Dona Teresa, on whom the county was bestowed by her father, Alfonso VI of Leon. Tarásia, as she was always called, was styled queen as the daughter of an emperor, but, as was customary, took her husband's rank. After he was killed in 1112, she governed as queen for sixteen years, and was so recognised by more than one pope.

The territory of Portugal had been founded, or at least claimed, in 868 by one Vimara Peres, a count of southern Galicia. The 'portus' was in Roman times the point at which travellers from the province of Lusitania crossed the Douro to go to the north-west. When the Roman Empire in the west was overrun in 410, the Sueves, part of a Germanic people from the Elbe, were installed in the districts of Oporto and Braga. They built a fort on the site of the city of Oporto. In about 550, the Suevic kings were converted to orthodox Christianity by St Martin of Dume. He came to govern

thirteen dioceses, both in the kingdom and beyond. Portugal thus consists of the
Suevic provinces and the territories south of the Douro incorporated in the church of
St Martin. In 585, six years after his death, the Suevic monarchy was overthrown by
the Visigoths, a Germanised faction of the late Roman army. The Suevic rulers have
left a concentration of place-names in the districts of Oporto and Braga unique in the
Iberian Peninsula, but have contributed only a few words to the Portuguese language.

The Goths governed Suevic Portugal until 660, when they imposed a restoration
of the Roman provinces by returning the area south of the Douro to Lusitania. Their
monarchy of Toledo was in turn overthrown by the Muslim invasions of 711 to 712,
when Roderic, the 'last of the Goths', was defeated and killed. The annexation of the
Iberian Peninsula to the caliphate of Damascus was soon followed by the emergence
of a Christian kingdom in the northern mountains of the Asturias, a miniature resur-
rection of the Gothic state. In 756 the Muslim state became an independent kingdom
with its capital at Cordova. Some Arab contingents were implanted in southern
Portugal and nomadic Berber peoples roamed the meseta or undertook military service. In 838, one Mahmud ibn al-Jabbar, a Christian from Mérida, departed with his
followers to find a refuge at the crossing of the Douro with the consent of the Asturian
king. He was killed two years later, and his name is preserved at Mafamude, now a
southern suburb of Oporto. The bishops of Braga and Dume fled, but the diocese of
Iria, later Santiago de Compostela, probably survived. In the absence of any documents, we must suppose that northern Portugal was inhabited by a free society of
shepherds, fishermen, monks and hermits. There are no Arabic place-names in the
Minho. In the ninth century, Muslim Cordova was rent with dissension and posed no
immediate danger.

More serious were the attacks of the Vikings or Norsemen, who in 842 raided
southern France and reached Galicia. They entered the estuaries in their long-ships to
plunder the towns upstream, robbing churches and taking prisoners for ransom.
Their second major expedition was in 857, and their attacks were repeated at intervals
until 1015, when they sacked Tuy on the Minho. These raids explain the building of
defensive castles on the rivers and may have been the context of Vimara Peres' occupation of Portugal. Ten years later, in 878, Count Hermenegild Guterres, of the
Asturian royal house, occupied Coimbra, then a largish city, and while the Asturian
rulers remained pent in their mountain fastness, the western pioneers had advanced
far to the south.

In the tenth century the Muslim rulers of Cordova recovered and by assuming the
title of caliph obtained volunteers and mercenaries from North Africa. By about 920
the frontier returned to the level of Viseu. The first king *in* Portugal, though not *of*
Portugal, was Ramiro II (930–51), a grandson of Hermenegild Guterres, who as prince
governed the western frontier. He favoured the monastery and castle of Guimarães,
built for Dona Mumadona Dias in about 950. One of the oldest Portuguese families,
who took their name from Maia, north of Oporto, liked to claim descent from him.
Other settlers, Gascons or Basques, were brought to strengthen the long and exposed
frontier. The Asturian kings advanced to Leon, which became the centre of an empire
stretching from the narrow territory of Navarre and Castile to the much deeper
expanse of Galicia and Portugal in the west. King Ramiro II proved to be the last effective ruler of the old Asturian house. From 951 the Muslim caliphs were in the ascend-
ant: the defence of the west fell on counts, who held their castles from the crown.

Linguistically, Portugal was united to Galicia, but distinct from Leon, and even more so from Castile. The counts of the west were at first few, with vast and scattered possessions. They were drawn towards Santiago by its wealth and by royal favour. The patronage of the Christian reconquest was asserted by the apostolic see of Santiago. Roman Braga remained unrestored, for Lugo in Galicia claimed to have inherited the metropolitanate of the west. The shrine of St James had been discovered only in about 820, but it was endowed by successive kings and was the *de facto* head of the church. There was a bishop of Oporto, but the Christian faith was held together by monasteries under the patronage of local families. The first notable Portuguese churchman was St Rudesind or Rosendo (916–77), a cousin of Ramiro II, born at Santo Tirso, and elected bishop at the age of sixteen. He briefly held the see of Santiago, but was removed by the next king and retired to his foundation at Celanova, now in the Spanish province of Ourense. His father had vast possessions. His will was confirmed by two dozen counts, but in Portugal itself, there was rarely more than one count, and the local families had relatively small and scattered domains. Their holdings were linked together by the rivers Douro, Câvado, Ave and Lima, and their affluents were used by boats and ferries, whence the inland 'ports' that exist as place-names. A single road, the 'Moorish way', led to Coimbra; by it luxury goods were obtained from the cities of the south.

Muslim power reached its zenith between 980 and 997, when the vizir al-Mansur marched through Portugal to sack Santiago. After he died in 1002, the puppet caliph could no longer control his armies. The Caliphate was abolished in 1032, when Cordova disintegrated into its several parts: the *taifa* states. But al-Mansur's campaigns had brought about the collapse of the old Asturian house. The count of the Portuguese, Mendo Gonçalves, Mumadona's grandson, was tutor to King Alfonso V, who married Mendo's daughter, Elvira Mendes. In 1028, Alfonso was killed by a bolt while besieging Viseu. He left a young son and a daughter, Sancha. But a new dynasty was about to be launched from Navarre, where King Sancho III the Great (1000–35) annexed Castile and entered Leon. His second son, Fernando, killed the young king of Leon and married his Leonese sister Sancha, thereby legitimising his claim to the whole empire.

Fernando I (1037–65) was the first king of Castile, holding Leon and the west through his marriage to Sancha. They acquired great wealth as their war-lords exacted tribute from their bickering Muslim neighbours. Neither of them much liked troublesome counts, preferring to govern through their own appointees, judges or vicars, whom they could remove at will. It was only in 1057 that Fernando occupied Lamego, south of the Douro, and in the following year Viseu. In 1064 he crowned his achievements by taking Coimbra after a long siege. He died in the following year, having entrusted it to one Sisnand Davides who had negotiated its surrender.

Since Portugal and Galicia were united by language, it may be asked why they did not form a single country. The attempt was made when King Fernando died and divided his realms between his three sons. He gave Castile to the eldest, Sancho II, and Queen Sancha gave Leon to the second son, Alfonso VI. For the third, Garcia, a new state was formed from Galicia and Portugal, with its capital at Santiago. Garcia was barely of an age to govern, and brought with him his father's retainers. His parents had espoused the Cluniac reform, which planned to remove the monasteries from the influence of local families. Therefore, he was soon in trouble in Galicia, where his bishop was murdered, and where he seized the properties of the greatest landowner of the Douro valley. The influence of the counts of Portugal had long been waning. There had been two long minorities and the last count appears to have played no part in the conquest of Coimbra. However, by 1071 Count Nuno was recognised, married and had a daughter, but Garcia drove him into rebellion and he was killed near Braga. Garcia was removed by his brothers and took refuge with the Muslims in Seville; Sancho then defeated Alfonso VI, who sought refuge in Toledo. But Sancho was murdered and Alfonso VI was recalled to rule over Leon and Castile. When the deposed Garcia emerged, he was arrested and held in a castle in Leon until his death. Coimbra was not yet part of Portugal and Sisnand Davides, who was styled vizir and who enjoyed his authority for life (1064–92), took over the administration, appointed a bishop and chapter, and drew settlers to replace the Muslims who had left.

Under Alfonso VI, Sisnand flourished. He was married to the daughter of Count Nuno Mendes and served as judge when he was at court. He was styled count when he participated with the men of Coimbra at the conquest of Toledo in 1085, and was made its governor. However, as he would have maintained Alfonso's pledges to the Muslims, he was soon dismissed. His government paved the way for the unification of Portugal with Coimbra, and the foundation of Portugal as a nation.

The path was not smooth. The diocese of Braga was refounded for Bishop Pedro (1071–91), but it had been despoiled of its land and had to face the jealousy of Santiago and Toledo. Both opposed the restoration of the ancient metropolitanate. When Bishop Pedro finally obtained the distinction, it was from an anti-pope and he was deposed for his pains. The Cluniac reform was now inseparable from the Peninsular empire. It was also closely related to the ambitions of the ducal house of Burgundy. Alfonso VI was married five times but had only one natural son, who was killed at the age of fourteen. The succession passed to the only daughter of his second wife Constance, a niece of Abbot Hugh of Cluny. She duly secured the appointment of a French monk, Bernard, as archbishop of Toledo, with the position of primate *ex officio* and permanent papal legate. For the French, the ancient Hispanic church was contaminated by Islam, and the Cluniac reform included the appointment of French bishops, the adoption of the Franco-Roman liturgy, and even the French style of writing.

If the conquest of Toledo raised Alfonso VI to triumph, it brought a swift retaliation. The Muslim clergy appealed to the new power which had taken over the Magrib, the Almoravids, who crossed the Straits of Gibraltar and heavily defeated Alfonso VI just outside Badajoz on 23 October 1086. The Duke of Burgundy responded to his appeal, but the Almoravids had already left when he arrived. He therefore arranged for Constance's daughter, Urraca, now eight, to marry his brother-in-law Count Raymond, thus ensuring a Burgundian succession. Raymond and Urraca were installed at Santiago as count and countess of Galicia. The Almoravids, scorning the *taifa* princes who paid tribute to the Christians, refused to defend them unless given political power. The ruler of Badajoz, who had welcomed the Almoravids in 1086, appealed to Alfonso, offering him the lower valley of the Tagus, Santarém, Lisbon and Sintra, in return for protection. The Almoravids responded by sending a detachment to assassinate him. In Coimbra, Sisnand was already dead, and the governorship had passed to his son-in-law, Martim Moniz, from the Douro valley. A Portuguese named Sueiro Mendes seized Santarém, but Lisbon and Sintra were lost, and it fell to Count

Raymond to attempt to take them. He gathered the notables of Galicia, dismissed Martim Moniz, and was defeated somewhere near Lisbon. Raymond was not the successful young commander defending the western frontier Alfonso had hoped for. The solution was to send his cousin Count Henry, who signed a contract by which he was to bring Raymond to the throne and be rewarded with Toledo or its equivalent. It is unknown if Alfonso was aware of this bargain, but Count Henry was duly married to Alfonso's illegitimate daughter, Tarásia, and the couple went to occupy the vacant castle at Guimarães at the end of 1095 or early 1096. Tarásia was not born Portuguese, but her mother held a castle in the Bierzo and she was related by marriage to Sueiro Mendes of Santarém. She thus struck roots in Portugal, while her half-sister Urraca would abandon Galicia to succeed their father, the Emperor, in Leon. Count Henry's wider ambitions came to nothing, since Count Raymond died before Alfonso VI.

For seventy years, the Muslim *taifas* had offered no serious threat, but the African intervention made it necessary to strengthen Coimbra with castles south of the Mondego. Lamego and Viseu were left without bishops, their resources being assigned to the defence of Coimbra. Count Henry brought a Frenchman, St Gerald, to be archbishop of Braga and another, Maurice, to Coimbra. Count Raymond had tried to secure Santiago for a Cluniac, who died, and the see was then left vacant, but administered by Raymond's notary Diego Gelmírez, whom he later made bishop. If Count Henry had held the pretensions of Santiago in check, the rivalry with Braga and Toledo was revived by Gelmírez, who succeeded in placing his French chaplain Hugh at Oporto.

When the old Emperor died in June 1109, Urraca succeeded to Leon. She was already a widow, with an infant son, who was declared king by the Galicians. She was hastily remarried to the King of Aragon. The Burgundians exercised their influence in Rome to bring about an annulment. Count Henry was excluded and eventually settled for the promise of the border town of Zamora: he was killed in May 1112, apparently while going to obtain it. Tarásia, who had governed Portugal during his absences, was left with three children, the future Afonso Henriques being about three years old. She reigned until 1128, relying on the barons of the Douro and the knights of Coimbra. There was no legal impediment to the succession of a woman, but she needed someone to wield the sword of state for her. The southern frontier was now insecure, threatened by Almoravid campaigns. In 1116 she was besieged for ten days in Coimbra. It did not fall, but the forward post of Soure lay abandoned for seven years. Thus Tarásia entrusted her defence to Fernando Peres, the second son of the Count of Galicia, who not only managed the frontier but acquired for her part of the Galician province of Ourense. Her half-sister Urraca ended her disastrous reign in Leon in 1126, being succeeded by her young son Alfonso VII. In May 1128, Queen Tarásia and Count Fernando Peres were expelled after a token resistance at São Mamede near Guimarães, and her young son Afonso Henriques was acclaimed in her place. She issued no more documents, but lived in exile, probably at Allariz in Ourense, until her death in November 1130.

The modern visitor may find vestiges of the old county north of the Douro. The castle of Guimarães, the cradle of the nation, has been enlarged and rebuilt, and the small church where Afonso I was baptised is preserved. The ancient castle of Lanhoso on a mountain-top near Braga dates from Suevic times and recalls Queen Tarásia's refuge there from the invasion of Gelmírez and her half-sister, and the cathedral of

Braga has the tombs of the queen and her husband. Most of the castles and monasteries have been rebuilt or abandoned, but survive in transformation, and there are a number of early churches. The founding nobility is supposed to have comprised some thirty families, who were not counts, but 'rich men', *ricos homens*, able to raise and feed their contingents. Afonso I also had the support of the Templars, who defended Soure, and of the Cistercians, who abandoned the grand political aspirations of Cluny to undertake the resettlement and cultivation of the reconquered areas. For them, Afonso I founded the monastery of Santa Cruz in Coimbra. His great feat was the conquest of Lisbon aided by the Anglo-Norman crusaders of St Bernard in 1147. The first bishop of the see of Lisbon was Gilbert of Hastings. Nothing is known of his previous life, but he quarrelled with the Templars about jurisdictions and revisited England in 1151: his problem was settled in Rome by Adrian VI, the only English pope, in 1157. Without the great port, the monarchy of Portugal might possibly have survived but it could not have achieved fame as the initiator of the European Discoveries.

In 1146 a new African movement, the Almohads, or Uniters, landed at Mértola and occupied Seville in 1147. The brunt of the Portuguese defence then fell on the Military Orders, bands of knights subject in theory to the papacy. The Templars made their permanent headquarters in Tomar, and the Order of Santiago made its headquarters at Palmela, south of Lisbon. Beja was taken in 1162 and Évora by an adventurer known as Gerald the Fearless in 1166. The same Gerald attempted to take Badajoz. When Afonso intervened he was wounded in the leg and captured by the Leonese: his military career ended, and he associated his son Sancho I with his rule. In 1179, Pope Alexander III recognised his kingship and his hereditary rights: he died in 1185, leaving a vast fortune in gold and coin.

Sancho I was able to use the services of another band of crusaders to capture Silves in 1187. It could not be held however, and in 1191 the Almohads recovered most of the Alentejo. The African dynasty was itself vanquished only in 1212 at Las Navas, opening the way for the Christian conquest of Seville in 1248. The Portuguese had taken Alcácer do Sal in 1217, and most of the Algarve between 1240 and 1245. The knights of the Temple and Santiago lacked the resources to resettle so vast an area. Therefore, as at Lisbon, those Muslims who could do so departed, and those who remained became 'free Moors', *mouros forros*, who retained their mosques, officials, usages and charities. Although coin was used for larger transactions, between 1140 and 1150 it consisted of gold and silver from the mints of the Almoravids, or *morabitinos*. No coin of value was issued until the time of Sancho I, perhaps from 1188. His successors, less affluent, regularly reduced the content of precious metal. As the Reconquest proceeded these revenues dwindled.

Northern Portugal was still an agrarian monarchy, where the barons and communities were entrenched in a profusion of local practices and privileges enshrined in charters, or *forais*. Since the frontiers were now far away, much of this law became irrelevant. From about 1245, the Reconquest was over, though in Spain, where Castile and Leon were finally reunited, the Muslim kingdom of Granada survived until 1492. Portugal, like Galicia, participated in the conquest of Seville, but although Fernando III was styled a saint, the title of emperor was not restored. For Portugal, the important consequence of the taking of Seville was the opening of the Straits of Gibraltar to merchant-shipping, not merely armed fleets of crusaders. Italian merchants soon set up a regular service by Andalusia and Lisbon to the ports of Flanders and England. The transition from barter and taxation in kind to a monetary economy ensured the growth of Lisbon as a trading-centre and led to the prevalence of royal law over local customs. This process was stimulated by the deposition of King Sancho II in favour of his brother Afonso (III), who had emigrated to France and married the Countess of Boulogne. The change was inspired by the clergy and authorised by Rome, and had the support of the Military Orders and the citizens of Lisbon, who had begun to emerge as a power in the land. In 1254, King Afonso summoned his parliament, or Cortes, at Leiria, calling for the first time not only his nobles and clergy, but commoners representing the towns. The commoners did not obtain control of the discussions, but were able to negotiate the value of the various coins in circulation.

Portugal and Galicia had taken part in the conquest of Seville, but it fell to St Fernando's son, Alfonso X, to seek the title of emperor, which the papacy refused. He had been brought up in Galicia, and was regarded as the patron of Galaico-Portuguese literature. His preoccupation with learning and his failure to win the imperial title disillusioned the Castilians, who repudiated him. He gave an illegitimate daughter as queen to Afonso III of Portugal, and agreed to settle on their infant son Diniz the areas reconquered by the Military Orders in the Algarve, establishing the present frontiers of Portugal. The long reign of King Diniz (1279–1325) thus saw the completion of the Portuguese state.

His favourite residence was Leiria, near which he planted the great pine-forest, the Pinhal d'El-Rei, which served the double purpose of preventing the encroachment of sand-dunes and providing timber for the royal ships. He is remembered as the 'husbandman', Rei Lavrador. He founded the 'General Studies', the University, in 1290, for the purpose not only of training the clergy, but also of ensuring that his administrators knew the law. This had the effect of creating the new class of letrados, men of letters, who in time were to supersede the old nobility in the administration of justice and the machinery of government. Like his grandfather, Alfonso X, he composed poetry and also gathered the Cancioneiros, large repertoires that preserved the amatory, or satirical verse, of the previous hundred years. His illegitimate son Pedro, the first Count of Barcelos, composed the genealogies of the leading families, the Linhagens, and may be described as the founder of Portuguese prose, though its orthography was still unfixed. Diniz's queen, Isabel of Aragon, was sanctified for her piety and her influence in curbing the quarrels of Diniz's sons.

Diniz's heir Afonso IV (1325–57) fended off the ambitions of his illegitimate but older brothers, and contributed to the defeat of the Africans in their last attempt to recover their possessions in the Iberian Peninsula at the battle of the Salado in 1340. He is now chiefly remembered for his part in the murder of his son's mistress, Inês de Castro. She was a Galician and came to Portugal in the train of the prince's bride Constance, who died in giving birth to the eventual heir Fernando; Inês bore several children to Pedro. Afonso IV was well aware of the problems posed by illegitimate pretenders. His advisers persuaded him that by killing Inês he would be rid of the influence of her brothers and restore his son to his senses. She was murdered at Coimbra in January 1355. Her two sons survived. When Pedro came to the throne he is supposed to have sworn that he had been legally married to Inês, and even had her crowned posthumously. Their story is recorded in stone in the extraordinary carved tombs at Alcobaça. In fact, the masterpiece owes something to Castro influence. Pedro was not inconsolable and the Castros played a part in the affairs of state, though a less catastrophic one than Afonso IV had feared.

The first function of a king was not now to win victories in the field but to dispense justice. Pedro revelled in his power to execute justice in a permanent assize that filled the ten years of his reign. When he died, Lisbon was rich and active from the numerous ships that brought goods from Italy and the north. The custom-house of Lisbon remained one of the essential sources of income of the state.

Both England and France looked to the Iberian Peninsula for allies in their long struggle for Aquitaine. In Castile, King Pedro 'the Cruel' was defied by his illegitimate half-brother Henry, Count of Trastámara, who won the backing of France, murdered Pedro with his own hand, and made himself King Henry II of Castile. In Portugal, King Pedro I was wise enough not to be involved, but the young Fernando who succeeded him in 1367 allowed himself to be persuaded by Andeiro, a Galician loyalist, that he might easily acquire Galicia and western Leon. He was promptly invaded by Henry II, who entered Braga. Fernando's adviser, João Afonso Teles, accepted the peace made with papal mediation at the village of Alcoutim in the Algarve, by which Fernando undertook to take a Castilian wife. But instead he married Teles's niece, Leonor: she was already married, but her husband fled to Castile. She bore Fernando a daughter named Brites. John of Gaunt, governor of English Aquitaine, espoused the legitimist cause in Castile by marrying Pedro the Cruel's daughter. Andeiro persuaded him to make alliance with Fernando, and this led to the conclusion of a pact at the small village of Fagilde near Braga, where the event is commemorated by a plaque. The treaty of 10 July 1372 did not engage the English crown, but it forms the keystone to the Anglo-Portuguese Alliance. Before it could take effect, Henry II again invaded Portugal and laid siege to Lisbon. Fernando then submitted and renounced the agreement with John of Gaunt, but he evidently did not regard himself as being committed by a decision taken under duress, and on 16 June 1373 the first Anglo-Portuguese Treaty of Alliance was formally concluded in London.

Seven years passed, and both Henry II of Castile and Edward III of England were dead. The change of rulers was a signal for a new trial of strength. In 1380 the English treaty was confirmed, and John of Gaunt undertook to send his brother, the Earl of Cambridge, to assist in a war with Castile. Cambridge arrived in Lisbon in July 1381 and his little son was betrothed to Fernando's daughter, Brites. But the English troops proved unruly, and Fernando unilaterally came to an agreement with John I of Castile, who supplied ships for Cambridge and his men to be repatriated. When Fernando died in 1383, he left his young daughter pledged to Castile with her mother as regent. His disreputable union with Leonor Teles had been strongly disapproved of by the Lisbon guilds, and her presence was sufficient to provoke a movement in favour of King Pedro's natural son, John, Master of the Order of Avis. At the *cortes* of Coimbra in April 1385, the jurist João das Regras made out the case for John, who became Defender and King as John I. He at once renewed the English connection with the Treaty of Windsor created on 9 May 1386, from which the Ancient Alliance is formally dated.

When the Castilian king attempted an invasion in August 1385, he was heavily defeated at Aljubarrota and the Castilians were driven from the field. John's general was Nun'Alvares Pereira, the 'Holy Constable'. A small company of English archers participated in the victory, which secured the independence of Portugal. John of

Gaunt did not become king of Castile, but when he came to Portugal he married his daughter, Philippa of Lancaster, to King John at Oporto; a union which confirmed the Alliance and assured the continuation of the new dynasty. Their children are called, by Camões, the *ínclita geração* or Illustrious Family, of whom the best known is Prince Henry 'the Navigator', the originator of the Portuguese discoveries and of the expansion of Europe. Philippa left a noble memory among her new subjects. She died in 1415, just as her husband and elder sons set out to conquer the North African port of Ceuta.

King John I reigned for nearly half a century. He rewarded liberally his Holy Constable and other adherents, many of them ennobled gentry who replaced the old families tainted with disloyalty. He subordinated to the crown the Military Orders, which in Castile became private armies in the hands of rival factions. The border war with Castile continued until a truce was made in 1411. By then he was even more in debt than the profligate Fernando. The coin was debased, and his resources were overdrawn. It was in these circumstances that he embarked on the conquest of Ceuta. It had once formed part of the Roman empire and its annexation thus seemed a legitimate extension of the Reconquest. It was a prosperous emporium, now exposed by a quarrel between the Nasrids of Granada and their former allies in North Africa. John's natural son Afonso was of military age and so were three of his sons by Philippa; Duarte, Pedro and Henry. Ceuta fell in a day, on 21 August 1415, and King John named Henry as its governor, introducing the title of duke for him (of Viseu) and his brother Pedro (of Coimbra). The crusade against Islam was thus linked with the first expansion of Europe and the Discoveries. Henry, later called 'The Navigator', had inherited his mother's piety, while his elder brother was sickly and bookish, and Pedro was more independent than their stern father liked. Ceuta, far from being a trading-centre, was now isolated and required to be garrisoned and supplied at a heavy cost. Henry began to consider other ways to confront Muslim North Africa, sending his squires to occupy the Madeiras in 1425 and the Azores from about 1427.

King Duarte (1433–38) limited his father's munificence by ruling that grants of land could be transmitted only to legal male heirs with the sanction of the crown, the royal house being excepted, including the family of Afonso, who had acquired by marriage the vast estates of the Holy Constable. Prince Henry persuaded the king to authorise a new campaign against Tangier, directed by himself. His large army was cut off and to save it he was obliged to promise to return Ceuta, leaving his younger brother Fernando as hostage. In Portugal it was held that Ceuta could not be surrendered for one individual, however exalted, and Fernando died a prisoner at Fez, being considered the 'Infante Santo'. Prince Henry then settled at Sagres in the Algarve and devoted himself to the exploration and commerce of the southern Magrib, the islands and West Africa. Madeira produced timber, wine and sugar, but the trade, including African slaves, was largely in the hands of merchants.

King Duarte's son, Afonso V (1438–81), was a child of five, and the regency was shared between his Aragonese mother and Prince Pedro, Duke of Coimbra. They soon divided, the queen looking to Castile, the church and Afonso who aspired to be made duke, while Pedro had with him the *cortes*, Lisbon and the guilds. She departed for Castile, appealing to her relatives, but without result. Pedro continued as sole regent, securing his position by marrying Afonso V to his daughter. He had travelled to England, the Low Countries, Hungary and Italy, and brought Henry information about the Orient, but he was not the man to indulge his brother's crusading zeal. When he prolonged his tutorship after King Afonso's fourteenth birthday, his rival and half-brother Afonso, made Duke of Braganza, opposed him, drove him into open rebellion and killed him at Alfarrobeira outside Lisbon in May 1449. The new duke claimed to be part of the royal house and was the richest landowner in Portugal with estates in all parts of the country.

After the disaster of Tangier, Prince Henry was never again a military commander. His voyages to the southern Sahara revealed peoples beyond the reach of Islam. From his headquarters at the Vila do Infante near Sagres he obtained knowledge of the West African coast and its navigation and trade. Merchants, including Italian adventurers, collaborated in the commerce, which soon brought in 'Guinea gold'. In 1455 the gold *cruzado* or 'crusader' was minted for Afonso V, whose reign was marked by many mintings of good standard. In 1453 the Turkish conquest of Constantinople ended the Roman Empire in the East. Rome and Europe were shocked and there was talk of a new crusade, but little sign of action. In 1454 Pope Nicholas V granted Portugal the monopoly of navigation in the south Atlantic, a claim contested only by Castilian pretensions to the Canaries. Afonso V began his military career by seizing the 'little castle', or Alcácer as-Seghir, between Ceuta and Tangier. His wealth enabled him to remunerate his nobles, who became dependent on royal pensions rather than the tribute levied on their subjects. When Prince Henry died in 1460 at his Vila do Infante, he left no grand palace but was in debt. The flow of Guinea gold benefitted the crown and the traffic in slaves, and the products of the land went to the traders. Henry's heir was his nephew Fernando, the younger brother of Afonso V, now Duke of Beja and second Duke of Viseu, and the father of Manuel I, 'the Fortunate'. Fernando did not intend to leave Beja and entrusted the trade and exploration to one Diogo Gomes, who received a monopoly of trade in return for exploring a hundred leagues of coast a year. The headquarters of the enterprise was shifted to Lisbon, where the doings of the merchants could be more closely scrutinised.

Crusading and chivalry brought Afonso V 'the African' to a sorry end as an elderly knight-errant. His sister had married Henry IV of Castile and left a young daughter Joana as their heiress. Her claim was contested by Henry's sister Isabel, who married Fernando, the prince of Aragon. There followed a campaign of defamation against Joana. Afonso V, a widower, was persuaded to espouse his niece and her claim. He then went to France to seek the support of Louis XI, who eluded his pleas. He abdicated, but changed his mind and returned to Portugal just as his son John II had been acclaimed. He resumed his reign, but was a broken man, and it fell to John II to negotiate: Joana forfeited all claims in Spain and remained at a monastery in Aveiro as the 'Excellent Lady' until her death in 1530.

John II (1481–95) was regarded as the 'Perfect Prince'. He managed relations with Spain adroitly, took charge of the Guinea trade, founding the trading-castle of Mina, or *al-mina* (Arabic for 'the port'), in 1481, and despatched Bartolomeu Dias, who explored the coast from the Congo to the Cape of Good Hope. Dias placed a stone marker, or *padrão*, at the Great Fish River and saw the Cape on his return. John II gave it the name of Good Hope, a clear proof of his intention to reach India. He sent Pero da Covilhã and Afonso de Pavia to ascertain the way to India and Ethiopia by land, but in 1492 Columbus, whose schemes he had rejected, put in at Lisbon after discovering what he believed to be the Far East. John II was at first angry, but then negotiated the

Treaty of Tordesillas in June 1494, which annulled the Portuguese monopoly of navigation in the South Atlantic, and established a north-south demarcation. It had the effect of reserving Brazil, still undiscovered, for Portugal. Thus, the way was prepared for the opening of the sea-route to India, though it had not been launched when John died in the Algarve in 1495. John had imbibed Italian ideas of the nature of royal power and justice, sending his lawyers to study in Italy. He embodied the Macchiavellian Prince, requiring the Duke of Braganza to do homage to him and then executing him in Évora on a charge of treason. The son from his marriage to his cousin Leonor was killed in a riding-accident at Santarém. John would have preferred his throne to go to his natural son Dom Jorge, but his wife secured the succession of her youngest brother Manuel, John's cousin. She had the lawyers with her, and the solution that had brought the house of Avis to the throne was ruled out.

The young Manuel (1495–1521) was doubly Fortunate, *Venturoso*, in coming to the throne as a ninth child, and in acquiring the wealth of Africa and the East. Vasco da Gama, son of the captain of the small port of Sines, was sent on his epoch-making voyage in 1497. He had perhaps not been expected to cover all East Africa, but found an Arab pilot at Malindi and seized the opportunity to reach Calicut. Portugal was suddenly rich, with a monopoly of trade over all the Orient. This permitted Manuel to embark on a building programme of unprecedented scale for its size, complexity, and originality. King Manuel chose Pedro Álvares Cabral, the heir of an old military house, to command a fleet of thirteen ships to follow up Gama's discovery. On the outward voyage, on 3 May 1500, Cabral discovered the coast of Central Brazil which duly fell to Portugal.

The great flow of wealth from the sale of oriental spices did not long outlast Manuel's reign. A few early fortune-seekers like Tristão de Cunha loaded ships and returned very rich. But those who went as governors or soldiers often died in the East. If merchants at Cochin prospered, soldiers at Goa, the seat of a new Luso-Indian race founded by Manuel's nominee Afonso de Albuquerque, seldom returned to enjoy the fruits of their exertions. King Manuel's court rejoiced in his good fortune: his nobles were drawn to Lisbon by pensions and by proximity to royal favour. The king attempted to improve the education of his subjects, using part of his wealth to enable Portuguese to study in Paris and Italy. However, his resources did not suffice to populate Brazil, man the string of castles in the Magrib, and maintain the Christian native kingdom of Congo, as well as the captaincies scattered from the Azores to the Spice Islands. In the East, Afonso de Albuquerque took Malacca, and Portuguese ships reached Canton. The Celestial Emperor then closed his vast domains to them but they went on to discover Japan. It was little wonder that the known globe seemed about to become one.

The chief obstacles were France, which refused to acknowledge the division of Tordesillas, and later England. Although private enterprise took the profits from the distribution of spices in Flanders, the cost of the fleets and of defence was borne by the state, and ships were made larger and less seaworthy. Collaboration with Spain was necessary. The union of Castile and Aragon, and the conquest of Nasrid Granada in 1492, followed by the discovery of the West Indies and Mexico, made Spain a great power, and the grammar of Nebrija, also published in 1492, fixed the Spanish language and made it an instrument of empire. In 1500, Manuel married a Spanish princess, whose son, had he survived, might have inherited both crowns. On the death of Isabella in 1504, the succession passed to her daughter Juana and her husband Philip, heir to the Emperor: their son Charles, born at Ghent in 1500, would inherit the whole.

King Manuel contracted a final Spanish marriage in 1517 and died in 1521, leaving a large family, the heir of which was John III, a youth of nineteen. His cousin Charles V had inherited Spain and the Holy Roman Empire. It then seemed natural for John III to marry the young Emperor's sister, and for Charles V to marry John's sister, though King John had to find an enormous dowry. In 1519, the Portuguese Magalhães, or Magellan, now in Spanish employment, set off from Seville to make the first circumnavigation of the globe. However, he was killed in a skirmish in the Philippines, and did not see the results. They were to open a dispute about the Spice Islands, since there was no demarcation in the East corresponding to the line of Tordesillas: In 1529 John III paid a large sum to settle his claim. Meanwhile, the price obtained for pepper, sugar and other exotic rarities declined steeply.

Beyond other considerations, Portugal and Spain were held together by the hope of evangelising the whole known world: Goa would become the Rome of the Orient. John III was a quiet and pious man, dominated by his Spanish wife, Catherine, who did not forget that she was the sister of the Emperor and, like other Castilian queens, did not learn Portuguese. The court was bilingual, and many of the plays composed by the dramatist Gil Vicente were in either language or both. But Gil Vicente died in 1536, and the royal theatre disappeared. Printing had appeared by 1489, but the first printers were itinerant artisans who found a larger market in Spain. John III welcomed two Spanish institutions, the Inquisition and the Jesuits, who appeared in Portugal in 1542.

The expulsion of the Jews from Spain in 1492 brought many to Portugal. King Manuel had granted them a period of grace during which no investigation of their beliefs was made, but his son was not prepared to compromise and the only active tribunals of the Inquisition were in Évora (for a time), Lisbon, and Coimbra. The Jesuits acquired their first college at Coimbra and soon exercised a powerful influence in the University predominating in the early evangelisation of Brazil, and to a lesser extent in the East.

King John had already in 1529 considered and rejected a plan to abandon some of the forts in the Magrib. In 1535 he reluctantly joined the Emperor in the conquest of Tunis. It was successful, but had the effect of drawing the Barbary 'pirates' into the western Mediterranean, and of stimulating the Sa'adi revolt in the southern Magrib, which took the Portuguese outpost of Agadir. By 1549 it was necessary to scour the prisons to settle Brazil, and to abandon the minor African forts and recruit in Andalusia for the defence of what remained. The jollity of Manuel's court gave way to pious gloom: John and Catherine had nine children, most of whom died in infancy. Only a daughter Maria, betrothed to Charles V's heir Philip, and a sickly son named John survived. Prince John reached his majority at fourteen, and was knighted at a tourney at Xabregas, the parade-ground outside Lisbon. He was duly married to the Emperor's daughter, Juana, who was received with great festivities. He died of a fever soon after the marriage, and a son was born posthumously in 1554 named Sebastian. He became king at the age of three when John III died in 1557. The Count of Castanheira, King John's minister for a quarter of a century, was dismissed and the regency was shared between Catherine, the queen-grandmother, and Cardinal Henry,

King John's younger brother, the sole legitimate male survivor of his house. The Cardinal was a man of some learning and a patron of the Jesuits, who had founded a college, later a University, in his see of Évora. Under Jesuit tutors, Sebastian was encouraged to see himself as a crusader in Africa, and showed no disposition to marry and beget an heir to the throne.

There had been various projects to record the achievements of the Portuguese, though nothing was published until João de Barros, a high official in the overseas administration, produced the first part of his *Decades of Asia* in 1552, and was hailed as the Portuguese Livy. The poet Luis de Camões, born in Lisbon in 1524, had become famous at court for his mastery of traditional verse, and of the Italian sonnet and eclogue. He sought a protector who would enable him to compose and publish an epic to rival Virgil and Homer. In 1552, he was involved in a street brawl which led to his being sent to India. He spent fifteen years in the Orient, hoping to find a viceroy who would become his sponsor. He left for Mozambique with his *Lusiads* largely written and published his book in 1572, with a dedication to King Sebastian. The intention was doubtless to divert the young king's attention from Africa to the East and to persuade him to marry. But Sebastian persisted in his obsession, thinking to impose a client king in the Magrib. After raising a large army, he invaded Morocco, where he was defeated and killed in the disastrous Battle of Three Kings in August 1578. His death and the captivity of many of his nobles led to the accession of his great-uncle, the Cardinal-King Henry. The only other male member of the royal house was Sebastian's cousin, the illegitimate António, Prior of Crato, who had met with the Cardinal's disapproval. Philip II, who had succeeded the Emperor Charles V in Spain, was the grandson of King Manuel and had been married to Sebastian's aunt, Maria, now deceased. In default of a legitimate male successor, he had a passable claim to the throne of Portugal. There were many that disliked the prospect, but the Anglo-Portuguese Alliance had been shaken by the Reformation and by the influence of the Jesuits and the Counter-reformation. Henry died in 1580, the same year as Camões, and left the kingdom in the hands of five governors. Philip II martialled many lawyers to support his claim, and sent the Duke of Alba and his army to defeat the ill-prepared force of Dom António to the west of Lisbon.

King Philip made a long stay in Portugal and promised at the cortes of Tomar to preserve Portuguese institutions, and to be represented by a member of his house, reconciling many to the conquest. A series of impostors pretended to be Sebastian, having survived the battle, but they were easily dealt with, and the Prior of Crato fled to Paris, hoping to find support. Preparations for the famous Armada of 1588 provided work for the shipyards of Lisbon. When it failed, Queen Elizabeth sent Sir Francis Drake and Sir Edward Norris, with a large expedition, to put the Prior of Crato on the throne. However, this was botched by stopping to besiege Corunna, which had no interest in the Prior, giving Philip time to organise the defence when they landed much too far from Lisbon at Peniche. But, if Philip was half-Portuguese, his son and grandson were not, hence Philip III came to Portugal only once, and Philip IV not at all. Philip II gave Lisbon churches, not palaces; Oporto was given its own court of appeal, and the kingdom of the Algarve was given its own governor. But the Council of Portugal, which sat in Madrid, took decisions affecting the Portuguese. Some of the nobility were attracted to Spain and were intermarried with Spanish families. But from 1590, Portuguese patriotism was aroused by the publication of its writers, especially Camões, whose *Lusiads* became a breviary of Portuguese nationalism. The sole institution of authority in Portugal was the City Council of Lisbon, or Senate, composed of the lower nobility and lawyers, with a representative of the guilds. Portugal had acquired the enemies of Spain, and the union was unhappy for her commerce. In 1639, new taxes were imposed to pay for the suppression of the Catalans during their revolt. On 1 December 1640, the rule of the Philips was ended by the removal of the Spanish governor, the Duchess of Mantua, and the head of the house of Braganza was called to become King John IV.

The wars that followed the Restoration of Independence lasted from the accession of John IV until 1668. John IV was concerned not only with the defence of Portugal but also with the recovery of northern Brazil and Angola from the Dutch. It was only after his death in 1656 that the war on the eastern frontier intensified. It was believed that no invading army could safely advance far into the interior without finding its supply-lines cut. The Spaniards threw a large force at Elvas, which was saved by the battle of the Lines of Elvas in January 1659. The result seemed to justify military theory, and Queen Leonor was able to marry her daughter Catherine to Charles II, an admirable match if a less than perfect husband. The death of Philip IV of Spain in September 1665 and the succession of the mindless Carlos II enabled the Earl of Sandwich to negotiate a truce which became permanent in 1668.

The Restoration of 1640 provided Portugal with a monarch, the wealthiest nobleman in the land, but with no army, no money, no allies and no foreign relations. The Dutch seized the opportunity to occupy northern Brazil and to take Angola, its principal source of labour. The English, the 'Ancient Allies', were about to abolish their monarchy as the Portuguese restored theirs. But, more positively, Brazil had grown rapidly in population and trade, as the Portuguese Orient diminished. The Brazilians also wanted independence from Dutch interlopers, and the Jesuits, who had once seemed to be the instruments of Spanish policy, were now anxious to be the opposite. Padre António Vieira became a statesman of the Restoration, and his vehement sermons made him the best prose writer of his day. John IV had married an Andalusian, Leonor de Guzmán, who was eager to be queen. Spain, for all her influence in Rome, had more enemies than allies, yet the problem of the Restoration was not to find friends, but to ensure that they were effective. Despite the difference of religion and regime, the Ancient Alliance was revived with the Anglo-Portuguese Treaty of 1654. This was negotiated with the Commonwealth and brought Portugal military aid in return for commercial concessions. Many ancient privileges, some long obsolete, were also confirmed. Although the treaty provided that the English should have their place of worship and cemetery, the Inquisition opposed the concession, and the burial-ground was not used until 1717. But the English recovered the right to have a 'judge-conservator' of their privileges, originally a judge of the customs-house empowered to give quick decisions. However, by the seventeenth century there were resident merchants and a consul. Oporto had long traded with England, but it was only after the Restoration that wine from Oporto replaced 'Lisbon wine'. There was no tribunal of the Inquisition in Oporto, its cases being dealt with at Coimbra: from its inception until its suppression in 1820, only one English name occurs, that of an Irishman named King.

King John summoned *cortes* frequently because of the pressing needs of defence. He died in 1656, but it was only in 1668 that the Spaniards were persuaded to recognise Portuguese independence. The *Lusiads* had inspired the *letrados*, the lawyers of the Restoration, with a tale of Portuguese greatness. Its first English translation was by Sir Richard Fanshaw, who served as envoy extraordinary to Lisbon in 1662, 1668 and 1681. He played a prominent part in the English Restoration and in the marriage of Charles II to Catherine of Braganza, the eldest daughter of John IV and Leonor. She was the only Portuguese Queen of England, and it was in England that she spent the years 1662 to 1692. In Portugal, her brother, Afonso VI, proved incapable of ruling, and was replaced by her more personable brother, Pedro II, who also married his French queen. If the English connection prevailed in policy and trade, the declining Spanish influence in dress and manners yielded to that of Louis XIV's France. But, the freedom of Portugal to express herself in her own way was provided by the tide of gold flowing from Brazil. In the last years of the seventeenth century, bands of explorers from São Paulo, the *bandeirantes*, began to find alluvial gold in the rivers of the interior, the Minas Gerais, or 'general mines'. In 1662, Portugal had given Catherine an immense dowry, Tangier, Bombay, and half a million in coin. By the end of the century however, Portugal, the poor member of the European family, emerged as the most courted. The marriage, though childless, did something in England to keep the balance between Protestants and Catholics. It was overset by Charles' brother James II, and Catherine returned to Portugal in 1692, acting briefly as regent during the illness of Pedro II: she died in 1705.

King Pedro had only a daughter by his French wife. He then married Maria Sofia, daughter of the German Elector-Palatine, who gave him four sons and two daughters: the heir John V was born in 1689. In 1700, the death of the last of the Spanish Hapsburgs precipitated war between France and Austria. The prospect of a union of the French and Spanish crowns alarmed the other European powers, and England joined Austria and Holland to prevent it. In 1702, John Methuen, the son of a Wiltshire wool-merchant, returned to Portugal as minister to persuade King Pedro to join the Grand Alliance against France. In December 1703, he took the opportunity to conclude the treaty by which he is best known. It ensured the admission into England of Portuguese wines at a lower rate of duty than French wines, provided that Portugal admitted English woollens. This assured Portugal of a very large market, and Portuguese fears that the English taste for port might be sated proved unwarranted. The Methuen Treaty is often represented as fatal to the Portuguese woollen industry by abandoning the protectionist policy of the Count of Ericeira. But Ericeira had died in 1690, and Portugal could now afford luxury goods. The sheep of the Estrela provided country cloths and blankets, even if they did not compete with fine woollens. The growth of a prosperous English colony in Oporto was itself a protection for the wine trade.

If Methuen knew of the flow of Brazilian gold, he could hardly have guessed at the volume it would reach under the new king. John V was soon married to Maria Ana, daughter of the Austrian Emperor Leopold I. He had neither his father's ability, nor his enthusiasm for the war in Spain. The war of attrition produced nothing more than a brief allied occupation of Madrid, and the death of the Emperor and succession of the Austrian pretender to Spain made Austria seem as formidable as France. The struggle ended with a Bourbon on the throne of Madrid, with the promise that the crowns of France and Spain should never be united. The supply of Brazilian gold and diamonds reached its height in the decade of 1720 and had dwindled before John's death in 1750. He was however, too wealthy to be troubled with trade-figures. The old

Brill!

nobility had been strengthened by the generals and ministers of the struggle for Independence and now devoted itself to diplomacy and colonial administration. The king was pious and generous to the church and, wanting to rival the rulers of France and Spain, known as 'catholic' and 'most Christian', he became 'most faithful'. He wanted a permanent Cardinal independent of Braga, to which end the Patriarchate of Western Lisbon was created. He also wanted a small monastery as thanks for the birth of his first child, which then grew into the enormous pile of Mafra, remote as the Escorial and even larger. Architects were brought in from Italy and elsewhere, who, if they were not in themselves great geniuses, left good schools in Portugal. His piety led him to surround himself with clerical ministers, whom he rarely changed and his later years were gouty and stagnant.

He was succeeded by his elder son Joseph I, born in 1714 and married to a daughter of the first Bourbon king of Spain in a double union, his sister Barbara of Braganza being united to the Spanish heir. Such unions bode ill in 1383 and 1542, but the danger was supposed to have been averted by Afonso Henriques' 'cortes of Lamego', which forbade a foreign prince from succeeding to the throne. But the prohibition and the 'cortes of Lamego' were a fabrication invented after 1640, and as Spaniards say: 'laws go where kings will'. Joseph had been brought up in indolence and devoted himself to religion, the opera and the chase. He was rudely shaken, and so was the whole capital, by the devastating Earthquake of 1755. It occurred on the morning of All Saints' Day and lasted about ten minutes, being followed by an immense tidal wave, which inundated the waterfront. The air was filled with smoke from many fires and dust from collapsed buildings, and the waterfront Palace was completely destroyed with all its contents. The Castle and cathedral were damaged, as were half the forty parish-churches and the forest of monasteries and convents. Estimates of the number of dead are varied and unverifiable. Of the nobility, a score died, and of the British residents, seventy-seven, including forty-nine women. In crowded tenements the toll may have been high. King Joseph was at Belém. The only active minister was Sebastian José de Carvalho, better known as the Marquis of Pombal, who is supposed to have taken charge with the direction: 'Bury the dead and feed the living'. Many of the parish clergy kept their heads, but there were those who thought the catastrophe a punishment for sin. The controversy about divine intervention and natural causes had international repercussions.

Pombal remained in charge of the government for the rest of the reign, while Joseph approved of everything he did. It was regalism as absolute as Louis XIV's. Pombal had been minister in London and Vienna, and his Austrian wife enjoyed the favour of Joseph's queen, her compatriot. The wealth of Brazil had declined, and Pombal had to impose restraint and discipline. The Lisbon Baixa, the Lower Town, was rebuilt in the simple style, Pombaline, named after him. He set up new industries, and curbed the privileges of the English and other foreigners. A national Port-wine company was set up and the area where the wine could be grown was demarcated. He cowed the nobility by executing members of the Távora family and the last Duke of Aveiro on a charge of attempted regicide. Disagreeing with the Jesuits who believed the Earthquake a divine chastisement, he eventually suppressed the Society for opposing the royal settlement of the boundaries in South America. He retained the Inquisition, with his brother as inquisitor (it was too valuable an instrument to lose), ruthlessly repressed popular protests in Oporto against increases in the price of wine, and burnt the village of Trafaria near Lisbon when its fishermen opposed him. He personally reformed the University of Coimbra to eradicate all trace of the Jesuits and modernise the curriculum and could claim to have created a new class of clerks and accountants. Oddly enough, he was venerated by the republicans of 1920, who built his memorial column at the top of the Avenue of Liberty in Lisbon.

When King Joseph died in 1777, his daughter Maria I at once dismissed Pombal, who spent the last years of his life at Pombal defending himself. Maria was born in 1734 and in 1760 married her father's younger brother, Pedro, seventeen years her senior. Their domesticity and devotion is exemplified in their palace at Queluz and the basilica of the Estrela. The new regime is often called the *viradeira* or 'turnabout'. The victims of Pombal were released, many after years of confinement, and the new first minister was the Marquis of Angeja, a member of the old nobility. Other aristocrats obtained promotion to the rank of marquis, making them level with Pombal. However, Pombal's minister of Marine, Martinho de Melo e Castro, remained and succeeded Angeja, and Pombal's son survived as leader of the Lisbon council. Lisbon society is graphically if egotistically described by William Beckford, the prototype of the wealthy dilettante, ostracised in England for his imprudent conduct and scandalous views. Refused a title and sent to Lisbon, where he spent most of 1787, he was befriended by the Marquis of Marialva who introduced him to his numerous kinsmen. Their efforts on his behalf were opposed by the British ambassador, Robert Walpole, whom Beckford conceived of as a personal devil. In addition to singing and wining and dining, Beckford posed as a convert to Catholicism, and was taken only too seriously by his Portuguese friends. He left unsatisfied and unconverted, his departure a relief to Walpole and to most of the British community. His overt detestation of his compatriots contributed, however unwittingly, to confirming the aristocracy in their predilection for France.

Queen Maria's reconciliation was marred in 1788 by the deaths of her consort and their heir Prince Joseph. The revolutions in North America and France distressed her; she lapsed into a melancholy madness which made her incapable of governing. Her indecision turned into insanity, and in 1781 she entrusted her authority to her surviving son John, who became Prince-Regent in 1799. She died in Brazil in 1816.

Prince John was betrothed to Carlota Joaquina, the eldest daughter of Charles IV of Spain and Maria Luisa of Parma, a mismatch, since John, who had not been brought up to rule, inherited his mother's mild temperament, while his bride, whom Beckford saw as a lively child, inherited the vehemence of her mother Maria Luisa. Though nurtured in Portugal and the mother of two sons and five daughters, she never forgot that she was an infanta of Spain. The hapless Charles IV entrusted his authority to Godoy, a young guards-officer favoured by Maria Luisa. When the King of France was executed, Charles or Godoy declared war on the French republic, and the Portuguese sent a contingent to Catalonia. The Spaniards were overrun and concluded a humiliating peace at Basle, leaving the Portuguese to return as best they could. Prince John was no soldier, and the only member of the house with military training was the Duke of Lafões, whose experience dated from the days of John V: Pombal had sent him to Vienna, where he spent twenty years before returning in 1777. He is chiefly remembered for the foundation of the Portuguese Academy of Sciences in 1779. At sixty-eight he had married the daughter of Marialva. At eighty he was ready to be first minister and commander-in-chief.

The volte-face of Godoy made Spain a puppet of the French republic, and exposed Portugal to demands for indemnity, the cession of part of northern Brazil and equality of treatment with the English. The demands were reinforced by the rise of Napoleon. Many French aristocrats were now refugees in Portugal, and to some, now their heads were no longer at risk, his presence seemed an improvement. A Portuguese fleet joined the British in the Mediterranean, which Napoleon denounced as an outrage that would make Portugal weep tears of blood. The English contingent sent to reinforce Portugal consisted largely of French and other refugees.

The defences of Elvas were not seriously tested until Napoleon, having reduced the sorry Charles IV of Spain and his minister Godoy to servitude, pressed them to invade Portugal. Godoy was more willing to invade Portugal than to admit French revolutionaries into Spain, and he arranged a pre-emptive invasion before the French should have time to participate. When Charles IV declared war on 27 February 1801, the aged Portuguese commander called for resistance. The Spaniards were repelled at Elvas and Campo Maior, but overran Portalegre, Castelo de Vide and other places in what was nicknamed the 'War of the Oranges' because Godoy sent Queen Maria Luisa a branch of Portuguese oranges as proof of his triumph. Peace was made at Badajoz in June, and the Spanish conquests were returned, with the exception of Olivença. In the treaties that ended the war, the return of Olivença was not included and it remains a piece of Portuguese *terra irredenta* in Spain.

Godoy's ploy did not deceive Napoleon or Talleyrand. In the brief peace of Amiens in 1802, Napoleon sent General Junot to Lisbon to press his demands against Britain and to form a party.

The Ancient Alliance was now threatened by a power stronger than Spain. Portugal could not be defended without external aid, and many in England doubted whether she could be defended at all. This dilemma continued until 1807, when Napoleon had intimidated the eastern powers and resumed his demand for the expulsion of the English from Portugal. Prince John was now guided by his Council of State, which included various shades of opinion. The English Alliance was supported by Dom Rodrigo de Sousa Coutinho, who foresaw that the royal family might have to withdraw to Brazil. The neutralist position was held by António de Araujo, who was confident of his ability to negotiate with the French. His attempts at appeasement continued as Junot began the march from France across Spain and arrived at Abrantes. It would have been unthinkable for the royal family to abandon Portugal until the last moment. The fleet was made ready and British ships blockaded the Tagus; in November 1807, the royal family embarked for Brazil.

The winter of 1807 saw General Junot install himself in the vast house at the top of the Rua do Alecrim called the palace of Quintela, or House of Millions, built by the holder of the state leather-monopoly. The city was soon reduced to need by the British blockade. Junot declared the Braganzas deposed, and seized the reins of government from the Council of Regents left by Prince John. In Spain, Napoleon captured the royal family, and Madrid rebelled against him: the Spanish patriots were shot by Murat on 2 May 1808. The resistance at once spread to Oporto, where Bishop Castro formed a Supreme Junta. The Asturians appealed to London, and Wellington, with an army gathered at Cork, was sent to the Peninsula. He decided to disembark on the south bank of the Mondego at Lavos between 1 and 5 August. The Portuguese army, virtually disbanded by Junot, was hastily reassembled, and took an inland course as

Wellington followed the coast and defeated the French at Roliça on 17 August, and Vimeiro on 21 August. Junot sued for peace, but General Dalrymple, who accepted the Convention of Sintra, had outranked Wellington, allowing the French to depart with their loot in British ships. This led to the famous enquiry, in which Wellington defended himself and emerged as commander-in-chief. It fell to General Beresford to administer the terms of the Convention, to his own disgust. He was appointed Marshal of the Portuguese army in March 1809; he at once integrated it with the British.

In 1809 the second French invasion took place, when Marshal Soult entered Oporto. Many deaths were caused when the bridge of boats across the Douro collapsed. The Anglo-Portuguese armies forced Soult out of Oporto and pursued him up the valley of the Cávado: he was back in Spanish Galicia by the end of May. Napoleon retorted by forming the 'Army of Portugal' with three divisions and a total of 60,000 men under Marshal Masséna. Its mission was to drive the British into the sea, and impose Napoleon's brother Joseph whom he made King of Spain. Wellington and Beresford assembled their forces on the Beira frontier. The explosion of the magazine at Almeida, coupled with lack of cavalry, obliged them to fall back first on Coimbra, where the combined army won the battle of Bussaco, and then on the prepared Lines of Torres Vedras, which covered the Lisbon peninsula. After his losses at Bussaco on 27 September, Masséna was in no position to risk a frontal attack, and on 14 November fell back on Santarém. Wellington's plan to abandon the centre was thus justified, but it was only in February 1811 that he resumed the pursuit.

The Alentejo had been relatively calm until Masséna abandoned the assault on Lisbon and scoured the region south of the Tagus for supplies. Wellington pursued Masséna and detached Beresford to recover the Alentejo and reduce Badajoz which had again fallen into French hands. French forces in the Alentejo were not formidable, but it was on the cards that Soult, with his 'army of Andalusia', would intervene to relieve Badajoz. Elvas was in no danger, but the French had attacked Olivença and Campo Maior, where Major Talaia resisted for eleven days in March 1811. Beresford recovered it, thus ending the French occupation of Portuguese soil, a feat which the Prince-Regent recognised by creating him Marquis of Campo Maior: an inscription on the walls commemorates the event.

Delayed by lack of cavalry and guns, and want of pontoons to cross streams swollen in a wet spring, Beresford was unable to reduce Badajoz before Soult gathered the 'army of Andalusia' to relieve the place. The last and bloodiest battle of the campaign was fought not in Portugal but at Albuera, a few miles south of Badajoz, the siege being suspended. The site was selected by Wellington. Beresford had integrated the Anglo-Portuguese forces, but the Spaniards remained independent and Wellington contracted for a given force on a given day. It arrived only hours before the battle and was placed in front of the village of Albuera. On 16 May Soult, advancing with great speed, flung his force of Polish cavalry against the hastily prepared position, and for a time the outcome remained in the balance. By the afternoon, the French had withdrawn and did not return; the number of British casualties was over 4,000, and of French reported nearly 6,000. The carnage was not exceeded until the battles of the Great War. Though Albuera is not numbered among Wellington's victories (he was not there), its importance lay not only in its bloodshed: if Soult had relieved Badajoz, he would have been able to launch a fourth invasion of Portugal.

The battlefield is now marked by a ceramic showing the disposition of the troops: it notes the commanders as Soult for the French, Castaños (who was not present), Blake, the Irish catholic serving Spain, and Beresford for the allies, without indicating that Beresford was in overall command.

For the Portuguese, this, with Wellington's minor victory at Fuentes de Oñoro, concluded the French invasions. The Anglo-Portuguese army continued through Spain and the Pyrenees to Toulouse, where news came of Napoleon's flight from Paris. The Prince-Regent remained in Brazil, where his mother died and he became King John VI in 1816. His regents, except those guilty of collaboration, were restored by Dalrymple without ascertaining his wishes, and without regard for the Supreme Junta in Oporto. It fell to Beresford to bring about a reconciliation. He had improved the pay of the Portuguese army but Portugal, having lost its monopoly of Brazilian trade as a result of the opening of the Brazilian ports, could not meet the cost of reconstruction and of defence without a reform of the taxation system, which only the King could enforce. When Napoleon escaped from Elba, no Portuguese contingent was sent to Waterloo since royal consent could not be obtained in time. Castlereagh interrupted diplomatic relations on the grounds that if Portugal was a European power, either John or his representative must have full powers in Europe. But John was involved in the affairs of South America and required his army for service there. He lingered in Brazil, fearing to leave it while republican machinations engulfed Spanish America. He intended his acclamation to declare a United Kingdom of Portugal and Brazil in all the Portuguese possessions. But this plan was frustrated by the outbreak of a rebellion in Pernambuco in northeast Brazil. It was the work of a few zealots with 'French ideas' and was easily suppressed, but nobody knew if it had ramifications through masonic secret societies.

The presence of the royal family held Brazil together, instead of allowing it to dissolve into its component parts like the Spanish American empire. In Spain, the so-called liberals had organised the short-lived *Cortes* in Cadiz in 1812, where self-appointed delegates proclaimed a pseudo-republican constitution which Fernando VII swept away as soon as he was liberated from France. In Portugal, a crude conspiracy was organised by General Gomes Freire, who had served Napoleon throughout the war. It was revealed to Beresford, who informed the regents. In Portugal, treason was the gravest of crimes, and after a treason-trial or *inconfidência*, Gomes Freire and his military adherents were executed. Beresford had done his duty in reporting the matter and had pointed out the danger of making martyrs, but his advice was disregarded and the liberals depicted him as a monster. The opposition was quietened for a time, but Beresford was made doubly unpopular. In 1820, the Spanish army in Andalusia rebelled against being sent to South America: the rebellion seemed to have failed, but when Galicia rose up Fernando VII caved in. In both countries the armies were in arrears of pay and the government had no funds. Beresford still commanded a group of English officers, now promoted to high rank. On hearing the news from Spain, he sailed for Brazil to urge John VI to give him full powers and money: he was granted the former, but the latter only in insufficient quantity. Many Portuguese felt that they were in danger of becoming a colony of Brazil. Before he could return, the revolution had been declared in Oporto and had spread to Lisbon, where he was forbidden to land. Wellington, in Cambrai, thought the journey to Brazil foolish, but he was far away and regarded himself as above mere politics: Beresford could hardly avoid being of the number of staunch monarchists.

Dissatisfied officers and lawyers, who knew the inadequacies of the old regime, made the revolution of 1820, which was led by Fernandes Tomás, who had served in Beresford's commissariat. The effect of the French invasions had been disastrous in central Portugal. Although the British Parliament had voted relief, it was insufficient and the means of distribution was lacking. The cost of keeping the army together far outstripped the available resources. Wellington believed that there was the ability to pay, but it had disappeared in the opening of the Brazilian ports: he had known a Lisbon full of affluent refugees and merchants enriched by supplying the armies. There was no income tax and it would have required the presence of the king to impose one. Part of the untaxed nobility was at the king's side in Rio de Janeiro.

The first liberal government of 1820 debated a constitution similar to that of Cadiz of 1812, hoping to face King John with a fait accompli. It adopted an indirect system of election in which all citizens met in the parish-church to choose electors, who then met in the provincial towns to choose deputies. Like other forms of popular government, it was easily manipulated. Brazilians were appointed from those in Portugal without reference to Brazil: when Brazilians objected, Tomás airily bade them good-bye. There was much discussion about whether sovereignty resided in the Nation 'originally' or 'essentially'. King John was finally induced to return in July 1822: he had no choice but to accept the constitution, though his wife refused to do so. Their elder son Pedro was left to govern Brazil, and in September he proclaimed himself Emperor of Brazil rather than accept a republic. In Portugal, Tomás died, and the Cortes ended in confusion.

King John had done his best to swim in the turbulent sea of politics, holding Portugal and Brazil under the same royal house with similar but not identical constitutions. The French had already intervened to restore Fernando VII to his native absolutism, and Carlota Joaqina, banished to Ramalhão near Sintra, controlled her younger son Dom Miguel, who proclaimed the restoration of John VI at Vila Franca de Xira. King John had promised to grant a moderate constitution, but in April 1824 Miguel used his influence in the army to proclaim a pure absolutism. King John retired to an English warship, summoned Miguel and dismissed him from his command, sending him to exile in Austria. He then recognised his elder son as Emperor of Brazil, reserving for himself the style of 'Senior Emperor'. He died in 1826, when the question of the succession and the constitution was in abeyance. He left his unmarried daughter Maria Isabel to preside over a council of regency.

There seemed no doubt that Pedro was his heir, but the Portuguese were reluctant to be ruled from Brazil, and Castlereagh had espoused the view that Portugal should be governed by a present ruler. It fell to the Emperor Pedro to grant the Charter, a constitution by which his daughter Maria da Glória, a child, would inherit Portugal and marry her uncle Dom Miguel, who would swear to uphold it. Miguel returned from Austria by way of England and became Pedro's lieutenant, being effusively greeted by the absolutists in February 1828. Pedro duly abdicated the throne of Portugal, leaving the liberals to undergo persecution in the north. Miguel showed no desire to marry his niece, but declared himself king with the backing of Carlota Joaquina. Beresford was probably the only person who could have controlled Miguel, but Canning decided to take sides with the liberals. When Carlota Joaquina died in 1830, Miguel's government showed neither ability nor goodwill. In France the absolutist regime of Charles X, was overthrown by the July Revolution, which brought the liberal Louis-Philippe to the throne: he made a clean sweep of the chambers, local government and diplomatic service. Wellington would have recognised Miguel and have sent Beresford as ambassador, but his government fell in November 1830.

The Brazilians grew tired of their Emperor, and he abdicated in favour of his son Pedro II, a child. After two abdications, Pedro was now free to claim Portugal for his daughter, Maria II. A Portuguese regiment with liberal sentiments had been exiled to the Azores and thus provided the springboard for Pedro to raise an army of liberal exiles and mercenaries to liberate Portugal from the Miguelites. It landed on the beach of Mindelo north of Oporto, and occupied the liberal city, which the Miguelites did not defend. But the liberals were soon besieged there. The 'War of the Two Brothers' lasted from July 1832 until May 1834, the cities being 'liberal' and the countryside strongly traditionalist. The protracted siege of Oporto was a stalemate, but the liberals contracted the sea-captain Charles Napier who destroyed the Miguelite navy. At the end of June 1833 they took Lisbon, and the Miguelite cause fell into decline. Maria II was recognised as queen, her uncle withdrew to Santarém, and his general capitulated at Évora-Monte in May 1834. Miguel left Sines in a British ship and reached Genoa, where he at once repudiated the treaty made in his name. His brother Pedro, III of Portugal and I of Brazil, died of consumption on 24 September.

Maria II was married, left a widow and remarried to Ferdinand of Saxe-Coburg-Gotha, a cousin of Prince Albert, who gave her eleven children: she died in giving birth to the last in 1855. The leading liberals were the Duke of Saldanha, who had seen service with Beresford in 1811 and attempted his last coup in 1877, the Marquis of Sá da Bandeira, its most respected figure, the Duke of Palmela, the diplomat of the moderates, and Mousinho da Silveira, a reformer of the eighteenth-century school who abolished the remaining feudal privileges without promising the earth and died almost forgotten in Paris.

Liberalism rewarded its followers by creating desk-jobs and selling off crown estates. Its most dramatic act was the dissolution of the monasteries enacted by J J de Aguiar in May 1834. In the England of Henry VIII the seizure had greatly enriched the aristocracy, but in the Portugal of Maria II there were few who could buy: the number of monastic buildings was large, but the occupants were few. Many notable houses became local government offices or barracks. The most scandalous result was the purchase of the great Convent of Christ at Tomar by Costa Cabral, otherwise Count of Tomar: other fine buildings were allowed to crumble. The assembly of vast quantities of monastic documents enabled the liberal historian Alexandre Herculano to rewrite the history of Portugal. He convinced himself that the way to regeneration lay in participation in local government and was himself mayor of Belém; he died in scholarly disillusion. The legacy of division was slow to heal. Its effects colour many of the novels of Camilo Castelo Branco, and Eça de Queirós's last novel gives a satirical account of the wealthy exile Joaquim, who becomes weary of the pretentious folly of life in Paris and returns to discover the joys of the Minho he had lost. In fact, under the old regime, many local services were performed for a pittance, but the liberals rewarded their followers by creating posts which added to the existing deficit. Banks and financiers made their appearance: they served the interest of the few without contributing much to the development of industry in an insolvent state. The radicals, under the leadership of Passos Manuel of Oporto, advocated a return to the high principles of 1820 and, winning the elections of 1836, were known as Septembrists. In an orgy of reforms, Passos Manuel dismissed superfluous officials. Maria II feared for the future of her throne, attempted to dismiss the Septembrists and then accepted their reassurances, thus giving them an increased majority. The Chartist generals attempted a revolt in the north and a Miguelite leader Sousa Reis, the Remexido, harried the Algarve. In 1840, Costa Cabral, a former radical turned Chartist, swept the board. With the aid of Marshal the Duke of Terceira, he restored the Charter of Dom Pedro, arranging elections in the lower house and creating thirty peers to carry the upper. Portuguese titles of nobility had been few, but in the nineteenth century, they proliferated. Politicians are commemorated in a plethora of street-names, but liberalism looked constantly for majorities in the upper house. The indiscriminate creation of political life-peerages contributed to bringing down the monarchy in 1910.

What brought down Costa Cabral was not only corruption but a law forbidding burial in churches and imposing public cemeteries. This aroused the rural population of the north, which joined in the rebellion of 'Maria da Fonte' (Maria was the quintessential countrywoman). The immediate impulse was to burn government files and documents, and drive out parasitical pen pushers. It was a mixture of civic sense and innocence in protest against the succession of political intrigues and military 'pronouncements'. Politicians were not slow to join in the hue and cry against Costa Cabral. In the confusion that followed, Queen Maria attempted to install her husband as commander-in-chief, with the Duke of Saldanha as head of the government, in a sort of royal coup. She succeeded only in uniting the liberals of the north, the Patuleia, who with the aid of Sá da Bandeira occupied Setúbal. Britain, France and Spain agreed to intervene to save the throne by removing Saldanha. There followed a reaction in favour of Costa Cabral, who governed from June 1849 until April 1851, when a fresh scandal, blown up by the press, obliged him to retire.

In 1851 the political scene was stabilised. The Regenerators were the party of the Charter, with an Additional Act bringing in direct voting and annual budgets. From 1851 to 1856, Saldanha governed, bringing in Fontes Pereira de Melo as minister for Public Works. Fontes undertook to modernise what is now called the infrastructure. Travellers from Lisbon to Oporto still went by sea, and it was only in 1856 that the stretch of railway from Lisbon to Santarém was opened and carried on to Elvas in 1863. The northern line reached Gaia in 1864.

When Maria died in 1853, she was succeeded by her eldest son Pedro V, born in 1837, with his father Fernando as regent until he came of age in September 1855. There seemed good hopes of a long reign by an intelligent, conscientious and popular prince married to a German princess, Stephanie, or Estefania. She died a year after the marriage, and Pedro V himself succumbed to an outbreak of cholera in 1861, leaving the throne to his brother Luis. Their father survived until 1885, devoting himself to his palace at Sintra and to the opera. Dom Luis was the complete constitutional monarch: he had not been educated to rule, and translated Shakespeare, explaining the difficulties to the British minister, who knew no Portuguese. Lisbon and Oporto became great modern cities. They were on the main shipping-routes to the Mediterranean, South America, Africa and the Orient, and the steamship sealed their pre-eminence. It was confirmed by the completion of the railway system. Lisbon acquired piped water, gas and public transport: its Avenida was extended from the old Passeio Público or Parade, largely owing to the energy of Rosa Araujo, mayor from 1877 to 1893. Oporto built its Crystal Palace to stimulate agriculture and industry, and installed *Americanas*, or horse-trams. All this required extensive borrowing abroad, of which few other cities were capable.

The Regenerators relied on local big-wigs to win elections for them. The opposition consisted of the Historicals, who preserved the radical tradition of 1820, and smaller parties, who remained subdued until 1876 when they merged and took the name of Progressists. Fontes formed his last and longest government in September 1872: it lasted until his death in 1877. Young men found his style pompous and Victorian, but he had done much that was overdue. There was widespread illiteracy, not only in the countryside, and still only one university, though Passos Manuel had set up technical colleges in Oporto, and King Pedro in Lisbon. The newspapers preserved a tradition of free speech, but were firmly attached to the politicians. There was steady emigration to Brazil, especially from the crowded north. The returned 'Brasileiro' is a figure in the novels of Camilo. One such returned to Santo Tirso and bought the ancient Benedictine monastery: others simply erected nouveau-riche mansions.

The separation of Brazil left Portugal in control of large parts of Africa, including Angola, which had the first European city in southern Africa, Luanda, founded in 1572, and Mozambique. Missionary zeal had declined after the expulsion of the Jesuits and defeat of the traditionalists, and Portuguese emigration was very largely to Brazil. In the nineteenth century, the movement against the slave trade became general, despite the opposition of Brazil, Cuba and the southern United States. Sá da Bandeira and others joined in the campaign, but the Portuguese navy was depleted and it fell to the British to create a naval protectorate round the African coast. The question of territorial demarcation became serious only when Germany sought a share, having overthrown the French empire in 1870; intelligent Portuguese perceived that the balance of Europe had been overset. By 1884, Germany had acquired footholds on both coasts of Africa, and summoned the conference of Berlin to adopt the criterion of 'effective occupation'. The British and Portuguese had failed to reach agreement about the navigation and control of the river Congo.

The Progressists had still not found a programme. Both parties represented the middle classes, now adorned with life-peerages. There were newspapers for workers from 1850, but it was not until 1876 that a socialist party began to emerge. The deposition of Isabella II in Spain in 1868, and the short-lived Spanish Republic of 1873, unleashed ideas of a pan-Iberian federation: it had few supporters. The interventions of the army had now been eliminated and King Luis presided over the alternation of the main parties, whose chiefs rarely troubled the country with their presence outside of the great cities. These were adorned with new buildings, avenues, theatres and museums while much of the country, poorly served and apathetic, supplied them with cheap food. The French republic attracted the young intelligentsia of 1870, such as Eça de Queirós and Antero de Quental, who combined poetry with idealistic philosophy. The radicals played a prominent part in the commemoration of the tercentenary of Camões' death in 1880, when they began to complain of the failure of the Regenerators to defend Portuguese rights in Africa. King Luis' role as constitutional monarch exposed him to accusations of indifference: he died in October 1889, and was succeeded by his son, Dom Carlos, then thirty. In the same year, Brazil expelled the Emperor Pedro II and became a republic. This encouraged Portuguese republicans who adopted the 'religion of humanity' or positivism, as enunciated by a minor French thinker, Auguste Comte, in 1842. The Brazilian republic, borrowing recklessly to achieve progress, devalued its currency, reducing the flow of remittances to Portugal.

In 1890, the Ancient Alliance was shaken by Lord Salisbury's Ultimatum, which, though ignored by British historians, remained a wound in Portugal for many years. The dispute about navigation had been transferred from the Congo to the Zambesi. When the Progressists sent an expedition to the disputed area, Salisbury delivered his Ultimatum demanding Portuguese withdrawal, instead of negotiating, precipitating a crisis in Portugal, for which the republicans blamed the young king who was in no way responsible. The British Ultimatum was followed a year later by an attempt at a republican revolution in Oporto. It was easily suppressed, but the republicans trained their sights on King Carlos, who with his elder son, was assassinated by anarchists in the Terreiro do Paço in 1908. The younger son Manuel II ruled for two years, but the monarchist politicians were too divided and discredited to save the regime, which fell to a republican revolution in October 1910.

The republic adopted a new flag, anthem and currency, abolished titles of nobility and created two new universities. King Manuel settled in Twickenham, where he died in 1932. The new regime balanced its budgets for a year or two, but soon relapsed into deficits and loans. Portugal participated in the war of 1914 to 1918, sending a division to Flanders. It is a land of war-memorials; various towns have their 'Ruas dos Combatentes' in honour of those who fought. Had the war been lost, Portugal would have forfeited her share of Africa. The socialists were now Africanists, whereas in most countries the parties of the left were 'anti-colonial'. The 'effective occupation' of Portuguese Africa was completed, and much was done to develop the potential wealth of Angola. But in the confusion of the post-war period, the republican movement was divided and its governments were as unstable and debt-ridden as those of the past. Spain, which had remained neutral, was ravaged by anarchism, but Portugal preferred more orthodox forms of socialism. The prevailing atmosphere of intrigue, ineptitude and violence was curbed in May 1926, when General Gomes da Costa proclaimed the situation untenable, removed the President and dissolved *cortes*. He was soon replaced by General Carmona, who was elected President in March 1928 and re-elected in 1935 and 1942. The financial situation required a further loan, which the League of Nations would provide only if given power to control the finances. This was repugnant, and led instead to the appointment of Dr António Salazar, a lecturer in economics at Coimbra, as Minister of Finance with full control of expenditure. He presented a balanced budget, and was made Prime Minister in 1932, repeating his performance annually until 1968, when he was obliged by a stroke to retire.

In his New State, Dr Salazar attributed the problems of Portugal to its professional politicians: he thought that a stable economy, with a balanced budget and surplusses prudently invested in industry, communications, education and other essentials, would lead to political stability. Cortes were replaced by a National Assembly in which the National Union would supplant political parties. The syndical organisation was fitted into a corporate system, which included employers and workers, with government mediation. The French 'Popular Front', imitated in Spain, plunged the neighbouring country into civil war from 1936 to 1938. Dr Salazar sympathised with the rising against the communist-dominated Spanish republic. In the War of 1939, he maintained a difficult neutrality, fencing off Hitler's attempts to intimidate or coerce the Iberian states. The Portuguese railways subsisted without coal, there was little petrol, and the supply of food was controlled. In the later stages of the war, Portugal granted the Allies the use of the Azores as an air-base under the Anglo-Portuguese Alliance. Competition for wolfram at inflated prices brought Portugal a modest affluence. Ancient buildings were restored, to the benefit of tourism, which, as in Spain, became a major activity. One of the most important windfalls for Portugal was the Gulbenkian Foundation: the estate of Calouste Gulbenkian, who owned five percent of Iraqi oil-production and died in a Lisbon hotel in 1955. His art collection is second only to the Janelas Verdes, and his fortune supports art, education and other activities on a scale unknown since John V.

Dr Salazar was often considered a dictator, though he could have been dismissed by the president at any time and had no inclination to become head of state. His policy of preserving a united, larger Portugal, including all the overseas possessions, was severely jolted in December 1961 by the Indian invasion of Goa. It caused little stir outside Portugal, but quickly led to the formation of independence-movements in Portuguese Africa, mainly communist-inspired and with roots in France and elsewhere. Portuguese Guinea was easily infiltrated from its French neighbour, while in Angola there emerged three movements: the half-castes of Luanda adopted Marxism, a Baptist enclave in the Congo looked towards the United States and the largest native people, the Ovambo, adhered to the Union for the Total Independence of Angola or UNITA. For Dr Salazar the demands of these disparate groups offered no basis for negotiation and he decided to stay.

He himself was incapacitated in 1968, when President Tomás asked Dr Marcelo Caetano to form a government. Caetano had been a theorist of the New State but foresaw the need for reform and now attempted to open the economy and to admit less dogmatic members to the National Assembly. The war-effort in Angola made for ever-increasing demands on the national budget and Dr Caetano found himself on narrowing ground. The long eclipse of the socialists permitted them to shift from zealous champions of colonialism, which had brought down the monarchy, towards 'anti-colonialism'. The continuance of the war in Africa upset the bureaucratic tradition of advancement in the army and called for more rapid and general promotion. The crucial moment now appears to be that when communist Russia and the United States voted together for the first time to declare Angola a 'threat to peace'. Arms were poured into the hands of rival groups and Cuba stood in for Russia as a supplier of men. However, the crunch came in Guinea, where the former governor, General Spínola, concluded that there was no other solution except negotiation. Some younger officers, attracted by Marxist dogma, took a similar line and in September 1973 formed the so-called Armed Forces Movement, the MFA, in Portugal. It soon collected a body of adherents under the leadership of men who had served in Guinea. It met with no opposition from the chief of general staff, Costa Gomes. He was joined by General Spínola, who was no Marxist but was about to publish a book to show that any solution must be political. In March 1974, Dr Caetano replaced both men, thus precipitating a small attempt at a coup which failed. It was soon followed by the revolution of April 1974, when the Armed Forces Movement occupied Lisbon with tanks and carriers, and President Tomás and Dr Caetano were expelled to Madeira and thence to Brazil.

The revolutionaries adopted as their emblem the red carnation. The communist leader Alvaro Cunhal returned from Czecho-Slovakia and the socialist Mario Soares from Germany. The MFA imposed a Marxist commander, Brigadier Vasco Gonçalves, and set up a domestic striking-force under the command of Otelo Saraiva de Carvalho, a young officer back from Guinea. General Spínola's idea of a federation with the colonies was soon thrust aside in favour of unconditional independence. Banks, insurance companies and large industries were seized, and the large estates in the Alentejo were handed over to workers' activists. Their incapacity to produce food led to a crisis that took some years to resolve. Attempts to 'cleanse' the civil service were resisted, and it was the influence of the bureaucrats that brought out the ineptitude of the system. Crude attempts by agitators in uniform aroused the opposition of the countryside in the north. In 1975, the striking-force was disbanded and the MFA reduced to a less active role. The Constituent Assembly declared Portugal a socialist state in April 1976.

General Costa Gomes, elected president of the republic, oversaw the abandonment of the former colonies, which led to the return of thousands of former emigrants, the *retornados*, and their families. They came largely from Angola, which lapsed into a civil war that continued intermittently for a quarter of a century until the assassination of Jonas Savimbi and his family. The refugees were accommodated in tourist hotels requisitioned to house them. In June 1976, Costa Gomes retired and was promoted marshal. He was followed by General Eanes who pursued a more moderate and firmer policy. The tourist industry had failed, and by the end of 1977, there was extensive unemployment.

The carnation revolution had been welcomed effusively in Lisbon after the preoccupations of the war years. It was the work of a minority and found the opposition in disarray. In January 1980, the Democratic Alliance of Sr Sá Carneiro formed a majority, though it was still saddled with the military council which could exercise a veto, and could not muster sufficient strength to amend the constitution. On the eve of the presidential elections of December 1980, Sá Carneiro was killed in an aeroplane crash. His successor Sr Balsemão was defeated by the Socialists of Mário Soares and it was not until 1989 that it became possible to amend the constitution. Already in 1985, a more moderate regime under Sr Cavaco Silva had privatised some seventy enterprises seized by the state. The communists had been reduced to a small number of constituencies in which they were entrenched. In much of the south, the Socialists prevailed, while the north inclined towards conservative positions.

Although Dr Salazar had provided Portugal with considerable reserves of gold, the prospect of intermittent insolvency, which had overshadowed Portugal until he applied drastic remedies, now reasserted itself. The formation of a new European block, under the aegis of France in alliance with Germany and pledged to an economic equalisation of western Europe, presented itself as the most viable immediate prospect. Following the failure of British attempts to form a peripheral combination, Portugal applied for entry into the European community, and after some delay was admitted to membership in 1986. This was during the premiership of Dr Mário Soares and was opposed only by the Communist Party, now in full retreat. Dr Soares became the first civilian to be elected to the presidency of the republic since 1925. The application to join had been lodged in 1977 and was followed by prolonged negotiations, which involved the simultaneous entry of Spain. Relations with Spain had not been easy after the April revolution but, on the death of General Franco, the Spanish monarchy had been peacefully restored in the person of King Juan Carlos, and the central authority was relaxed to placate the linguistic minorities. Both countries had heavily devalued currencies, still insufficiently doctored by the growth of tourism. In 1993, an agreement was reached by which the land-frontiers were thrown open and travellers could pass freely between the two countries. In Spain, the monarchy was a better guarantee of independence than a written constitution, and both countries could boast of internal stability, marred only by acts of terrorism in Spain perpetrated in the name of the Basques.

For Portugal, the material benefits of joining the European Community were considerable. She acquired a system of motorways, paid for by tolls, a modern train service (after the closure of lines thought unremunerative), and an array of telephones, television and computers. An extensive building programme provided some remedy for unemployment and gave work to many Africans, particularly from the Cape Verde Islands. The Adjacent Islands were accorded limited autonomy, and Madeira benefitted from the visits of numerous Scandinavians. Much tourist investment was concentrated on the Algarve, where the airport of Faro became busier than that of Oporto. The slowing down of emigration for work in northern Europe and the application of industrial methods to agriculture led to a movement away from the land, not only towards the two great cities but also towards smaller places, particularly in the north, where villages became towns and towns developed into cities with shopping streets, high-rise buildings and lots for the sale of cars. The religious flocked to Fátima, which became a sizeable town. Universities, public or private, sprang up with an all-but English profusion. Day-long television provided *inter alia* a menu of soap operas made in Brazil, and those who could run played football, while those who could not watched it or read about it. These changes were not without cost. They were followed by increasing imports of industrial goods and of foodstuffs, while industry, farming and commerce were exposed to external competition as never before.

The former secretary-general of the socialist party and mayor of Lisbon, Jorge Sampaio, was elected president in 1996 and re-elected for a second term in 2001. The old century was closed with an international commemoration to mark the fifth centenary of Vasco da Gama's opening of the sea-route to India in 1498. It took place on the eastern side of the capital where an extensive area was redeveloped round the new railway station of Oriente, and the Vasco da Gama bridge was built to link Lisbon to the South Bank by a long causeway. Oporto has its new airport named after Sá Carneiro and work was started on the underground system to relieve the city's traffic problems. The grid of international motorways was brought to completion. The delivery of Macau to China completed the programme of colonial withdrawal, while the campaign for autonomy for East Timor was brought to a successful conclusion. Signs of disquiet at the policies of the socialists followed, however, as the moment approached in 2002 for the abandonment of the escudo in favour of the euro. In the parliamentary elections the socialists were defeated by a moderate coalition, which found the national cupboard bare. Yet Portugal retained her capacity for civility and hard work in her enviable natural setting and climate.

3

Before Portugal

There were innumerable generations of inhabitants of Portugal before they recognised themselves as Portuguese, or even Lusitanians, the name given by the Romans to the people of central Portugal. The first Stone Age or Palaeolithic takes us back a hundred millennia, when the present climate and landscape did not yet exist. The range of primitive artefacts, from stone bludgeons to the refined laurel-leaf blade, can be seen in the Museum of Archaeology and Ethnography at Belém and in numerous local collections. Although Portuguese archaeology goes back to 1865, new sites are constantly being revealed. A project for a hydroelectric scheme in the valley of the river Coa, an affluent of the Douro, was halted because of the discovery of scrawled drawings on the flat rock. The preservation of this ancient art became a question of national concern, and the small town of Vila Nova de Fozcoa acquired a tourist attraction it previously lacked.

The existence in Portugal of cave-paintings of the Magdalenian age, like those of Altamira in Northern Spain and Lascaux in southern France, was unknown until 1963, when the caverns at Santiago do Escoural, near Montemór o Novo in the Alentejo, were explored. These underground galleries have fourteen sketches of animals and humans, supposedly done in about 15000 BC. Most of Portugal escaped the rigours of the last glaciation, and the drawings at Escoural do not reveal any sign of the despair at the disappearance of the reindeer and cold-weather fauna which it is possible to read into the art of Altamira. To the amateur eye they resemble the drawings at Fozcoa made in the light of day, when men had abandoned the life of the caves, and drew in the open on flat surfaces eroded by the small river. In the period between 8000 and 7000 BC, the valleys of the Tagus and Sado to its south were frequented by men who hunted and also gathered shellfish on the shore. The middens were noticed in 1865, and those at Flor da Beira in 1935, with others on the Sado. They are mounds of discarded shells, which also contain the bones of animals and human beings. Some three hundred skeletons have been found, pointing to continuous rather than dense occupation. The former owners of the bones dwelt in the open or behind wind-breaks or rock-shelters: they decorated themselves with perforated sea-shells. There is evidence of similar settlement on the Mondego.

The New Stone Age or Neolithic refers in Portugal to the sixth to the third millennia before Christ. It brought agriculture and the domestication of animals, the use of pottery as well as the use of boats, already known in the eastern Mediterranean. The sites are numerous and scattered. The caves at Escoural have produced plain pottery as well as the cardial, decorated with patterns made by the sea-shell from which it takes its name. It occurs on the coast from Sagres to the Mondego. The mild climate of the west favoured primitive agriculture more than the extremes of the central meseta. There is some concentration of sites in the interior of the modern Alentejo and in the Lisbon peninsula.

What the traveller is most likely to observe are megaliths, large single stones or groups erected from the fourth to the second millennia. A single stone is known by the Celtic term menhir: a group makes a dolmen. The Portuguese place-name 'anta' corresponds roughly to a dolmen and may be a rock-shelter, a passage-grave or a single stone. The dolmens are sometimes called 'orcas', first noted in 1734. They may bear geometrical patterns and sometimes human figures. Single menhirs are neither so large nor so numerous as in Brittany, but the blocks of stone attain enormous size, and were transported over long distances. They imply much manpower employed over a long period. Four *orcas* found at Satão near Viseu in 1896 include one showing a hunter apparently lassoing a deer or goat. A menhir at Outeiro, near Reguengos de Monsaraz, is nearly twenty feet high and is estimated to weigh eight tons. Another, at Abelhoa, Reguengos, incised, but now fallen, was about twelve feet. They are fairly frequent in the vicinity of Évora. Cromlechs, or rings of menhirs, supposedly for tribal gatherings or rituals, were discovered as recently as 1964, at Almendres, Évora. This is a collection of 95 stones of different sizes, about two yards apart, arranged in an oval. Another at Portela de Mogos, some eight miles away, has 36 stones in an irregular oval. Passage-graves consisting of a round half-buried chamber entered by a trench or passage lined with slabs appear to have reached the Alentejo from southeastern Spain. A few occur in the Algarve, but there are more in the centre: at Palmela, south of Lisbon, there is a group of four, and at Estoril (Alapraia, Cascais) four more, with others at Sintra, some of them now lost. The beehive hut or *tholos*, a round chamber with a corridor entrance and adobe roof, is represented by 26 examples, two from the Algarve and the rest from the Alentejo and Lisbon area.

In the third millennium BC, navigators from the Mediterranean had settled on the southern coast of the Peninsula, coming in search of metals, particularly copper and gold. They built defended settlements placed on hills near the sea or river, but a little inland. There is a cluster of about a dozen in the region of Torres Vedras. It is possible that the oldest city in Portugal (though no proof can be expected) is near the village of Vila Nova de São Pedro, on the north side of the Tagus between Lisbon and Santarém. When I first saw it, it had been lately excavated in 1961, but by 2001 it was much overgrown with many spring flowers. It stands on a hill with extensive views over the rolling valleys and is ringed by a solid dry-stone wall, with ten semicircular bastions, of which half have been destroyed. It has yielded three small statuettes, fragments of bell-beakers and a potter's kiln with crushed pots beside it. There are plentiful signs of agriculture: querns, sickles, hoes, and traces of wheat and beans. There are clay loom-weights and combs, and a button, but little sign of metalworking except a pile of copper ore. The early bell-beakers suggest a date of 2000 BC. The use of bronze for axe-heads is controversial, but brings us close to 1000 BC.

At this point a use was found for iron, to the great relief of shipbuilders, foresters and those who were ambitious to rule, as mentioned by Homer. It must have travelled fast, aided by the Celtic migrations. Until about 750 BC, Iberian founders continued to forge their wares in bronze. Carved stone stelas from Beja depict the sword with scabbard and belt and what appears to be an anchor hanging from a rope. Others show the round bronze shield and helmet considered typical of Lusitanian warriors. The Celts, arriving by land from central Europe in waves, differed from all previous immigrants. Others had been single merchants or small groups who arrived in the south, probably by sea. The Celts came in bands if not tribes, bringing their families and flocks. They entered by the eastern Pyrenees and fanned out, following the course of the Douro, since travellers never ventured far from water, to the northwest, where they imposed themselves on the indigenous peoples. The intermingling is not consistent. It may have begun in the eighth century, but the prevalence of Celtic toponyms and the establishment of the hill-top *castros*, of which many are known and which distinguish the north-west, place it in about 500 BC. They continued to be occupied in Roman times, and the names applied by the Romans have led us to believe that the Celtic component was large in comparison to the indigenous. This may not be the case. Meanwhile, the south had cities, which responded to the influence of the Phoenicians, who, having vanquished the Greeks in Sicily in 535 BC, excluded their rivals from the Straits of Gibraltar and stimulated the emergence of urban communities. The chief was the empire of the Turdetani at Tartessos or Tarshish in the neighbourhood of Seville near the Phoenician emporium of Gades or Cádiz. The coastal ports and fisheries of southern Portugal, Balsa (Tavira) and Ossonoba (Faro) in the Algarve, Salacia (Alcácer do Sal), Olissippo (Lisbon), and the cities of the interior, Beja and Évora, together with Mértola on the Guadiana, fell in the zone of Punic influence. The Punic merchants or their agents probably knew what we now call central Portugal.

The passage from pre-history to history is marked by man's ability to record the sounds he utters. Herodotus says that the first Greek to reach the Iberian Peninsula was Colaios of Samos: if so, he picked up the word Iberia from the river Ebro and applied it, however inexactly, to the whole Peninsula. But the first to write in the Peninsula itself were the Tartessians, who used a modified form of Phoenician script: a stone from near Almodóvar, on a stream that flows into the Guadiana at Mértola, has a sketch of a person inset in an inscription in Punic letters, which can be read but not understood. Such memorials are probably related to the evolution from collective to individual burials. The shrine at Garvão near Ourique has revealed a large array of pots, together with strips of worked gold and silver probably brought as votive offerings by pilgrims: it is ascribed to the third century BC or shortly before the Roman conquest of Carthage. Another shrine, which was in use long after the Romans had subdued the area, is that of Endovelicus at São Miguel da Mota at Terena, Alandroal, which has preserved some forty pieces of statuary in Roman style, many of them fragmentary, but including an excellent figure of Endovelicus himself. He carries a staff, and is considered a god of medicine: he was perhaps a hero of the Lusitanians, like the rebel Viriatus, revered long after Augustus had made Lusitania the name of a Roman province.

In the north, the great *citânias* or hill-top cities, were also iron-age settlements which remained in use after the Roman conquest. Of the many *castros* which are concentrated in the north-west, much the largest is the *citânia* of Briteiros between Braga and Guimarães. It has two hundred huts, mostly round, but some rectangular, with outhouses, and partly arranged in streets. It is surrounded by three circuits of walls, too low to be effectively defended against an enemy, and large in relation to the probable size of the population, but perhaps sufficient to protect flocks or herds from thieves or wolves. The small *citânia* of Sanfins, not far away, appears to be less roman-ised. Possibly Briteiros provided labour for the cluster of Roman villas that appeared round Braga, forming the nucleus for the city and the seat of the Suevic monarchy, which lasted from c. 410 to 585 AD.

One of the proto-historical features of Trás-os-Montes is the *berrões*, or granite figures of pigs, of which the best known is the Porca de Murça, which stands in the middle of the town and is used to advertise its wine. Although called the Porca, or Sow, its status as a Boar is easily recognisable. It is not unique; in 1974 J R Santos was able to trace some forty, more than half in Trás-os-Montes, including the 'town pig' in Bragança, and a dozen in Zamora in Spain. They are akin to the Spanish *verracos*, figures of cattle found in Spanish Extremadura. The animals are types that may be wild or may be domesticated. The boars are often shown with tusks and a dorsal hairline. The carvings show considerable craftsmanship. One has been found in the middle of a small circular pit entered from a stone-lined channel, like a beehive hut. Another is associated with a Roman coin of the fourth century AD, when the ability to work granite accurately was known. The probability is that the figures were made when most boars were wild, but that the possibility of domestication was also being realised. In the *Odyssey*, a millennium BC, the pig-man Eumaeus kept the royal sows fifty apiece in twelve pens, while the boars slept outside, and accompanied them when taken to graze. The king feasted passing heroes on pork.

The numerous representations of native warriors with helmets, plastrons or padded coats, and round shields, come from the north. Those who go in search of the famous Lusitanians will look in vain for a *civitas*. They were more than a simple tribe with one tribe-stead. They were warriors who fought their battles with the Romans in distant Andalusia and did not hesitate to follow leaders named Punicus and Caesarus, demonstrating that they knew of Punic and Roman military practice. Nor were they completely illiterate, but left a very small number of inscriptions in Roman script. Perhaps these refer to barbaric gods, but no single shrine has appeared like that of Endovelicus in the Alentejo. They could hardly have overcome legions if they did not have the gift for rousing other peoples to defend their freedom. When Augustus bestowed the name of Lusitania on a vast area, it was not to commemorate his recent victories in the Asturias and Cantabria, but the epic campaigns of Caesar against Pompey: the Lusitanians were still sufficiently organised to offer their services to the Roman commander Sertorius, who was murdered in 72 BC.

When the Romans defeated Carthage in BC 202, they took over what they called Ulterior, the Further Province, on which they were to confer, in the course of time, their laws and customs, and finally their religion. Their great monument is the lan-guage. In the sixteenth century, it was still possible to compose a sonnet that might be read either as Latin or as Portuguese. In 1947, when the Duke of Palmela was granted an honorary degree at Cambridge, the Public Orator delivered a couple of lines that were both Latin and Portuguese; he went no further. Modern Portuguese still uses the vocative case. British children learning Latin may have wondered why the Romans should address a table as '*O mensa*', though they probably accept Shakespeare when Caesar cries '*Et tu Brute!*'. To educated Portuguese, to call anyone '*O José*' sounds polite, but a bare '*José*' is brusque or peremptory, – or so my elderly mentor in Coimbra taught me.

Rome's second gift was a landscape cultivated with the vine, the olive and wheat. The cities have been constantly rebuilt. Lisbon, or Olissippo, was on the site of an indigenous *oppidum*, probably the Castle of St George. Vestiges of Roman temples have appeared between this high point and the Baixa. A *cryptoporticus*, covered galleries for shops and storage, stood on a corner of the present Rua da Prata, and a theatre, found after the Earthquake of 1755, was built over but partially recovered when the concealing construction was demolished in 1961. It remains in the Rua de São Mamede, and has yielded an inscription of the time of Nero. In 1981, traces of a tank for fish-curing were found in the Rua dos Bacalhoeiros. Similar plants were built in Carthaginian times along the coasts of the Peninsula and North Africa. Mosaics and other remains are preserved in the Museum at Belém.

Outside Lisbon, the principal monuments from Roman times may be briefly summarised. The best known is the temple at Évora, often called 'of Diana', but probably related to the cult of the Emperors in the second century. The most completely excavated Roman town is Conimbriga, which gave its name to Coimbra: it is now Condeixa, some ten miles to the south. Once a Celtic village on a tongue of land, it became a comfortable *oppidum* with an elaborate water-system, a forum, shops and temples; the excavation still proceeds. Not far away, in Coimbra itself, the Museum of Machado de Castro is built over the large *cryptoporticus*, rectangular compartments of massive stone on a scale sufficient to supply a large garrison and accessible from the Museum. Adjoining the city of Viseu is the so-called 'Cave of Viriatus', an octagonal walled camp: it has yielded only one coin of 41 BC. The greatest Roman bridge is that at Chaves, which crosses the Tâmega and is still in use: it has inscriptions of 79 and 104 AD with the names of the ten neighbouring peoples who collaborated with the Seventh Legion in building it. At Belmonte, near the Serra da Estrela, there is part of a large square building, whose purpose is not known. Idanha a Velha, the ancient Egitania, was a garrison town and preserves an arch and part of the walls, as well as an early Christian basilica. There are also arches at Bobadela (Oliveira do Hospital), Évora and Beja. Braga was fully walled in the middle ages, but now only sections remain. Part of the outer wall of Évora exists and Braga has the 'Fonte do Idolo', dedicated to a pre-Roman deity by a donor with a Roman name.

The Romans entered Ulterior from the south and, apart from mining operations which required roads and bridges and were perhaps not so profitable to the miners as to the state, the main sources of wealth, whether from agriculture or trade and fishing, were south of the Tagus. In the Algarve, Milreu, at Estoi, was the centre of a vast estate: part of the plan survives, together with the apse of a large Christian basilica of Byzantine times.

Myrtilis, now Mértola, has its Roman section, and was the port on the Guadiana for the large *villae* of the lower Alentejo. The best preserved of these is at Pisões, a few miles from Beja. The copper-mines at Aljustrel were important: the inscription recording their regulation is now at Belém. Miróbriga, beside Santiago de Cacém, had a fine acropolis with two temples, streets, shops and the only circus found in Portugal. Salacia, now Alcácer do Sal, on the Sado, was an important port, referred to by Pliny as 'imperial city', and was perhaps more prosperous than Lisbon. Setúbal was probably Caetobriga. The site of Troia on a spit of sand was an offshoot of Salacia: in 1850 it still had houses with the ground floor intact, as well as fish-tanks, a cemetery and the remains of a Christian church of the fourth or fifth century. Much has been lost to the encroaching sand.

A very rough test of Romanisation is provided by mosaics, which were often installed by owners of *villae* or estates. Some 168 are recorded: of these, 21 are from the coast of the Algarve; 55 from the upper Alentejo between Beja and Évora, and from the Tagus; some 20 are from Lisbon and the area between Alcobaça and Tomar; and only ten from Braga and the valley of the Douro. The only large Roman city in Roman Lusitania was its capital Mérida, founded by Augustus and now in Spain, having been deserted in Muslim times.

Roman Ulterior consisted of the Carthaginian south, with the ports of Ossonoba (Faro), Myrtilis, and the Atlantic coast. The characteristic Phoenician and Roman fish-tanks are found at Miróbriga, Tróia, Salacia and Lisbon, but not apparently further north. There the Celts built or took over the hill-top forts called *castros*, which abound in northern Portugal and Spanish Galicia. There were also Celtic groups in the Algarve and at Miróbriga and perhaps Évora. The war-like Celts alternately raided the southern cities and served them as mercenaries. The Phoenicians had traded in the interior and recruited men from the tribes. The only remaining evidence of the earliest Roman occupation may be a group of small forts or command-posts near Beja. Serious warfare, north of the Tagus, with Viriatus and his troops, began in 159 BC and lasted ten years. Viriatus became the prototype of the hero of national independence, but was killed by treachery.

In 137, Decius Junius Brutus marched northward through central Portugal, crossed the Douro and reached the Lima, which his men would not pass until he went first, believing it to be the Lethe, from which no man returns. The Roman general continued north and fought a battle that earned him the title of Callaecus, the Galician, a name later applied to the whole area north of the Douro. Thereafter, the Romans held the south securely, the centre less firmly and the north tenuously. They may have used the port of Salacia and concentrated their troops at Morón, at or near Santarém, which they knew as Scallabis. The vast camp at Viseu may be of early date. The first historical figure of note to visit both Portugal and Britain was Julius Caesar, who collected enough tribute to buy his way to the consulate. He pursued the natives to an island off the coast, which may have been the salt-marshes of Aveiro. He or his family conferred the titles of Liberalitas Julia on Évora and Felicitas Julia on Lisbon.

The completion of the Roman conquest was the work of Augustus, who waged the Cantabrian Wars and founded Mérida as the capital of the province of Lusitania to reward his veterans in 26 to 13 BC. It was perhaps the only large settlement of Romans, and became the only great monumental city in Ulterior, with a full range of Roman constructions. From collecting tribute, the Romans passed on to the stage of controlling the whole country and using the army to impose order. The Seventh Legion was raised by Galba and placed at Leon, where it had its own land and peasantry and was steadily Hispanised. The army built roads and bridges and conducted mining operations on a large scale. Gold was obtained from quartzite in a belt extending from near Oporto to the Cantabrian coast. At Jales and Três Minas in Trás-os-Montes vast quantities of earth were shifted. Roads, bridges and milestones, some dedicated to Jupiter, are numerous, but the evidence of Roman leisure, theatres, circuses, hippodromes, temples and civic ostentation, is slight. Aqueducts were scarcely needed, but mosaics and funereal slabs are few. The ancient *citânias* show evidence of continued occupation into Roman times. For Pliny, writing before AD 79, places north of the river Vouga were still tribal territory: Conimbriga was a Roman town, and Aeminium, the present

Coimbra, a forward post of Romanisation. The treasure from the north was probably conveyed to Mérida and Seville by a road which avoided the mountains of Northern Portugal. There was much mining activity for less prized metals in the mountainous area of Beira. The regulations for the copper mine at Aljustrel in the Alentejo are dated 117 to 138 AD.

The temple at Évora was of rectangular shape on an elevated platform with twenty-six columns, of which half still stand. The city walls can be traced and show the modest dimensions of a provincial capital. Its beauty is enhanced by the view over olive-groves and wheat-fields and the distant mountains. The remains of Conimbriga, now Condeixa, of roughly the same period, point rather to a comfortable *oppidum* for town-dwellers. In the Alentejo there are remains of numerous *villae*. That at Torre da Palma had mosaics showing the family's horses with their pet names: they are now at Belém. The *villa* of the Atilia family at Pisões, Beja, had spacious rooms decorated with marble and mosaics and the usual conveniences for bathing in hot and cold water. The estate at Milreu has mosaics on maritime themes, which were frequent.

In the nineteenth century, it was believed that Rome was the model city-state, which conferred its system of government on municipalities far and wide, and even that these *municipia* were the origin of the medieval *concelhos*. It does not now seem likely that Rome conquered the Iberian Peninsula with the object of founding *municipia*. The Romans came for wealth and land, and those who settled set up the form of government to which they were accustomed, allowing the tribes to manage their affairs, or have them managed in *conventus*, administrative centres to co-ordinate tribal interests. In the north, these were never superseded. The last province to be formed was the Antonine New Province of Gallaecia, which dates from c. 210 to c. 220. It consisted of three *conventus*, each with its local capital, of which Braga came to be the chief administrative centre. The border between it and Lusitania was the river Douro.

By the end of the third century, the emperors were no longer Hadrians and Trajans, but generals who subordinated the empire to their armies with the complaisance of the wealthy senators. The remoter provinces were neglected and disappear from view: in 175 AD, the governor of Lusitania was honoured for resisting an invasion from Africa, of which nothing is known. In 261, Franks and Germans sacked Tarragona in eastern Spain and reached Africa: the scare caused some to bury their treasure, but did not lead to any general erection of fortifications. Large landowners had their own armed guards, who warded off bandits and kept peasants down. Municipal office, once regarded as the foundation of freedom, was made compulsory. The imperial cult can have been no more than a formality. The strange altars at Panoias in Trás-os-Montes were for some oriental cult of a barbarous nature.

The emergence of Christianity from the state of persecution took place at the beginning of the fourth century with the conversion of the Emperor Constantine I. The first known bishop of Lisbon was one Potamius, in 357: like Constantine, he had adopted the Arian version, later considered heretical. Braga had a bishop named Paternus at the end of the century. Braga became the seat of religious orthodoxy: it still occupies a special place in Portuguese religious life. It is not now possible to identify the earliest surviving Christian church in Portugal, perhaps the small building at Troia, or the large structures that remain at Idanha and Milreu, or even a chapel on one of the *villae*. Although Portuguese cities like to trace their origins to Roman *municipia*, these civic bodies had been crushed by taxation and other pressures.

Defensive walls, not monuments, were the order of the day. Among the walled cities of Portugal were Évora, Beja, Santarém, Coimbra, Viseu, Oporto, Braga and Chaves. Some were rebuilt in the middle ages and all were later reduced to only small sections: the only remaining complete Roman circuit is at Lugo in Spanish Galicia.

The founder of the last imperial dynasty was Theodosius, a Gallaecus, who made Christianity the only legal religion throughout the empire: he died in Milan in 395. Braga was engaged in imposing orthodoxy in the west when the Rhineland frontier collapsed in December 406. A stream of Vandals ran riot in the south and in 430 crossed into Africa, where they founded a kingdom at Carthage. In the confusion, the Suevi, German peasant farmers from the Elbe, were settled in the districts of Braga and Oporto, where they built their 'new castle' on the site of the present city. They were the only ones of these groups who remained permanently in the land assigned to them. Like other barbarians, they avoided cities, unless to sack them, and built their royal hall at Dume, the seat of a former villa outside Braga. The only cluster of Germanic place-names in the Iberian Peninsula is confined to Braga and Oporto, the present Minho. Their kingdom lasted 170 years, but they vanish from view from 465 until about 550, during which period not even the names of their kings are known. They were pagans, but adopted Arian Christianity when the Goths became their neighbours in Spain.

Although Rome ceased to govern in 450, when the last of the line of Theodosius was assassinated, the Eastern Empire of Byzantium recovered North Africa in 535 and sent priests and merchants into the Peninsula. The conversion of the Suevic monarchy was accomplished by St Martin, a Pannonian, who built his abbey at the royal site of Dume. He introduced the monasticism of the Desert Fathers, and when he died in 579, left thirteen dioceses, divided into two synods, one for the Suevic kingdom and the other for Lugo and Galicia. The Sueves had annexed part of Roman Lusitania between the Douro and the Tagus, though not Santarém or Lisbon. North of the Minho their influence extended only to the district of Tuy. Their kingdom thus broke down the old Roman boundaries and largely foreshadows the modern Portugal.

The monarchy of the Sueves was overthrown by the Goths in 585, and the dioceses south of the Douro were returned to Lusitania, but this change was soon followed by the Islamic invasions of 711, which put an end to the Gothic kingdom of Toledo.

4

Islamic Portugal

The sudden collapse of the Spanish Goths in AD 711 arose from their own dissensions and from the dynamic expansion of Islam, which had conquered Egypt in 642, been held for a time at Carthage, and then at a bound reached the Straits of Gibraltar, reducing Eastern Rome, the Byzantine Empire, to a shadow of itself. The Greeks had occupied North Africa for less than two centuries and had revived the western church both in Lusitania and in the Suevic kingdom of Braga. They had been driven out by the Goths before 615, but rarely regarded the rulers of the west as anything more than a barbarian division of the Roman army that had seized power and perpetuated itself. The Gothic kings of Toledo lived in some state, but they and their nobles were no better landlords than the absentee Roman senatorial order they had replaced, and were much closer at hand. A faction seeking to overthrow Roderic, 'the last of the Goths', sought aid from North Africa. The first invasion, of Berbers, killed Roderic and seized Toledo and its treasure: the second, of Arabs, occupied Seville and overcame the last resistance at Mérida. The two Muslim forces then joined and toured the provinces, receiving the capitulation of governors and counts: it is supposed that they reached Portugal and Galicia before being recalled to Damascus, but the evidence is slight. The caliph in Baghdad had not authorised a permanent occupation, and could hardly have envisaged that his successors would continue to govern in Portugal until about 1245, and in Spain until the fall of Granada in 1492. The difference is significant. We cannot expect to find an Alhambra or a Generalife in Portugal because the Christian Reconquest had been completed there before the Nasrid kingdom of Granada was founded. The only Portuguese province with an Arabic name is the Algarve. To northerners it is the deep south, but from an Arabic orientation it was the far west. The *garb* is the sunset and is also the name of Morocco, the Magrib.

At first, the invaders did not much care about the north-west, but thought of pursuing the conquest into Gaul. They formed a 'military colony', which made use of the Gothic faction that had brought them, but did not restore the monarchy. Many of the conquering Berbers returned to Africa. The only large group of Arabs to settle in southern Portugal was the contingent from Egypt, which was divided between the Algarve and Murcia – itself a word derived from Misr, the name for Egypt. They were assigned farmsteads, the Roman *villae*, and were required to appear when mustered to receive the caliph's pay. In 754, the military governors gave way to a prince of the deposed caliphal house of the Ummaiyads: he set up a dissident kingdom which rejected the new rulers of Baghdad and, though his reign was marked by numerous revolts, began the process of introducing the style of life familiar to his dynasty in Syria. Its symbol was the palm-tree, but it comprehended a whole system of agriculture, the fig, orange, lemon, almond, asparagus, egg-plant and the method of irrigation and water-tenure that goes with them. Roman agriculture was reformed from the ground.

If the records of the Asturian monarchy are sparse and there are no documents of the eighth century from northern Portugal, historians writing in Arabic tend to follow royal campaigns and ignore the provinces, much as the Romans did. The geographers give some account of the land and its products, but follow tradition without regard for actuality. Muslim rule adopted patterns already set: Roman cities became Muslim cities, and the former provincial capitals of Saragossa and Toledo became the fortresses of the frontier. In the case of Lusitania, Mérida was the scene of many upheavals until it was replaced by the Berber garrison town of Badajoz; both are now just outside Portuguese territory. But, under the Ummaiyads of Cordova, administration was in Arabic, and it was not possible to obtain employment, or at least promotion, without a knowledge of the dominant language. Converts adopted Arabic and many who were not converted used Arabic names. The discovery of St James' tomb at Santiago in about 820 provided Galicia with a shrine which influenced the whole Christian Reconquest: the news may have drawn Mahmud ibn al-Jabbar to settle at the crossing of the Douro, the present Mafamude, in 838. A generation later, while Cordova was convulsed in a long *fitna*, Vimara Peres began the reorganisation of Portugal, and Hermenegild Guterres occupied Coimbra. When Cordova recovered, Coimbra was lost again, and in the time of Ramiro II the frontier was at or near Viseu. Behind this area, Muslim territory was divided into *kuras*, townships with their adjacent territories, smaller than Roman provinces, but larger than pre-Roman *civitates*. Muslim campaigns, unless mere raids, were expeditions mounted from Seville or Toledo against the Christian capital of Leon. In the west, there were long periods of relative tranquillity during which the 'Moorish way', the *caminho mourisco*, was open to trade. This was broken by the assault of al-Mansur who marched through central Portugal with a fleet from Alcácer do Sal to sack Santiago. He died in 1002, and the caliphate of Cordova was itself extinguished in 1032.

It is with the *taifa* states of the eleventh century that Muslim Portugal begins to take shape. In Coimbra part of the walls remain: they were regularly repaired after the Christian conquest in 1064, but the concept of the *couraça*, an approach up a steep slope under the shadow of the walls to a gate placed on a small platform, is redolent of Muslim practice, and the main gate now called the Arco de Almedina was used by Sisnand Davides. He occupied the palace of the Muslim governors, later replaced by the royal palace and donated to the University.

The Cluniacs and other French clergy succeeded in expunging most signs of Islam and of the old Hispanic church. The only building of the kind to have survived with a minimum of alteration is the church at Mértola, standing on a platform high above the Guadiana. Its altar replaces the *mihrab*, but its general disposition, its slender columns and arches, bear witness to its parentage. An inscription says that it was founded by a Portuguese after the conquest, but this may mean founded as a church. The ruined castle that crowns the hill is mainly of Muslim times, and various inscriptions have been found, one with a date equivalent to 1202 AD.

The most substantial and beautiful of the Muslim relics in Portugal are the walls and gate of Silves, adorning a steep slope above the little river Arade, once navigable, and now reduced to a trickle. It is built of rose-red sandstone and is in effective contrast with the rich green and blossom of the orchards and fields below. The present circuit of walls and massive gate was built or extended to shelter the inhabitants and the country people from round about. The buildings within are levelled to the ground, but their purpose is identifiable and the vast underground cistern would hold water enough to outlast any siege. Silves reached special prominence in the late eleventh century when it was the residence of the princes of the Abbadids of Seville, whence its royal standing. After the collapse of the caliphate of Cordova, the secretaries sought service with the *taifa*–princes, who competed for the most talented scribes and poets. Their flowery poems proved their command of language, and their works were collected by anthologists, of whom the best was ibn Bassam of Santarém. He had served the rulers of Badajoz and died in 1147, the year of Afonso I's conquest of Lisbon. In Lisbon, ibn Muqana liked to watch the sun rise as the Pleiades sank below the horizon like a spray of jasmine in flower, as he mingled his wine with water to drink with his noble friends before the muezzin chanted his 'God is great'. The aesthetic sense extends to places. Silves was a nostalgic memory to the poet king of Seville, al-Mu'tamid, who recalled the beauty of its castle, the Palace of the Varandas and its pleasures, where he had spent his youth. His bosom friend and vizir, ibn Ammar, who was born at Silves, compared its gardens to a flowered dress and its river to a white arm stretched upon a green tunic. The prohibition of wine was evidently not strictly enforced. But ibn Mu'tamid died in miserable exile at Agmat in the Magrib in 1091. He, like the *taifa*-princes of Badajoz, had been dismissed and deposed: those of Badajoz had been summarily assassinated. An austere age had begun. The Almoravids sent members of their royal house to govern the great cities, especially Seville, where their main cavalry was usually based: royal expeditions took long to prepare and were infrequent. A forward force at Badajoz regularly raided Christian territory. The Almoravids soon succumbed to their own dissensions and in 1147 they had already lost the Magrib to a new movement, that of the Almohads. Beja fell to an attack in 1162, and the adventurer Gerald the Fearless took Évora.

Although the tangled streets below the University in Coimbra have an air of antiquity, like the Alfama in Lisbon, they are medieval without much distinction of religion or style. Long after the Reconquest the builders continued to practise procedures they had learnt from their forebears. When Lisbon fell, not all the Muslims left: many artisans and countrypeople stayed behind and became 'free Moors', keeping their own laws and customs. Lisbon has its Mouraria but its aspect has changed completely. Tavira has one, and Beja has a 'street of the Moors'. I had some difficulty finding it until a policeman in a car kindly led the way: it is a line of attached cottages, such as many towns and villages in the Alentejo have. Not all Magribian cities are cramped tangles of streets. It has no single Islamic building, but the shape of the ducal former palace and the hermitage of Santo André built for King Sancho suggest that they were made by hands that had travailed long before in the same way. The foremen had their way of setting up arches and buttresses, which they did not quickly abandon. The museum at Beja has a rich and varied collection, but few inscriptions in Arabic: the language was easier to expunge than habits of craftsmanship. The fine geometrical coloured tiles called 'mourisco' are rather the result of a revival of an older industry, which King Manuel I is thought to have brought from Seville. The little town of Olhão in the Algarve with its white-washed boxes of houses has all the appearance of a set for an oriental film. Yet its history seems to go back only to 1695, when a band of independent-minded deep-sea fishermen built their own parish church amidst their cabins and boatyards. Its name is Latin, derived from *oculus* in the sense of a spring of fresh water. Loulé, north of Faro, looks much less 'mourisco', but its name is the Arabic 'Ulā', or higher, meaning further from the sea.

The last Muslim city to fall was Tavira in the Algarve, which yielded to the Templars in 1242. Many of the inhabitants who could do so fled, but others stayed to become 'free Moors'. Like those of Lisbon, they had their governor, mosque, scribes, school, baths and prison, lived together and went out to work in the fields, paying their own taxes, with a tithe for the king and the obligation to supply him with wine. The 'king' was represented by a group of knights of the Temple or some other order who had not sufficient retainers to work the countryside and had no intention of doing so themselves. The wine was included to ensure that they were supplied. This state of affairs continued until the fifteenth century, when the fall of Constantinople and Eastern Rome to the Turks filled the west with alarm. The destruction of the old communities was a slow process: as late as 1541 fears of collaboration with the Turks led to a prohibition against Muslims dwelling anywhere within range of the sea, though an exception was made for property-owners. The fear was lest the Turks land and mobilise an army: it was probably inspired by trepidation in Spain where the process of assimilation was much less advanced.

Those who were once Mouriscos had children and grandchildren who were Mudéjares, having changed to a greater or lesser degree their language and their religion. The word is naturally commoner in Spain. For some, the Manueline, the most charac-teristic of Portuguese styles, divides into two: that derived from florid Gothic, which is northern, and the *mudéjar*, which is southern with roots in the Alentejo. W C Watson, whose *Portuguese Architecture* was published in 1908, affirmed that the Alentejo had seen no large immigration of Christians, and 'the Moors continued for long in their eastern ways of building and agriculture'. This perhaps overlooks the fact that in King Manuel's day the Portuguese were quite familiar with the Magrib and had no hesitation in adopt-ing forms of defence that seemed useful, such as the corner sentry-box with a pepper-pot top. Pérez Embid in 1955 published a book on Portuguese *mudéjar*, in which he dis-cerned common features in the palace at Sintra, the Loios at Évora, São Francisco, the royal palace of São Brás, Sempre Noiva and private mansions at Évora, Santo André and Santa Maria in Beja, and the castle of Alvito. All these except Sintra are in the Alentejo. He thought them marked by walls of clay or brick rather than granite, turrets with con-ical cupolas, columns rather than pillars, white marble, a lack of heraldic motifs, a var-iety of arches rather than lintels, crenellated parapets and other features. However, none of these structures seems to go further back than 1480, when King Afonso V had waged his wars in the Magrib and begun to receive gold from Guinea which enabled him to look further afield for models.

The residual architectural style of the south, preserved by craftsmen who had been trained in an ancient tradition, is evident in neat rows of attached cottages, white-washed and painted with a low wainscot in a single colour, and in the decorated chim-neys characteristic of the south. This distinguishes the villages from the granite cottages of Beira, or the European detached cottage in its garden of the Minho.

Although Arabic contributed to the vocabulary of place-names and words for objects, implements and articles of dress, its effect on the grammar of Portuguese is small. As styles change, Arabisms tend to diminish. Some words have been revived, such as *albufeira*, now applied to a reservoir, not simply a lagoon. Instead of words, however, the silent language of agriculture speaks, if not volumes, baskets of lemons, oranges, almonds, figs, artichokes and aubergines.

5

Architecture

Architecture is undertaken by those who have the means to engage in it. There are two styles for which Portugal is famous, that called Manueline after King Manuel I, who disposed of great wealth resulting from the opening of trade with the East, and the baroque of John V, which arose from the profusion of Brazilian gold and diamonds in the eighteenth century. Both mingle innovation with forms and practices of the past. It is unwise to look for a purity of style which obeys only some imaginary text-book. Buildings may be secular or ecclesiastic or both. There is a break with the past when rulers and nobles ceased to hold castles or towers and built palaces or mansions. There is no specific moment at which this occurs; King Manuel built the Paços da Ribeira in Lisbon in about 1500, without at once abandoning the castle of St George. Ecclesiastical architecture usually obeys traditional norms, but in a country with limited natural resources the building of a cathedral might take a century. The five great cathedrals of Oporto, Braga, Coimbra, Lisbon and Évora were built on the site of older religious buildings, and may be regarded as making a new start. The great monastic church of St Mary of the Victory at Batalha, near Leiria, one of the finest buildings in Europe, was begun to commemorate the victory of Aljubarrota in 1385 but was extended by the 'chapels' added more than a century later and left 'imperfeitas' or unfinished. In less wealthy places, it was usual to add new fronts to older buildings when need arose and resources permitted. By the eighteenth century, the existing cathedrals and churches could only be decorated, either with tiles or gilded woodwork. This is often described (and dismissed) as 'baroque'. In fact, the enormous palace-monastery of Mafra, perhaps intended to be the largest in Europe, explores a wide range of architectural and artistic possibilities of the age without indulging in either *azulejos* or gilt. It was the work of a south-German named Ludwig, trained in Rome where his name became Ludovice. He seized the golden opportunity to bring together the best available craftsmen. In some ways, Mafra is less 'baroque' than St Paul's in London.

When Queen Tarásia and Count Henry arrived at Guimarães, Portugal was an agrarian county limited to the region of the Minho, incorporating the territory of Coimbra since 1064. Guimarães was a monastery, to which a castle had been added for defence. The castle is a massive keep surrounded by ancillary towers. It was abandoned in the nineteenth century and was in some danger of being demolished for road metal, but is now carefully preserved. On the same site is the palace of the dukes of Guimarães and Bragança, built in the Flemish style of the fourteenth and fifteenth centuries and restored in 1940, perhaps too devotedly, for the double centenary of 1140 and 1640. Guimarães, or Vimaranes, was not a Roman town, but is only fifteen miles from Braga, the capital of Roman Gallaecia, and metropolitanate of the Christian church in 400 AD. Its cathedral was restored by Bishop Pedro and consecrated in 1089. Count Henry brought in Cluniac bishops, St Gerald 1196–09, and Maurice 1109–19, and the present church still follows a Cluniac plan. Perhaps because of its modest resources, it fits into the modern city with a more pastoral air than those of Oporto and Coimbra.

The Minho came to possess some twenty-seven castles, fifteen *torres* or towers (fortified manors), and forty-nine monasteries. Trás-os-Montes also had, or came to have, numerous castles, but having a much smaller population, few monasteries. Castles could be built only with the consent of the ruler, who appointed the *tenens* or governor. They often emerged from *torres*, built as strongholds adjacent to the landowner's manor for defence against invaders. They were granite cubes of two or three storeys with only slits for windows, and entered from a first floor. That of the Silva family overlooking the Minho behind Valença has been restored to make a comfortable dwelling. In the thirteenth century, the monarchy put an end to baronial struggles and King Diniz built castles for the defence of the frontiers, now fixed, or as residences for his nobility. His favourite castle was Leiria, now completely restored. Many of the 'Dionisian' castles were probably rebuilt on existing sites and embellished with open galleries at an upper level, a fashion used in the Muslim south, as in the lost palace of the Varandas at Silves and at Alcácer do Sal. A fine example of the tower, amplified by later galleries or arcades, is Bertiandos, near the roadside east of Viana do Castelo.

The leading families of the county of Portugal were thought by later genealogists to number thirty. They would often possess several scattered estates brought together by conquest, marriage or inheritance, and would be patrons of their own monastic church, or co-patrons with others. The two most prominent clans were the Maias north of Oporto, where there is a 'hill of Maia' but no surviving house, and the Sousas, a small stream in a broad valley east of Oporto. The Paço de Sousa belonged to Egas Moniz, the tutor of Afonso Henriques, who acquired enormous wealth. His tomb is in the adjacent monastery. The building was damaged by fire in 1926, but is now restored. A number of churches in the Minho probably date from the tenth century. The usual (monastic) church was a rectangular stone building, with a single nave separated by a triumphal arch from the sanctuary, lit by arched windows over the nave, and entered from a main western door set in arched columns with greater or less sculpture and surmounted by a rose-window. There were at first no transepts, side-altars, sacristy, choir or pulpit. There might be a narthex for women, and a free-standing bell-tower. After the Cluniac reform and the rebuilding of the cathedrals in grander form, churches were given additional naves and cloisters were added. The addition of a defensive tower or battlements occurs near the coast or rivers. The simpler form survives better in small or remote places. Not far from the Paço de Sousa is Cete, a tenth-century church enlarged for Tarásia and Henry, a long narrow building with a battlemented tower, a massive buttress and rounded apse. Other Romanesque churches are at Meinedo, Vila Boa de Quirós and the tiny church at Boelhe, only twelve yards long but adorned with stone figures and flowers. Roriz, near Santo

Tirso, is dated 1228, when cloisters were usual, but they have disappeared. East of Póvoa de Varzim is São Pedro de Rates, built in about 1110 on the site of an older hermitage: it has an elaborate doorway and a triple nave. Near Barcelos is Vilar de Frades, and south of the Câvado Manhente has a robust square tower for defence. Santa Maria do Abade on the Neiva also has an adjoining defensive tower: it is associated with Mafalda, wife of Afonso Henriques.

In Trás-os-Montes the population was more scattered. If Tarásia and Henry bestowed a charter on Constantim in 1096, it was soon overshadowed by royal Vila Real. The formation of the national frontier enhanced Bragança, only a few miles from the Leonese border. The great castle on the hill, with its street of dependents and suppliers, was extended and restored. Under its shadow is the first monument of civil architecture, the so-called Domus Municipalis or council-house, an irregular granite structure. It is open with round Romanesque arches instead of windows, and dates from c. 1250, though its appearance might suggest ancient Rome.

The cathedral of Oporto, dominating the city from a lofty hill-top, was the largest building in the north when it was begun, and occupied much of the walled city. It was still under construction in 1147, when the army of English and other crusaders put in and joined in the conquest of Lisbon. Its soaring central nave is flanked by two lower naves. It is lit by a large rose-window over a portal of later date.

The cathedral at Coimbra, the Sé Velha, is perhaps the finest Romanesque building in Portugal. The church restored by Sisnand was replaced after the Cluniac takeover and the site of the former mosque was used for the present stern and grand monument designed by French architects in 1160–80. It has a battlemented façade and Romanesque vaulting. The same French architects designed the cathedral of Lisbon, also on the site of the former mosque and begun a decade or more later. It conforms closely to the Romanesque tradition, with two massive side-towers and a large central rose-window.

The fourth of the great cathedrals, that of Évora, which was conquered in 1166, belongs to the following century. Its conical dome, adapted from Poitou and surmounting the crossing, had a prolonged influence in Portugal. It uses pointed arches and is regarded as completing the transition to the Gothic. These great buildings follow the course of the Christian reconquest and draw Portugal into the stream of European architecture. They do not necessarily replace earlier monastic traditions found in numerous Romanesque churches in the Minho.

Afonso Henriques moved his capital to Coimbra, where he built the great monastery of Santa Cruz. It was embellished in the sixteenth century, though rudely suppressed in 1834. It is splendidly refurbished. The great monastic achievement was the Cistercian abbey of Alcobaça, built in 1178, and later given a baroque portico. St Bernard rejected the ostentation of Cluny, and Alcobaça follows the example of Clairvaux in combining majesty with simplicity. Its structure introduces Gothic principles, achieving greater height by raising the piers on corbels. The nave and aisles are of equal height and lit by high windows. The eastern end is an apse with ambulatory and rounded columns set under tall narrow windows. The monastic dependencies are arranged round the church according to Benedictine principles.

Afonso Henriques brought in the Military Orders, beginning with the Templars, who were established at Tomar in 1160. The original round sanctuary or *charola* followed the Holy Sepulchre. Eight pillars carry a two-storeyed drum under a cupola.

King Diniz replaced the Templars with the Order of Christ. The fortress and chapel were extended in the sixteenth century, when the Manueline nave was added. The great cloister built in 1557–66 is the finest example of the high Renaissance in Portugal. Close by is the small church of the Conceição, of about 1530, a basilica of classical design. One of the great later medieval monuments of the north is the head-quarters of the knights of St John or Hospitallers admitted by Tarásia, who granted them an ancient hermitage at Leça do Balio on the small river Leça near Oporto. The present structure dates from about 1350: it continues the Romanesque tradition but uses the pointed arch and Gothic windows. It has the stout side-tower and battle-ments typical of earlier times. The building of castles for defence had now moved south to the Tagus and beyond. The castle of Almourol, built for the Templars on an islet in the Tagus, is a picturesque ruin.

The military architecture of the north used granite, but the expansion gave access to the limestones of the Coimbra region, which are lighter in colour: they are seen at Alcobaça. They are also more suitable for sculpture. The first masterpiece of funereal art is the tombs of King Pedro I and Inês de Castro, placed in Alcobaça in about 1360 (though the Cistercian order originally forbade statuary). The great monument of the fourteenth century is undoubtedly the abbey of Batalha. Its west façade is richly dec-orated, recalling the English Perpendicular, with a large flamboyant Gothic window. The nave with clustered pillars soars to a great height, and is austere, but the Founder's Chapel, with the tombs of King John, Queen Philippa and four of their sons, is decorated in rich Gothic style. It has a magnificent star-vault carried high on an octagon of piers lit by eight lancet windows. The chapter-house is a vast space covered by a single vault. The royal cloister is a Gothic arcade shaded with an intri-cate tracery or carved stone resting on slender columns. The church is in limestone with gables, pinnacles and flying buttresses, and the former battlements are replaced by balustrades of lace-like tracery. King Afonso V added a second more sober cloister. The added chapels had reached an extreme of intricacy when they were abandoned. In Lisbon many ancient buildings were destroyed by the Earthquake of 1755, leaving only the ruins of the monastery of the Carmo as a memorial. The last of the medieval cathedrals were Silves in the Algarve and Guarda in Beira. This last was begun in gran-ite in 1390, with massive towers and flying buttresses: it was not completed until the sixteenth century, when a carved altar-piece and other Manueline decorations were added.

Although the new churches in the south necessarily followed northern models, the craftsmen were the heirs of their Muslim predecessors. The palace of the dukes in Beja resembles a blockish, closed mansion like those of the Muslim south. Sintra is a clus-ter rather than a single piece of architecture, so too are São Bento de Castril and Sempre Noiva in Évora, the palace at Alvito and the Conceição and São Andrés at Beja. Buttresses are attached, cylindrical and capped with cones. There is some pre-ference for high windows placed well above street-level, often doubled and separated by a slender column.

Portugal began to welcome influences from the Italian Renaissance under John II, but it was only after his death that Vasco da Gama opened the sea-way to India. King Manuel built the new palace, the Ribeira, which was totally demolished in 1755. His largest achievement was the monastery of the Jeronymites at Belém, a huge rectangle with a fan-vaulted ceiling borne on slender twisted columns. The innovator was

Boytac, a Frenchman who had used similar methods in the church of Jesus at Setúbal in 1490. The unsupported star-vault at the crossing is an architectural feat. Boytac, followed by João de Castilho, designed the cloister in two levels, lit with round openings which break the light with tracery.

Just outside Lisbon, in the river itself, is the Tower of Belém (1515–20), which guards the entry to the narrows. It is a projecting platform backed by a square tower and adorned with heraldic and maritime devices. Its original design makes it the emblem of the city of Lisbon. The 'Manueline style' has a variety of adornments using plants and creatures as well as ropes and maritime symbols. These last reach their height in the famous window at Tomar. These elements are systematically organised, and Manueline is applied to a decorated aperture, particularly a doorway, treated like the frontispiece of a sixteenth-century book.

In 1509, Queen Leonor founded the convent of Madre de Deus on the eastern side of the city: it now serves as the Museum of the *azulejo*. As a nunnery, it has a plain exterior, though with a good Manueline doorway. As a royal foundation, it has a lavish chapel, much enriched in baroque style by John V. It is not in the classical tradition: the earliest church to display this is probably the small Conceição at Tomar, built in the form of a Greek cross on clear classical lines. The purely classical is not very common in Portugal. A simple outward form is usual enough, but Portuguese taste is for decoration, with plenty of scope for the minor arts of gilded wood-carving and coloured tiles.

The tide of prosperity did not outlast the reign of King Manuel. His son, John III, was faced with growing financial problems, and was pious, but necessarily restrained. His favourite residences were at Évora and Almeirim, over the Tagus from Santarém, of which nothing remains. He presented his palace in Coimbra to the University in 1537 and did not visit the north. From 1542, he was much influenced by his Spanish wife, the Spanish Inquisition and the Society of Jesus. The Jesuits sought to combat the Reformation by their preaching, and preferred an open church in which the preacher could be seen and heard, uninterrupted by columns or other obstacles. The purpose of decoration was to uplift and instruct, not to distract. The Jesuit college in Coimbra came to dominate the University. But the main contributions of the Jesuits came after the annexation by Spain: in Lisbon, São Roque, a former hermitage converted into a hall-church and embellished with Jesuit relics, is now a rich museum of sacred art. Their college in Évora was converted into a University in 1553–59, and their greatest achievement, the Sé Nova or new cathedral in Coimbra, was begun only in 1598. It follows general Jesuit principles, with a flat façade divided into compartments and adorned only with statues of the major saints and fathers. The interior accepts geometrical *azulejos*, but is often considered too chilly for Portuguese taste.

The palace at Sintra, an ancient complex which responded to the taste for coloured tiles or azulejos preserved in Spain and revived under King Manuel, is a wonderful meeting-place of styles. The most notable specimen of a country-seat of the Renaissance is the palace of Bacalhoa, across the river from Lisbon, where a mansion of simple outline has been enriched with an Italianate garden and a pool or tank decorated with glazed tiles. In the Minho, the transition from the medieval castle to the Renaissance courtly dwelling is best seen in the mansion of Bertiandos near Viana, where a defensive tower is enlarged by the addition of wings; two-storeyed residences of the sixteenth and eighteenth centuries, each with an open colonnaded gallery giving on to a lawn.

The Renaissance in Portugal appears in the sculpture of the Frenchman Chantereine in Coimbra, Lisbon and elsewhere. The purity of line appears in architecture only from the middle of the century, and is rather short-lived. The exuberance of Manueline decoration with its heterogeneous sources, gives way to the style known in Italy as Mannerist. It admits greater freedom to decorate by the use of light and distortions of shape to obtain effect. The great cloister at Tomar, built by Diogo de Torralva between 1557 and 1566, shows the classical revival at its finest, resulting from the mission of Francisco de Holanda, sent by John III to Italy to study with Michelangelo and others, but the King's hope of a new city of Lisbon was dissipated by his many problems. Three new dioceses were created in 1545, at Leiria, Miranda and Portalegre, but the great age of cathedral-building was over. At Guarda, an influential bishop made Manueline modifications to the ancient granite style, including a magnificent high altar or reredos in the Spanish tradition. An interesting curiosity is the small Augustinian church of the Graça at Évora, a pseudo-classical temple adorned with globes and sprawling giants.

After his victory of 1580, King Philip brought his Italian architect, Filippo Terzi, who designed the large church of St Vincent 'de Fora', outside the walls of Lisbon. It has a severe flat façade with a triple doorway between two flat towers joined by a balustrade, with niches for seven figures. Inside, the statuary is dramatised: St Sebastian is pierced by innumerable arrows, and the Fathers wear exaggerated mitres and flowing robes. The great age of the Spanish theatre was about to open. Since the Restoration of 1640 it has been made the pantheon for the house of Braganza. The obedient Orders, particularly the Jesuits, offered less resistance to Spanish rule than the secular church, and it was left to the nobility to found numerous monasteries and convents in Lisbon. The best design of the period is Santa Engrácia in Lisbon, a basilica in the form of a Greek cross. It has no towers, and the splendid dome remained unfinished until the twentieth century. It has flowing curves, and only simple adornment, and now serves as a national pantheon.

In 1640 the eighth duke of Braganza arrived in Lisbon to become King John IV. The Braganzas had left their possessions in the north to settle at Vila Viçosa, where in the final years of the sixteenth century they built an enormous palace of white Estremós marble, with a façade in three storeys and a slightly projecting centre. The whole is sober and harmonious, and is placed between a large *terreiro* and hunting-park the size of Richmond. John IV was obliged to devote himself to defence and administration, and had no resources to devote to architecture. It was only at the end of the century that his second son, Pedro II, enjoyed easier circumstances. The Wars of Independence had replenished the nobility with successful generals and ministers, some of whom built palaces near Lisbon, like the Marquis of Fronteira at Benfica. Such buildings are large, though not enormous, with two main floors and a projecting central section surmounted by a pediment. The entrance is by a staircase and is embellished, and the apertures large and balconied. There are ample gardens with statuary and a tank decorated with *azulejos*, as is the interior. The decorative arts of the tile-maker and the carvery of gilded architectural innovations were limited. Both sprang into new life as the tide of wealth from Brazil reached its zenith in the decade of 1720.

The great achievement of King John V was the monastery-palace of Mafra, built by Ludovice. Intended as a hermitage for a hunting-estate in sight of Sintra, it occupied thousands of men for a decade and its enormous size housed three hundred Capuchin friars and half as many novices. The façade recalls monasteries in Austria in Italian style. Its cupola is vast, and its effect grandiose. The palace quarters are modest, but there is a maze of cloisters, and the library is a vast storehouse of books, read or unread. It makes full use of Portuguese marbles, but avoids *azulejos* and the excessive use of gilt.

The Counter-Reformation appealed to reason and discipline, as the Jesuits had done, and also to the emotions through the senses, the eyes through the beauty of art, the ears through music and the nose through incense. It was appreciated that the unusual attracts attention, and the baroque alters reality in order to emphasise or awaken interest. The word baroque is attributed to the Portuguese *barroco* applied to an irregular pearl which called for an irregular setting in jewellery. When it was first applied to architecture remains obscure. In Aveiro the church of São João das Barrocas was built in 1722. It is attributed to João Antunes, who built Santa Engrácia in Lisbon in 1682, before the flow of Brazilian gold had begun. It has been called the first example of Portuguese baroque. But the plan of a Greek cross had been used at Santarém and in the Lisbon Bom Sucesso of 1626. Nor did Antunes persist with it in the Bom Jesus at Barcelos and at Aveiro. The tendency to a profusion of ornament is Manueline, and returns after a predomination of Castilian sobriety. The trend towards exaggerated and even imaginary forms of decoration is Mannerist, which uses light to focus attention. Mafra is often seen as not typically Portuguese. It perhaps attempted to outshine Philip II's Escorial and Louis XIV's Versailles. But the opulent King grew too portly for the chase and it was not much used. The most useful work of his age is the great aqueduct of 'Aguas Livres' or Free Waters, built between 1729 and 1748 to carry water over the Alcântara valley in a long channel supported by arches, with a pumping-station at Amoreiras, and in Lisbon ornamental fountains or *chafarizes* which embellished the city. The most attractive specimen of the baroque is the Royal Library conferred on the University of Coimbra in 1716–28, a rectangular hall of impressive height divided into compartments and lined with painted and gilded bookcases, and a full-length portrait of the donor in a grand setting like a high altar.

In Oporto, the constraints imposed by medieval walls lasted longer, and the growth of trade enhanced the value of land and led to the building of high and narrow houses. The churches were extended and decorated. The best examples are São Francisco and Santa Clara, where the wood-carver incorporates real or imaginary foliage and birds to create the 'church of gold', which was perhaps thought superior to all natural colours. Exotic timbers from Brazil were introduced to add to the native woods, pointing towards the English taste for Caribbean mahogany. At Braga, two magnificent baroque organs were added, together with decorated organ-lofts. At Aveiro, the convent of Jesus is a rich example of the new trend. The choir-stalls at Évora are made to match. In Oporto, the city emerged from its architectural subordination under the influence of Niccolo Nasoni, born in Tuscany in 1691, but resident in Oporto from 1725 until his death in 1773. His most famous and prominent work is the church of the Clérigos, built for a guild of priests between 1731 and 1749 in granite and on baroque lines, with a rear tower rising to 259 feet, the tallest in Portugal. It is entered by a divided stair, with access from the sides. The interior incorporates Nasoni's imaginative foliage and shell designs, recalling his work as painter, goldsmith and sculptor.

The renovation of Oporto was begun by its governor, João de Almada e Melo, a cousin of Pombal, who died in 1786, and his son Francisco. The old buildings were cleared, but not replaced by a general plan such as that of Lisbon. Oporto became prosperous after 1780, and the British consul John Whitehead obtained from John Carr of York a plan for the vast new hospital of Santo António in an Anglo-Palladian style: it was too costly to be completed, but with the enforced adjustments remains one of the most notable buildings in the city. Whitehead also designed the English factory-house of 1785–90. It is a simple and elegant building with an arcade on the street level, and strongly recalls the Adams brothers. The Almadas were also responsible for the law-courts (the Relação) and the prison. The last grand convent in the north was that of Santa Clara at Vila do Conde, built in 1777 on the bank of the Ave.

Pombal had risen to power with the Earthquake of 1755. The military engineer who had built the Lisbon aqueduct was summoned with others to restore or create the city's Baixa, the first piece of European city planning on a large scale. It employed geometrical lines, leading to the Terreiro do Paço, which replaced King Manuel's palace and was intended as the heart of government and commerce, with the equestrian statue of King Joseph as a centre-piece. Although adopted as the rational solution to a pressing local problem, the 'Pombaline' style was widely imitated and coincided with a return to favour of simpler lines. In the nineteenth century, its methods and objects remained, but the desire for embellishment was met by covering the exterior of houses with coloured azulejos. Many of the churches that had been destroyed were restored in the style of classical temples.

At the time of the disaster, the royal family had been at Belém. Plans for a new palace there were not executed, though the royal picadeiro or coach-house and stables, now the Coach Museum, is an excellent example of the simpler taste. Its place was taken by the Ajuda palace, planned just after Joseph I's death, but not begun until 1802 and, after many delays, completed only in 1835. Queen Maria I preferred Queluz, which had been given to her husband, Pedro III. The former manor was rebuilt from 1758 and extended when Maria became queen. The Portuguese Mateus de Oliveira had the collaboration of a Frenchman, J B Robillon. It is the best Portuguese example of the rococo. The exaggerated baroque decorations are reduced to order as garlands or posies, and the roof balustrades do not break the classical pediment. Its best features are its façades, its grand corner-staircase 'of the Lion' and its gardens. The rooms are unpretentious: even the throne-room is of comfortable size, and the music and cabinet rooms are modest. The object is to achieve pleasantness with only a touch of majesty.

Queen Maria's church in Lisbon is the basilica of the Estrela, where she and her husband are buried. It was built by Mateus Vicente in 1779–89, but also suffered interruptions. Its main external feature is a lofty cupola which, when illuminated, is visible from much of western Lisbon. It reduces baroque ornamentation to a minimum. The interior makes full use of coloured marble, and owes something of its proportions to the church at Mafra. It is the last great church to be built in Lisbon, though there are naturally many smaller and later parish churches. It appears to complete the long cycle of close collaboration between church and state. Lisbon still far exceeded Oporto, which was barely a quarter of its size. Fortunes were made by those who bought monopolies of trade under Pombal. When King Joseph's new opera-house was burnt down, it was they who united to replace it. The São Carlos was built in 1792–92 by Costa e Silva, trained in Italy and following the lines of the San Carlo in Naples. The Portuguese verdict, that its sobriety 'does not exclude true beauty', is too faint: it is a good building. Meanwhile, the reigning house disposed of Bemposta, rebuilt in plain style in 1793, but given a rich chapel. The English Huguenot Gerald Devismes, who had held the monopoly of Brazil-wood, built a palace at Benfica in semi-Palladian style which was considered English. Sintra was then coming into favour, and he acquired a house at Monserrate, replaced in 1865 by the oriental fantasy built for Sir Francis Cook, the textile magnate and collector.

In the north, the departure from baroque decoration is seen at Bom Jesus in Braga. Between 1784 and 1811, Carlos Amarante, a military architect responsible for the plain and austere Naval Academy in Oporto, built a church on an eminence reached by a divine staircase with a series of landings furnished with sacred statuary and balustrades. It uses the striking contrast between the dark granite lines and the white-washed walls, and is the favourite place of pilgrimage for the city. Not far away, the church at Falperra is also approached by a triple staircase, but its façade embodies many of the baroque themes dear to Nasoni. In Braga itself, the same architect is credited with the extravagant Palacete do Raio (House of the Mexican), with exaggerated pelmeted apertures and a pretentious doorway. It pleased the new rich with their imported wealth. He also produced the much quieter Braga city-hall, an admirable adaptation of baroque decoration to a traditional design.

During the period of the wars and absence of the royal family in Brazil, the thread of royal patronage was suspended. The Ajuda was still under fitful construction, and on his return John VI dwelt in the more modest palace of Bemposta, used by Queen Catherine of England in her retirement, damaged by the Earthquake, and later the Military College. Portugal had no academy of arts until 1836: architects had been sent abroad to study, usually in Italy, or were trained in the great royal undertakings of Mafra and the Ajuda. This made for highly proficient craftsmen rather than innovative artists. Those who worked on the Ajuda passed into the school of the new Academy as professors. It began in the large convent of St Francis (itself the successor to Raol's chapel of 1147). A link with the past was destroyed with the dissolution of the monasteries in 1834: many ancient buildings were converted into barracks or offices or fell into neglect. The convent of São Bento became the seat of parliament in 1834, but was given its present grand form only in 1876. The Passeio Público, or Promenade, was a walled garden dating from 1764 and enlarged in 1835, when it became the main public park: it occupied the site of the present Restauradores, and was demolished in 1879 to make way for the Avenida da Liberdade, the nucleus of modern urbanisation.

Queen Maria II's consort, Fernando of Coburg, had artistic tastes like his cousin Prince Albert: he devoted himself to the Pena Palace at Sintra, designed by his German adviser, Eschwege, in eclectic Gothic revival style from 1840. The Lisbon City Hall or Câmara Municipal was built in 1867–75 after a fire had consumed the Pombaline building: it is a piece of grand municipal architecture replete with the allegorical statuary typical of the genre.

The National Theatre in the Rossio is named after Queen Maria II or Almeida Garrett, the leading romantic writer, at whose behest it was built in 1842–46 to the design of the Italian Lodi: it has been restored after a fire in 1964, and lends classical dignity to the central square. In commercial Oporto, the statesman Passos Manuel, the first patron of the Lisbon Academy of Fine Arts, assured the development of the various colleges into what was to become the university. There was no royal palace in the city until King Pedro V bought the Carrancas, built from a substantial commercial fortune. In Lisbon, Pombal's College for Nobles became the Polytechnic School of Pedro V or College of Science, rebuilt in 1844 and later.

As elsewhere, Portuguese architecture of the nineteenth century is various and eclectic. If the builders of the Polytechnic were instructed to use the remains of the former college as far as possible, those of the City Hall were told not to be inhibited by expense. The Pombaline had become a norm, but this did not prevent the bull-ring in the Campo Pequeno from adopting a circular plan with a supposedly 'Moorish' structure and adornments, or Sir Francis Cook from constructing the oriental fantasy of Monserrate in 1865, any more than the Prince Regent's other tastes inhibited the Dome at Brighton. The movement of traffic required wider thoroughfares like the Avenida, and these imposed a discipline of size and proportion. Outside these constraints, former tenements made way for apartments or flats: the city fathers imposed urbanisation, and in the twentieth century a certain regularity was attained by the Valmor award, set up in 1916, for the best architecture of the year.

The growing need for public buildings was met in part by the use or adaptation of existing premises. The Lisbon Museum of Ancient Art, or Janelas Verdes, was a seventeenth-century palace owned for a time by Pombal, in which various collections were assembled in 1884. Modern Art had to share the convent of St Francis with the Academy of Fine Arts and the National Library. New departments of government were fitted into the Pombaline Baixa: the commercial centre he had built was soon invaded by banks and financiers. At Coimbra, the Museu Machado de Castro is the former Bishop's Palace. Urban expansion and the opening of new avenues engaged the attention of most professional architects. Other cities had followed Lisbon in planning, London with the Prince Regent and Paris with Haussmann in 1853. It was the latter who set the fashion for broad and leafy boulevards. Streets were to be straight and buildings conformist, if not uniform. The Avenida da Liberdade was planned in 1873 and opened in 1886, and the 'Avenidas Novas' after 1900.

The arrival of urban traffic – the famous yellow electric trams of Lisbon – straightened the streets without creating architecture. But the railway presented new problems, combining a palace with a shed. In London and in Paris various solutions were attempted. In Lisbon, the Rossio station in the middle of the city attempted to combine the Manueline with an enormous horseshoe. By its side, the same architect built the first of the 'palace hotels', the Avenida Palace. In Oporto, the terminus was the Benedictine convent bedecked with historical *azulejos* of great size: it was built in 1900.

Another stream of thought reverted to the Romanesque round arch and the medieval castle. The small Romanesque church of Cedofeita in Oporto was rebuilt or reproduced. In Lisbon, the opening of the electric railway linking the city with the fishing-village and summer-resort of Cascais in 1889–95 led to the development of wasteland at Estoril. Luso-medieval mansions sprouted on the beach in 1900, and mingled with anglicised Swiss cottages. The largest specimen of this Gothic revival was the Palace-Hotel at Bussaco, the fantasy of an Italian stage-designer begun in 1888. In Lisbon, the 'New Avenues' bear traces of a revival of the Romanesque arch even more prominent than in the council-chamber at Braganza of 1250.

Anachronistic castles might confer spurious authority on new fortunes, but excessive ostention did not long survive the fall of the monarchy and the war of 1914–18.

Beside the stream of foreign influences, there emerged a quest for essentially Portuguese elements of which the proponent was Raul Lino, who built the Tivoli cinema in the Lisbon Avenida in 1923. A decade later, Dr Salazar's 'New State' imposed financial restraint and discipline. The buildings of his regime reflected these circumstances. The style of the New State was not far removed from the simplicity of the Pombaline reconstruction, though it admitted in modest quantity such decorative motifs as the conical turret characteristic of the Alentejo. The culmination of the work of retrenchment and limited self-sufficiency was the 'double centenary' of 1140 and 1640, marked in 1940 by an assertion of national expression in the midst of a world at war. Never had Portugal so exerted itself in the preservation and reconstruction of ancient castles and historic buildings. It disliked the eclecticism associated with the nineteenth century. It rebuilt Dr Salazar's University at Coimbra in an austere style more practical than popular, and created the University City of Lisbon on spacious but restrained lines, to which the National Library and public record office of the Torre do Tombo have been added. Its emblem is the monument of the Discoverers and Prince Henry the Navigator at Belém. Its object was not to exclude or antagonise foreign influences: it welcomed the Armenian capitalist and collector Calouste Gulbenkian, whose Foundation gave Portugal its first great international gallery and museum. The headquarters were designed by an English architect in undecorated twentieth century style. A separate building simulating a factory houses the contemporary collection.

The public amenities that add to the attraction of Lisbon are largely the work of the nineteenth century. The public promenade was originally a garden, extended to make the Avenida da Liberdade, and ending in the Parque Eduardo Sétimo, founded to commemorate the visit of Edward VII in 1903. It is the largest in Lisbon and replaces a former fair-ground. The Estrela Garden was made in 1844 in front of the church, and contains exotic trees and bushes. The Campo Grande, or Alvalade, was a parade-ground for troops converted into a garden under Maria I, and much frequented for carriage-rides, with adjoining private gardens, now occupied by the University City. The eighteenth-century estate of Palhavã belonging to the royal house is now the headquarters and park of the Gulbenkian Foundation. Outside the city limits, the Parque Monsanto was a wooded and uncultivated area, popular for picnics. The Botanical Garden was formerly attached to Pombal's College for Nobles, later replaced by the Polytechnic and Faculty of Science. The Zoological Gardens at Benfica was founded in 1884 and occupied the estate of the Conde de Farrobo, a plutocrat of the time of Maria I. Other estates remain or have been converted to public or private use. Pombal's palace at Oeiras now houses the science departments of the Gulbenkian. The Quinta Nova at Carcavelos, built by an adherent of Pombal, houses the English School.

The first true public works of Lisbon were the public fountains, which distributed water from the Aqueduct of John V. They are also ornamental, such as the one that remains outside the Museum of Ancient Art, the Janelas Verdes. Medieval statuary, which reached its height with the tombs of Pedro I and Inês de Castro at Alcobaça, was almost entirely ecclesiastical and funerary. The first public statue of a monarch was the equestrian statue of King Joseph I in the Terreiro do Paço. It was designed by the great sculptor Machado de Castro, and cast in the military foundry, the first equestrian monument to be attempted in Portugal. It was followed by the modest monument to his daughter, Maria I, in 1798: she is attended by four allegorical figures, much in the taste of the time. The tradition was continued by Machado de Castro and others at the Ajuda palace, but the next public manifestation was the statue of Camões in the square named after him in 1867, though Oporto had commemorated Pedro IV, its own hero, in the previous year. The poet stands aloft, sword in hand, twice life-size, surrounded by eight contemporaries, picked rather at random, of normal size. The equestrian statue of Pedro IV in Oporto was by the Belgian Calmels. The Lisbon statue to Pedro IV, after lengthy discussions, was awarded to French artists, who raised him on a lofty column far above the Rossio, now the main square of Lisbon after the Terreiro. The Pombaline Terreiro was rounded off with the elaborate triumphal arch, which is far different from Pombal's intention, but gives it a grand and dramatic touch: its allegorical figures are by Calmels (1873). In the Restauradores at the beginning of the Avenida, the heroes of 1640 were commemorated with an obelisk surmounting an allegorical base concluded in 1886, and the liberal generals, the Dukes of Terceira (1877), of Saldanha (1909) and Marquis of Sá da Bandeira (1884), were given their place. At Belém, a column in late Manueline style was erected in 1892–1901 to carry the figure of Afonso de Albuquerque, the founder of Goa. Eça de Queirós, who died in 1900, was given his statue in the Rua do Alecrim in 1903. He was the first writer after Camões to be so honoured. Others have followed, notably Fernando Pessoa who occupies a table outside the Brasileira café in the Chiado.

6

Painting

Sacheverell Sitwell, who paid five visits to Portugal, says: 'in Portugal there are no painters', adding: 'what is lacking in Portugal where decorative painting is nearly always bad is the brush of a Tiepolo. There are moments when one longs for even a third-rate Italian painter. But Italy is the land of painting, and Portugal is no more to be reproached for want of that than England, for here too it is no part of our native genius.' I happen to be writing in the house of J M W Turner, R A and take these remarks for what they are worth. Sitwell is a child of the grand tour with a remarkable gift of reminiscence: everything he sees reminds him of something else. Perhaps Portugal ought to be Mediterranean, but it is not. Sitwell does not (I think) complain that there are no Scottish painters or no Icelandic painters. He loves Portugal, but has manoeuvred himself into being disappointed.

Greco-Roman pictorial art survives in mosaics rather than painting. Both forms were rejected by Islam, and the tradition disappears. Christian Europe inherited the Roman preoccupation with permanence and in the early middle ages preferred stone. Painting emerges between illumination and polychrome figure-sculpture: the former is minute and precise and the latter applies pigments to a stone surface without much subtlety. Early stone figures have little classical line, and the addition of colour does not make them more convincing. By the fourteenth century, the tombs of Alcobaça had acquired great narrative and decorative power, but have not the qualities of painting for which wood and ivory were more suitable. Queen Philippa brought the poems of John Gower to Portugal, but there is no evidence that she brought painting. Royal marriages were at times preceded by the exchange of portraits. In about 1428 van Eyck came to Portugal on a mission to arrange for Philippa's daughter Isabel to marry Duke Philip 'the Good' of Flanders. He was perhaps the first acknowledged great painter to visit Portugal. The first known royal portrait is that of Philippa's husband, John I, who died in 1433. There are a dozen manuscripts with miniatures dating from the twelfth-century Book of Birds (*Livro das Aves*) to the Missal of Lorvão of the fifteenth, with coloured drawings of rural work for each month of the year, a prelude to the art of painting.

The finest Portuguese painter of the fifteenth century is Nuno Gonçalves, whose style derives from the Flanders of van Eyck, not from Italy. He is first known as painter to Afonso V in 1450, and he died before 1493. The two triptychs of St Vincent, each of three panels, show the saint in gorgeous raiment receiving the obedience of members of the royal house, watched by representatives of the whole society: knights, Cistercian friars, lawyers, fishermen and others. The sixty-six figures show the generations of the Discoveries in all their similarities and differences. The work was painted between about 1460 and 1475 for a monastery. There are only two women, one an elderly nun and the other a young princess. It lay forgotten for centuries until it was discovered in a closet in the Monastery of St Vincent in 1895: it now holds a place of honour in the Janelas Verdes. Not all the portraits are certainly identified. They may not have all been living at the same time: Prince Henry's portrait is that in his chronicle: he died in 1460. If the boy prince is the future John II, he would have been ten in 1465.

Religious paintings from Flanders found their way to Madeira, which sent its sugar and wine to the Low Countries. The following royal painters, Jorge Afonso, his Flemish brother-in-law Francisco Henriques, and their sons-in-law, Gregório Lopes and Garcia Fernandes, are also in the Janelas Verdes: they continued the Flemish connection. The royal genealogy, a work of fiction, is by a Fleming, Simon Bening, and is in the British Museum: it was commissioned in the period between 1530 and 1534. King John III sent Francisco de Holanda to Italy to study art and architecture and in his time Portugal looked rather to Italy than to the north.

The most notable Portuguese painter of the first half of the sixteenth century is Vasco Fernandes, called Grão Vasco (c. 1475–1541). He spent three years in Lisbon, but returned to his native Viseu, where he is mentioned in 1501 and had a house from 1512 until his death. Many of his works are assembled in the provincial museum, adjoining the cathedral there. He worked for the churches of the vicinity as far as Coimbra. His most famous work is his St Peter enthroned against a Portuguese land-scape, in which the central figure looks suitably stony. In Lisbon, the school of João Afonso near the monastery of São Domingos passed to his son-in-law Gregório Lopes, whose 'Adoration of the Magi' arranges a variety of portraits before the Virgin and Child. Gregório's son Cristóvão Lopes (1516–94) portrayed John III and his wife Dona Caterina, and royal portraiture was crowned by the revealing picture of King Sebastian by Cristóvão de Morais. It is matched by the pictures of an unidentified princess and an elderly nun, also in the Janelas Verdes. The Spanish annexation of 1580 broke the golden chain of patronage, and Sanches Coelho became Sánchez Coello in Madrid: he had been a protégé of John III in Flanders and passed on to serve a Spanish princess.

The Portuguese nobility, itself partly lured to Madrid, was no substitute for royal patronage, which could ensure continuity if it could not create genius. Portuguese artists had often been attracted to Seville, on which the growth of Spanish America had bestowed a degree of artistic autonomy. The great Velázquez, born in Seville of Portuguese stock, studied there with Pacheco, no great artist but a devoted theorist. The Portuguese strand is resumed with Josefa de Óbidos (1630–84). She was born in Seville, the daughter of a Portuguese painter, Baltasar Gomes Figueira, who married a Spaniard but returned to Portugal when Josefa, the eldest of a large family, was an infant. Her father worked in Coimbra and she was educated in the convent of St Ann. Her first work on copper was produced in 1646, when the family settled in her father's native Óbidos. She was presented to King Pedro II when he visited the town, but her work was for convents of the district, among which she was regarded as a prodigy. She did not marry. She has left about a hundred and fifty works, many influenced by the taste of her clients. Her originality is unquestioned, and her children admirable. She is inclined to manage light for religious effect, but her still-lifes, reflecting accurately the nunnish taste for fruit and sweetmeats adorned with flowers and ribbons, are as true to her art as to her milieu. The works are scattered, but many are at the Janelas Verdes. They were exhibited in London in 1997, with a catalogue which removes some unnecessary myths. Her landscapes are attractive but few in number.

Domingos Vieira (c. 1600–78), known as 'o Oscuro' to distinguish him from a homonym, used black backgrounds to show up faces and decorations of figures of the court. But the Brazilian gold which brought opulence to John V can hardly be said to have done as much for painting as for architecture. This was partly because of the influence of French academicism applied to a very ecclesiastical society. Conformity, however needful in any society, does not make for originality or anything beyond competence in painting. King John V and his family were painted by G D Dupra, who was in Portugal from 1719 to 1730. The Cadaval family supported P A Quillard, and Jean Pillemont (d 1808) brought in French rococo, of which he has left specimens in the Oporto gallery of Soares dos Reis. His pupil Francisco Vieira (1765–1805), called Portuense to distinguish him, worked in Rome and in London with Bartolozzi, whose niece he married. He followed the portrait painting of Raeburn and Hoppner, and adopted the pseudo-classical style of Benjamin West, becoming a forerunner of the romantic taste for human beings set in an appropriate landscape. He died in Madeira in 1805 aged forty.

The greatest Portuguese artist since Nuno Gonçalves was Domingos António Sequeira (1768–1837), who studied with Francisco Vieira in Rome, taught there and returned to Portugal in 1795. He tried to set up an academy, but failed and retired to a monastery at Laveiras, painting his two studies of St Bruno, one now in Lisbon and the other in Oporto. His line is subtle and diaphanous, and while he excelled as a portrait painter, he liked allegorical subjects which combined the real with the ideal. In some ways he resembles Goya, whom he seems never to have met, but, instead of the violent pessimism and brutality of the Aragonese, his talent was for a softened and uplifting version of life. In 1805 he succeeded Vieira in the academy at Oporto, but in 1808 he welcomed the French invaders, earning himself six months under arrest. He portrayed Wellington and Beresford, and designed the monumental silver service presented to Wellington, now in Apsley House. His allegorical figures follow Italian neo-classicism, using luminous effects to enhance his portraits in what Turner would have recognised as the sublime. He welcomed the liberal revolution of 1820 but, after the traditionalist revolt of 1823, fled to France, like Goya. He returned to religious subjects, and spent the last decade of his life, 1827 to 1837, in Rome, enjoying considerable success. He has left many charcoal studies and sketches and is best seen in the Janelas Verdes in Lisbon.

The Royal Academy of Fine Arts which Sequeira had been unable to create was established in 1836, just a year before his death in Italy. Consequently, its first teachers were the painters engaged on the new palace of the Ajuda, who taught what was academically correct. This was certainly better than nothing, but it represented the taste of liberal politicians and declamatory historical scenes. Royal patronage was limited: Queen Maria II had no better judgement than Queen Victoria, and her husband Ferdinand lacked the flair of his cousin Albert. Liberal politicians liked portraits of others of their kind, against gloomy backgrounds. One can appreciate Sitwell's want of a Tiepolo.

The burgeoning taste for landscape discernible in Vieira Portuense did not flourish. The absence of the light colours favoured by Tiepolo is followed by a neglect of the water-colour with its wide range of new pigments which gave J M W Turner R A – an academic to the finger-tips – such a range for his genius. He never visited the Iberian Peninsula, though his younger follower James Holland did.

The portraitists and dramatic painters are A J Patrício and F Metrass (1825–61). The idea of the sublime being found in light, which turns everything into what we see, was slow to germinate. The best painter of the romantic period was Miguel Lupi (1836–83), born in Lisbon of Italian parents, who did some excellent portraits, though professor of historical painting. His pupil was Columbano, son of the caricaturist Bordelo Pinheiro, and the best-known nineteenth-century painter. He became director of the Academy's school in the former convent of São Francisco, where 'contemporary art', that is after 1850, was garnered: it is now called Modern Art, and contemporary has been transferred to the gallery added to the Gulbenkian Foundation. Columbano excelled in a wide range of subjects, though he was most at ease in the realism of his day. Malhoa is also a painter of the real, limited by the choice of 'genre' subjects done with earthy verve. The next master of portraiture was Enrique de Medina (Barros, b 1901). Almada Negreiros (1893–1970) was novelist, poet and artist: he is widely known for his portrait of the poet Fernando Pessoa in the cubist style. The twentieth-century movements, often emerging from Paris, were led by Souza-Cardoso (1887–1918), whose work is seen at his native Amarante and in the Gulbenkian extension. Carlos Reis (1863–1940) was the director of the contemporary museum, and Carlos Botelho (b 1889) enjoyed popularity for his stylised scenes of Lisbon.

From 1933, the award of prizes by the secretariat for propaganda played its part in stimulating artists. There are now fifty museums of different sorts in Portugal. Contemporary painting is concentrated in the Contemporary gallery attached to the Gulbenkian Foundation. It is rather rich in fantasy only distantly related to pictorial art. It follows the Pompidou factory in Paris and precedes by a couple of decades the extension to the Tate, Tate Modern. The Gulbenkian extension contains some good things, including an excellent canteen. But the best institution for contemporary art is the Serralves Foundation in Oporto established in a house and extensive gardens that reflect Paris taste of c. 1920.

7

Music

In an age when recorded sounds are available everywhere, what is heard in Portugal may or may not be Portuguese music. Discounting international sound, which is easily industrialised, and in which Portugal doubtless has its place, we can only say briefly what is typically Portuguese. When Ann Livermore wrote her *Short History of Spanish Music* in 1972, she remarked that she could not do a similar volume for Portuguese because you can't write about music unless you hear it. Now much more Portuguese music is available, for which a debt is owed to the Gulbenkian Foundation, particularly in the field of early church music which had hitherto gone unpublished. Church music emanated from the monasteries, and the tradition was abruptly broken at the dissolution of 1834, being only gradually restored. Secular music was performed at royal banquets and other occasions in the middle ages, and much of it went unrecorded. Some later music comes from the eighteenth-century opera, which flourished in the golden days of King John V. A detailed account of Portuguese opera by Manuel Carlos de Brito is available in English (Cambridge 1989).

The Galaico-Portuguese lyric goes back to the twelfth century, when the songbooks or *Cancioneiros* were formed. Under the learned Alfonso X (1252–84), the religious *Cantigas de Santa Maria* were preserved in Castile, while the secular tradition passed to his grandson, King Diniz of Portugal (1279–1325). The forms adopted in the songbooks fell into three main groups: the first, addressed by men to women; the second, put into the mouths of women, is amatory and plaintive, though almost always composed by men; and the third is satirical, denunciatory or comic. This convention lasted until about 1400. A new troubadour convention then arrived from Castile or Aragon (previously from Provence or Italy). The Portuguese style was more contemplative and discursive than the Castilian, which was ecstatic and introspective.

In the greater churches, the organ had prepared the way for orchestration and polyphony. The theatre of Gil Vicente, which prevailed at court from 1502 until 1536, calls for a wide variety of songs and dances, some of them regional. Camões' last play, *Filodemo*, performed by the poet and his friends in India in 1554, calls for half a dozen rustic instruments. After 1500, court music had grown in elegance: but the courtly lute, of Arab pedigree, was hard to tune and not portable, while the popular guitar (in Portuguese *viola*) was adopted by squires singing their serenades to girls outside houses or indoors. It was the guitar, not the lute, that crossed the seas to Brazil. Music was difficult to print, and was first done in the Iberian Peninsula at Valencia, where the lutenist Luis Milán published his *El Maestro* addressed to King John III because his court was an 'ocean of music' (1535). He had played his lute in Portugal, and was one of the earliest of the race of *virtuosi*.

Religious plays or pageants were presented by the Jesuits at least as early as 1619 when the discovery of India was glorified on the stage with music, but royal patronage disappeared from view under the Philips. The Duke of Braganza, Dom João, whom the Restoration in 1640 made John IV, devoted himself to the chase and to music at Vila Viçosa, and formed a vast library of contemporary European music. It was lost in the Earthquake, though a partial catalogue survives. Once King, his resources had to be devoted to defence, and it was only under his son Pedro II that royal patronage was resumed. Church music had not unnaturally fared better. The great Portuguese composer of the period was Duarte Lobo (c. 1560–1646) of Évora, who studied with Morales and Guerrero and whose work was published: of the same period was Manuel Cardoso, who lived until 1656.

It was the opulence of John V that led to a revival of Portuguese music on a grand scale. He married Maria Ana, daughter of the Emperor Leopold I, in 1708, and she at once introduced musical evenings on Sundays with music by ladies. Their eldest daughter was Barbara of Braganza who in 1728 married Fernando (VI) of Spain and became the patroness of Domenico Scarlatti, Antonio Soler and others. She was the pupil of Carlos Seixas (1704–42), the great keyboard composer of the period, son of the organist of Coimbra. Seixas never went abroad and was a member of John V's Chapel Royal and of the Patriarchal seminary founded in 1713 as the principal school of music in Portugal, much under Roman influence. A number of his harpsichord sonatas intended for royal concerts or the church have survived. Admired by Scarlatti, with whom he is compared, he died at thirty-eight, leaving only a few non-keyboard works. The opera made its appearance in Portugal from Italy soon after 1700. The *vilhancico* or traditional Christmas carol of ancient origin ceased to be sung in the royal chapel in 1715, when Roman usage was adopted. In the popular theatre Spanish plays with songs were offered in the one playhouse, and in 1711 the queen marked John's birthday with a 'comedy of music' with arias, recitatives and a small orchestra.

The Spanish *comedia* was only gradually replaced by the Italian opera, though John V sent many students to work in Rome. The first Portuguese masterpiece was the *Spinalba*, by Francisco António de Almeida (1739). The King's religiosity was shared by his subjects, and in music as in other things he preferred everything Roman. Another modification began in 1729, when Barbara's daughter Mariana Vitória arrived in Portugal to be married to Prince Joseph. She was then eleven, but had spent three years in France expecting to be married to Louis XIV. In 1740 King John had a stroke, followed by another in 1742. This did not deter the public opera from flourishing, principally in the house of the Rua dos Condes. In the Alto, the Puppet-house was fashionable, being licensed by the Hospital of All Saints from 1740. The puppet-operas were a sort of comic opera, with *sinfonia*, arias, duets and choruses in Italian style.

John V's career came to an end in 1750, when he was succeeded by Joseph and Mariana Vitória. It fell to the future Pombal to contract for Italian opera on a more lavish scale. The new Lisbon royal opera-house was completed only in March 1755, to be completely destroyed by the famous Earthquake seven months later. In the meantime Joseph had a theatre in his hunting-box at Salvaterra and at Ajuda. The music and production were Italian, but the words were supplied and printed in Portuguese.

The opera did not become a national habit: the only other city to have a house was Oporto, where it was improvised for a royal occasion in 1760 and the São João opera-house was inaugurated in 1798. Under King Joseph the Italian connection was resumed, but as Roman music was thought to be in decline, attention shifted to the less ecclesiastical centre of Naples. The greatest Portuguese composer of operas, João de Sousa Carvalho, born at Estremós in 1745, was sent to Naples where he composed his *Amor industrioso* performed on his return in 1769. The 'Portuguese Mozart' composed operas barely distinguishable from those of Wolfgang Amadeus, symphonies and religious pieces, before retiring wealthy, and dying in the Alentejo in 1799. He was remembered but not performed until about 1930.

Neither Mozart nor Dr Burney visited the Iberian Peninsula. But the Abade António da Costa met Burney and, in thirteen letters written to friends in Oporto, describes musical life in Rome, Venice and Vienna between 1750 and 1780. He admired the streets and buildings he saw. There was plenty of music, but many of the voices were poor and the fiddlers out of tune: much more care was taken in Portugal. By now Portuguese composers had entered the main stream with Domingos Bomtempo (1775–1832) and Marcos António da Fonseca, who called himself 'Portugal'.

One stream of contact between official music and the songs of villagers was military music. The royal band was military, John IV had his army band and in the time of John VI every regiment was required to have its band. Over the years they were joined by the firemen and others, and towns great and small provided bandstands for the entertainment of the public. The link between the music of the court and church and music for the family circle or social group is not easy to fix, or rather there are many links. The priest with his fiddle or guitar was a well-known character. He might perform *modinhas* or innocent ballads. Popular practice admitted the African *lundu* which, like the *fandango*, was not considered decent. The languid Brazilian *modinha* shaded into the drawing-room ballad as the pianoforte made its entry. Liberalism brought with it the national anthem, which acquired a special esteem, whatever its value as music. In the nineteenth century there were better communications and the differences of regional traditions came to be appreciated. The great Spanish collections of Barbieri and Pedrell have no precise parallel in Portugal, but there are numerous transcriptions and arrangements. In the Minho they tend to centre on the cheerful round-dance, the *vira*, accompanied by the squiffer or concertina, which has been carried to the Algarve. In the Alentejo, graver and more religious songs are found, together with male choruses.

The *Fado*, or 'fate', is not a national song, but is closely associated with low life in Lisbon, where it emerged early in the nineteenth century; its legendary exponent being Maria Severa in the decade of 1820: she died young, and the fado has been called 'the sad song of the south'. It may be contrasted with the ditties sung in English taverns in the seventeenth century: the themes are far less cheerful. There is also a Coimbra *fado*, a students' song which may be on a wide variety of themes: the legendary composer and performer was one Hilário. In both cases, the *fado* is a solo song to the accompaniment of a *guitarra* and *viola*. The Portuguese *guitarra* is not a 'Spanish' guitar, but a round and flat-backed instrument with up to a dozen paired strings. It is usually joined by the *viola*, the Portuguese guitar, which adds body to the tone. The rather jangling effect is indispensable. The theme of the song often concerns jealousy (*ciumes*) and domestic epics of one kind or another. The setting in low life was confirmed by a well-known painting by José Malhoa of 1910 and prevailed until about 1940, when the *fado* was given a fresh start by Amália Rodrigues, who possessed a good voice and continued to sing fados almost until her death. She made it respectable and gave it an international reputation, becoming in the process a semi-deity. The fado houses are still taverns or cafés, and there are those who can sing and also cook. They were originally in the narrow and popular streets of the Bairro Alto, but have spread to the Alfama and other districts.

8

Birds

Travellers who are also bird-watchers will find much to admire in Portugal. While the 'British list' has a little over two hundred varieties, the Portuguese exceeds three hundred, named by W C Tait in 1924, or two hundred and eighty named in 1973 by R Carey, who deals only with the south. The difference of nearly fifty per cent is partly because Portugal lies on a main migration route, receiving passengers from continental Europe on their way south and some African species on their way north. It is also due to the absence of any large industrial area and the survival of much countryside in the shape of mountainside, forests and open fields. There are several reserves, such as the coast north of Oporto at Mindelo, the National Park of Gerez-Penedo, the seashore of the Algarve, and the Berlenga Isles off the coast. Against this is the practice of eating birds, advertised in small restaurants with the sign: *Há pássaros*. There are two words for 'birds': larger kinds, such as chickens and above, are *aves*; small birds are *pássaros*, or with the diminutive, *passarinhos*.

There are eighteen warblers, thirteen gulls and eight terns: having no binoculars, I am not able to distinguish them. Birds not seen at all in the British Isles are: vultures, rare wanderers from the Spanish mountains; egrets; the purple gallinule, now confined to the reserve in the Algarve; and the serin, which can be heard in Lisbon. The azure-winged magpie is a native of China, found fifty years ago only at Montijo, on the south bank of the Tagus near Lisbon, but now reported from many places. Its spread will not surprise those who have witnessed the explosion of the magpie.

Among species now extinct in Britain are the stork, which is quite common and nests in towers, electricity-poles and elsewhere in villages: it is easily recognised and its clappering is a distinctive sound. The black stork is rare. The avocet is uncommon, and the great bustard survives in places in the Algarve and Alentejo. Cranes winter in parts of the Alentejo.

Birds extremely scarce in Britain include the hoopoe, bee-eater, golden eagle, osprey and kite. The hoopoe is a spring and summer visitor, common in the Alentejo, and the bee-eater also divides its time between Portugal and Africa: it occurs from the Douro southwards. The golden oriole is African and breeds in Portuguese orchards and clumps of trees: it is known as the *papa-figos* or fig-eater. The chough, in Portuguese the red-billed daw, is common where there are cliffs, and the raven has a special significance for Lisbon, since St Vincent's ship carries a pair fore and aft. Tame ravens used to haunt several streets in Lisbon itself. Portuguese starlings are usually unspeckled. Lesser predatory birds, such as hawks, buzzards and kites, are not uncommon.

The bird population is variable from decade to decade and place to place. The nightingale, now rare in England, is relatively common, while the song-thrush is much less so. The tourist influx into the Algarve has reduced the breeding areas of some species, but the cliffs of Sagres and the coastal strip are carefully protected. There is a Portuguese *Atlas* of breeding birds (1989), and G A and R S Vowles published a detailed *Breeding Birds of the Algarve* in 1994.

As a footnote to the fauna, the last bear is said to have been killed in 1650, and the Spanish lynx is also absent. The wild ass or onager was found in the mountainous north and in Galicia in medieval times, from which the word was applied to the African congener. It was called *camellus* in Latin, and *zebra* in Portuguese. Until recent times the ass was the poor man's horse everywhere, and the mule the regular means of transport. Wild deer are not now common. The wild boar is found in the National Park at Gerez, but the native wild goat appears to have been lost.

9

Fishing

Fish forms an important part of the Portuguese diet. Lampreys are found in the Lima and shad (*sável*) in the Tagus and Douro, and trout are bred in the numerous new reservoirs or *albufeiras*. But the sea is by far the greatest source. In ancient times the most important catch was the tunny. The Romans also relished *garum*, made of preserved fish. The chain of tanks and industrial plants of Phoenician times can be traced from Lisbon to the Algarve, and also extends to North Africa. After the discovery of America, the great fishery was the Newfoundland Banks, and a large sailing-fleet built at Aveiro and Figueira da Foz left Lisbon every year to catch cod, which was dried to make *bacalhau*. With the imposition of national limits, this fish is now imported. Sailing-ships are still built at Figueira and Aveiro, where the *Dom Fernando*, the largest of the nineteenth-century schooners, was rebuilt in 1998 to serve as a naval museum.

The usual sea-going fishing-craft is the trawler or *traineira*, with both sail and engines. The main deep-sea fishing is for the sardine, the tunny, and a variety of fish, some not easily translatable into English. Smaller trawlers serve for in-shore fishing and are joined by wooden rowing-craft which have elongated prows like crescent-moons and are painted in bright colours. The sheltered lagoons of the Algarve abound in shellfish and in decorative small craft.

The principal sea-fisheries from north to south are: in the Minho, Viana do Castelo, with its festival in the middle of August dedicated to Nossa Senhora da Agonia, who protects fisherfolk; Oporto draws its supplies mainly from Matosinhos, the fishing-village out of which the deep-sea Port of Leixões sprouted to accommodate ocean-liners; south of the Douro, Aveiro remains an active fishery but Figueira da Foz is now best known as a summer resort.

Nazaré was one of the fishing-ports associated with Alcobaça, and is famous for the customs of its fisher-folk and their tartan shirts and skirts. Until recently the boats were drawn up by teams of men and women or by oxen which waited by the beach: these have given way to tractors. Peniche is the largest port for catching and canning sardines. While Nazaré is open and exposed, Peniche has the advantage of two beaches, one sheltered from gales from the north and the other from the south.

The fishing-ports closest to Lisbon are Ericeira and Cascais. The cove at Cascais is sheltered from the Atlantic, and the catch is sold in the village, now better known as a holiday centre. South of Lisbon, Sesimbra is a picturesque village where the catch is brought into the Porto de Abrigo to be auctioned. It consists of sardines, bream, red mullet and *peixe-espada* or scabbard-fish. Octopus and squid are also brought in. Setúbal and the estuary of the Sado were ancient fisheries. The origins of industry in Setúbal developed from fish-canning. South of this, there is no important fishing-port except Sines until the Algarve, where most of the popular resorts are, or have been, fishing-villages. The first of these was Sagres, which is sheltered by Cape St Vincent and probably supplied Prince Henry and his men. The earliest discoverers sailed from Lagos. The broad bay shared by Lagos and Portimão is also a fishery, though Lagos now provides an elegant marina for pleasure craft. The capital Faro is not an important fishery though its Maritime Museum, which occupies the former harbour-master's office, is devoted to models of boats from the time of the Discoveries and also to the development of fishing in the Algarve.

10

Portuguese Wines

The name Portugal is indissolubly associated with that of Port-wine. Both words derive from the city of Oporto, which does not itself produce wine, but stores and exports the justly esteemed vintages of the Upper Douro valley, beginning some fifty miles to the east and continuing as far again to the Spanish frontier. It has enjoyed its reputation since the beginning of the eighteenth century and is still the most beautiful vineyard in the world. Port-wine became the country's leading export, and was widely consumed in Britain, serving even to restore the energies and spirits of university dons after the dispiriting exertion of teaching. Before 1680, the wine brought from Portugal was 'Lisbon wine', red or white. The change was due to a number of factors: the intermittent wars of England and France, which interrupted the trade in claret with Bordeaux; the Methuen treaty which stabilised the rates of duty; and the discovery of gold in Brazil, which made the 'Portuguese trade' eminently desirable. By then there were English merchants established in Oporto, and wine could be bought more advantageously there than in Lisbon. The wine obtained its unique quality by being 'fortified' with brandy, which strengthened it and made it keep better. Yet it was never more than a small proportion of Portugal's total production.

Even in 1930, port amounted to only 7 per cent of the total. Lisbon, the area between the ocean and the Tagus, had 20 per cent of all wine production, and Santarém, the Ribatejo, 15 per cent. Leiria, Braga and Viseu – the valley of the Dão – could also claim to exceed Oporto. Total Portuguese production ranked it with that of much larger countries: Italy, France, Spain and (for a time) Algeria. The vine is adaptable and now thrives almost everywhere. It prefers warm soil, with sufficient rain in the winter and spring, and a hot ripening-season. It does not like standing water, and though it flourishes on both banks of the Minho, it finds much of Spanish Galicia too wet. Nor does it enjoy tropical heat, such as is found in parts of the Alentejo. It has long been grown south of Lisbon at Palmela and Setúbal, and has more recently been extended into the eastern Alentejo round Évora. In much of Portugal the top-soil is thin, but it can send its roots down through broken schist to reach water: this is the prevailing condition in the Douro valley. There are some thirty varieties of dark grapes and as many more of green. In the middle of the nineteenth century all Europe was afflicted by the phylloxera disease, and resistant strains were brought in mainly from California. The resultant strains are fairly international, but Portugal has the advantage of possessing robust varieties of its own and is capable of a wide range of wines which respond to local conditions and practices.

Until the early eighteenth century, wine was drunk fresh, or *verde* (green), and not kept. It was then found that the addition of a touch of brandy made it stronger and made it improve with age. The practice was easily abused, and this was the reason for the formation of Pombal's national wine company, the Real Companhia, in 1756. It led to the demarcation of the Port-wine area, from which wine was genuine Port: wine from outside the area, however similar, was not Port. The first area has been considerably extended, but the principle remains. It was the first attempt at demarcation anywhere. The popular song used to bid: 'Come, come, drink some Port-wine with me/down at the old Bull and Bush.' The primacy of Port lasted until the war of 1939 to 1945. It was an after-dinner drink, and with the imposition of ration-cards, nobody in Britain invited friends to dinner. Sherry from Spain fared better, as an aperitif, and white Port was launched as an alternative.

Meanwhile, Portuguese table-wines were brought into prominence. The government instituted wine co-operatives from 1933, and producers in a given area collaborated to meet the best standards and used a common designation. The first large selling organisation was Sogrape, set up in 1942, which sold the rosé of Vila Real, adjoining the Port-wine area, in a distinctive bottle. Since Portugal joined the European Community the wine-producing areas have been aligned with continental practice. The main areas have 'Controlled' designations (DOC): they include Vinho Verde, Dão, Bairrada, Bucelas and Setúbal. These names are a guarantee of standard, but are themselves diverse. For instance, the wine of Carcavelos near Lisbon has a long history, but is now hard to find because urban development has diminished the area under cultivation: the same may be said of Colares, near Sintra. Dão comes from the valley of the name near Viseu, and is well known in Britain from the painting of St Peter by Grão Vasco that appears on the label. The Bairrada is a group of villages between Viseu and the sea, with no immediate centre, unless Mealhada and Cantanhede. Its wines are also distributed by Sogrape, but considerably varied by individual producers. Bucelas, north of Lisbon, has long been known for its white wine. Setúbal draws on the vineyards of the Palmela peninsula: its Muscatel was formerly much consumed in England at Christmas. There are two large companies at Azeitão.

Vinho Verde is the most famous wine of the Minho: it is also produced as far south as the valley of the Vouga. It is usually white, but there are kinds of a rusty red colour. It was 'green' because fresh, and consumed some three months after it had been made, drawn from the cask and with a strong head. It was not for keeping and therefore had no specific vintage. That from the Minho, Alvarinho, was akin to the Galician Albariño and was exported from the port of Viana. It was the usual tavern-wine in the north, but is now bottled and widely distributed. It is a refreshing drink with a low alcohol content, and admirable for a hot day. It is sometimes rather sharp, but the *vinho verde* made by my friends at Santo Tirso is not in the least acid. Though a neighbour of Port, its cultivation is completely different: the vines were trained up over trees and bushes, but nowadays it is more usual to suspend them on wires propped up on posts: this permits the ground below to be used to grow beans and other vegetables and allows the small-holder to make a living.

Many of the famous Port-wine firms now also produce table-wines. A historic vineyard adds greatly to the value of the land, and this is probably the strongest reason for the development of viticulture in the Alentejo, the least populated province of Portugal. Beside the 'Controlled Denomination' areas, there are wines of 'Regulated Provenance', which are also subject to close regulation in means of production, quantity and quality. Outside these distinctions, wines are 'Regional', denoting one or other of the eight prescribed regions, or simply classed as table-wines, *vinho de mesa*. In the twentieth century, the formation of the co-operatives made these bodies and the government responsible for maintaining quality. More recently, the emphasis has passed to selling organisations and to the private owner, who employ professional oenologists to advise them. While the large organisations are seeking to provide wines of equal standard to be distributed in large quantities, the producers are still looking for new combinations to capture the eye and palate. There are therefore both familiar labels that can be found abroad, and new labels that cannot. To those who are unwilling to learn the new language of 'masters of wine' whose metaphors are to me incomprehensible, one can play for safety, or can take a more adventurous line. In most ordinary restaurants, there is a 'wine of the house'. It often comes from the part of Portugal of which the owner is a native.

Innumerable varieties of Port may be tasted at the Solar do Vinho do Porto in Lisbon. But naturally, Port is best seen at its home – or at least resting-place – in Vila Nova de Gaia, just over the bridge from Oporto. The 'lodges' are not cellars, but vast dark sheds where thousands of casks lie patiently maturing or ranged in more or less cobwebby bottles in an atmosphere of medieval sanctity. The lodges welcome visitors, and most of them have bars in which to complete the tour. Those who attend congresses in the city are often entertained lavishly in this solemn and stimulating setting.

The seat of the controlling body is in the small town of Régoa, fifty miles up the river, where the headquarters, embellished with marble, has a large reserve adjoining it: the original building of the Pombalian Royal Company is in the Rua Nova, renamed after Pombal. South of the river, Lamego is the centre of making fizzy wine or champagne, which is said to equal the French prototype. The process involves several pressings by a modern mechanical process, and the maturing is done in cellars capable of holding a million bottles.

The best time to visit the Port-growing area is after the great heat of August and during the harvest-time of September, when there is much rejoicing. The old practice of crushing the grapes with the bare feet to the sound of rhythmic songs or music has probably vanished, or is at least very rare. By custom, the more generous owners feasted their workers at harvest-time. This is now less common, though a long tradition of hospitality and service protects the Portuguese from the modern phylloxera of greed.

Many years ago, a good friend presented me with a bottle of port so ancient that my great-grandfather might have drunk it. Perhaps it was a pity that he did not, for after I had admired it for a month or two I opened the bottle and drank it. I had left it until too late: its taste had gone and it was merely a liquid with no more taste or flavour than champagne. I suppose I should have kept it to look at.

Lisbon

Lisbon has a magnificent setting on hills at the mouth of the Tagus, which broadens into an inland sea, the Mar de Palha, before passing through a channel to reach the ocean. By convention the hills are seven, like those of Rome, but in fact the slopes are many and some very steep. On the height to the east stands the castle of St George, formerly regarded as the true seat of authority. It is separated from another height, the Alto, by a cleft, once an arm of the sea, and the city grew up between these and the water-front. It has now spread in all three directions on the north bank and has acquired suburbs on the other side, the Outra Banda. From a height, as the aeroplane approaches, it is a maze of red tiles and white walls, with the hills of Palmela and the sandy shores curving away toward the south. On landing, the missing dimension is restored and the vision becomes reality.

The airport at Portela de Sacavém is by modern standards near the centre: about four miles. It joins function with fantasy in the fashion of today, not architecture, but marbled like a bank with a façade of fountains. The taxi-rank is orderly, and there are buses; the underground, the Metro, is still on the way. The hotels are mainly near the centre. Lisbon sprawls but most of its inhabitants are flat-dwellers and its centre is compact; for the same reason, it is subject to traffic-jams in the busy hours and agreeably quiet at weekends. Much of the Baixa, the lower town, is easily covered on foot, and more of the city by the underground. The yellow trams which were one of the joys of Lisbon have been greatly reduced and replaced by long vehicles with trailers, or by buses of one or two decks. It is perhaps necessary, for, like all other cities, Lisbon has been overwhelmed by the proliferation of private cars. But it is a pity that Lisbon transport, like London buses, should be disfigured by aggressive and tasteless advertising. There are four elevators, three of them funicular, to avoid climbing the steeper places.

The castle of St George with its light fawn-coloured walls stands out above the city and is a useful landmark, being visible from many points. It also affords the finest view of the city and its setting. The castle ceased to be the seat of the kings in the sixteenth century, when the palace of the Ribeira was built. It was long neglected and owes its glistening appearance to the double centenary of 1940, which celebrated both the date when Afonso Henriques assumed the style of king of the Portuguese and the

1 The Castle of St George (António Sacchetti)

recovery of independence in 1640. It has a broad esplanade which surveys everything from the Baixa below and the Alto opposite to the inland sea and the distant hills of Palmela. Another fine viewpoint is half-way down at the charming *miradouro* of Santa Luzia, which takes in the inland sea, but not the Baixa.

From the castle parapet, the effects of the great earthquake and tidal wave of November 1755 are evident. The palace of the Ribeira was completely destroyed and in its place the engineers employed by Pombal built the Terreiro do Paço with its landing-stage and the network of straight streets by which he is remembered. The Alto opposite was almost unscathed, but the great monastery of the Carmo built by the Holy Constable Nun'Alvares Pereira, the hero of Aljubarrota, to end his days as a Carmelite monk, still stands in ruins with the bare ribs of its nave showing. The Cathedral, built after the conquest of 1147, has survived. The disaster made way for the first consciously undertaken piece of modern town-planning. The plain Pombaline style is in sharp contrast to the baroque which had been prevalent: it was solid and stable.

The hill below the Castle is so steep that it is climbed in places by flights of stairs impassable for wheeled vehicles, which use only the horizontal ledges. The way down to the level of the Cathedral is a tangle of streets, stairs and dead-ends known as the Alfama (the name is Arabic). The inhabitants were wise enough to use the gentler slope on the north side, the Mouraria. It is presented as the old 'Moorish' quarter but it is not known to have any building that goes back so far. In Camões' day the Alfama

2 Lisbon Cathedral

had the university, which was moved to Coimbra in 1537. It also had noble mansions, and barracks with unsavoury houses. More than one of its churches was destroyed in the Earthquake, but before that its better houses had fallen out of favour and become tenements. Its denizens hang their laundry out over the alleys, solace their poverty with pots of bright flowers and provide a precarious living for picturesque cats.

Lisbon Cathedral, the Sé, stands below the Castle and to the west of the Alfama. When Afonso Henriques took Lisbon, he appointed one of the Anglo-Norman crusaders, Gilbert of Hastings, to be its bishop. The present building belongs to the same tradition as those of Coimbra and Oporto, with a pair of massive towers and a rounded doorway overset by a recessed rose-window. It has suffered from the earthquake of 1755 and probably from previous tremors, but retains its austerity. The cloister was added in the fourteenth century. Unlike Braga, Lisbon had not been the capital of a Roman province and its metropolitan status was conceded only under King John I in 1393: the cathedral treasury has a dalmatic presented by the king. Following the tramline, which for a moment looks likely to enter the cathedral, the road passes the Aljuba, once the archbishop's palace and later a prison for women. It then comes to the Limoeiro, once the palace of the sons of Inês de Castro, and the place where John I came to the throne after killing the count of Ourém, and later the main jail. Some former noble houses remain, but in the sixteenth century the centre of Lisbon shifted to the present Baixa, with the building of the new palace of the Ribeira at the Terreiro do Paço, the centre of government, commerce, learning and entertainment until it was destroyed by the Earthquake. The present open square is the core of Pombal's reconstruction. Its centrepiece is the equestrian statue of King Joseph. According to the guidebooks, English sailors and visitors called it Black-Horse

Square. The King and his horse have a pleasant greenish patina: the plinth has a panel in praise of Pombal, which can be removed when the great man is under a cloud.

The open side of the square facing the river has marble steps of some dignity. The three arcaded sides house government offices. The massive triumphal arch which gives grandeur to the scene was added only in 1873: above it, Glory stands over the rivers Douro and Tagus in effigy. The Rua Augusta is one of four parallel thoroughfares running northwards to the Praça do Rossio. The buildings are of equal height and with identical apertures, though Pombal had not foreseen the growth of banking which has invaded the southern end of what was intended as the fashionable shopping centre. The north-east corner of the Terreiro has the Café Martinho, supposedly the oldest surviving coffee-house in Lisbon: it has souvenirs of the poet Fernando Pessoa.

The square of the Rossio is dominated by the National Theatre of Queen Maria II or Almeida Garrett, the romantic poet and dramatist who revived the somnolescent Portuguese theatre: the building was erected in 1846. The square is dominated by the column in honour of Queen Maria's father, Pedro IV, the ex-emperor of Brazil, and surmounts figures of Justice, Prudence, Strength and Moderation, with the shields of the sixteen chief cities of Portugal. There are flower-sellers and numerous cafés, and it is the best place to catch taxis, which are only hard to find when it rains. The square to the east, the Praça da Figueira, was the main fruit and vegetable market, the Covent Garden of Lisbon, until the stalls were removed: it now has an equestrian statue of King John I. The pavement at the north-east corner of the Rossio is a favourite rendez-vous for Portuguese Africans. Behind it is the church of São Domingos, erected after the Earthquake to replace the monastic church, the largest in Lisbon, said to have been frequented by Camões. By its side, the mansion of the Counts of Almada is the place where the heroes of the Restoration of 1640 hatched their conspiracy. The narrow street, now closed to vehicles, running north from the Theatre has the Geographical Society, founded in 1875, a club with a large Ethnographic museum relating to the Portuguese discoveries. Among other treasures, it possesses several of the *padrões* or stone markers which the early navigators placed on the shores of Africa to mark their achievements. An opening on the opposite side of the road was the Portas de Santo Antão, where the young Camões was involved in an affray which led to his being sent to India, where his father had been offered a lucrative post at Chaul. It is sometimes said that the poet languished in the Limoeiro (then the court prison) between the incident in June 1552 and the following February, when he accepted his rival's pardon: his own account confutes this. The incident is commemorated by a ceramic inscription round the arch.

The building adjacent to the Geographical Society is the Coliseu dos Recreios, the largest popular theatre. Another has been dedicated to the memory of Amália Rodrigues, the queen of the *fado*. A little shop called Eduardinho is devoted to the sale of *ginginha*, or cherry-brandy, made with the pink fruit; Eduardinho, or Teddy, whose favourite tipple it was, was a clown at the Coliseu.

At the western end of the National Theatre, the Rossio is joined to the square of the Restauradores, which has an obelisk to commemorate the conspirators of Independence. The only underground things now are the large car park and the Metro. Between the two squares is the Rossio railway-station, a piece of neo-Manueline built around two inverted horse-shoes and opened in 1890. By its side is the Avenida Palace, the first of the palace-hotels in the French style, by the same architect. The street level now serves only for information and tickets. A lift and elevators carry passengers to the platforms, which can be reached also by car or taxi from above. It was formerly the departure point for Paris but now the Rossio station serves only Sintra and the Western Line. Traffic to Oporto and Beira and to foreign parts uses Santa Apolónia on the east side, where there is access by taxi and space to hire cars.

The western side of the Restauradores is occupied by the Palácio Foz, a grandiose building erected after the earthquake and owned by the Marquis of Foz in 1889: he lavishly embellished the old Palace of Castelo Melhor until he lost his fortune from extravagance; it now serves to direct tourism and supply tourists with information. From it, the Avenida da Liberdade runs for the better part of a mile to the Praça do Marquês de Pombal, or the Rotunda, or Pombal, or simply 'o Marquês'. It was originally the Passeio Público, or promenade, and the present leafy boulevard was opened up in 1879 to 1882. The central avenue allows drivers to try their speed. The traffic-lights (in Portuguese 'semaphores') act as a sort of restraint but the hunters have the advantage, and if held up do not hesitate to sound their horns. The houses on the Avenida met the standard of elegance required in the later nineteenth century. The harmony has been rather altered by ostentatious banks, hotels and cinemas, but verdure and seats are there, and the serins sing in the branches above. Portugal is a land of war-memorials and a monument at the Rua do Salitre commemorates the bloodshed at La Lys in April 1917.

The western height, or Bairro Alto, can be reached without undue expenditure of energy by the funicular tram which operates from the Restauradores, called the 'elevador da Glória'. There is often a queue but the yellow tram waits patiently until it has a load and then grinds gravely up the steep track, doubled in the middle for it to pass its track-mate, rarely as full, coming down. It arrives beside the little park of São Pedro de Alcântara (which is nowhere near the suburb of Alcântara), with a view across the Baixa towards the Castle.

In London, the pavement artist used to show his skill by drawing portraits or landscapes in coloured chalks on the flagstones, but in Lisbon the sidewalks of the Avenida are decorated with black and white stone chips fitted together to make mosaic lines and scrolls. The art is not ancient, and has spread to a few other places. In the Avenida, it can be used to transmit messages. By the bronze statue of Simon Bolívar is an inscription in black and white mosaic, which declares that Corte-Real discovered America in 1480. The Liberator (who himself thought he had 'ploughed the seas' in vain) must be puzzled. It is not pure surmise, as Columbus' biographer Admiral Morrison asserts, but arises from a note on the Cantino map, which shows Newfoundland with the legend that: 'It was found by Gaspar Corte-Real'.

These decorated pavements are not confined to the capital. At Alter do Chão in the Alentejo the square in front of the castle is patterned in black and white zigzag, and at Vila Real de Santo António in the Algarve it is filled with long rays coming from a central point, while at Ponta Delgada in the Azores the geometrical frame contains an intricate carpet in stone.

Another view can be obtained from the 'elevador' of Santa Justa, a column in Eiffelian Gothic ironwork, which rises from the Rua do Ouro. The ascent on foot begins from the south-west corner of the Rossio and is closed to traffic. The Rua do Carmo has been renovated since the great fire of August 1988 gutted the department-store at the upper end. The former style has been preserved, but the shops have followed the vogue of the time. The Carmo turns into the Chiado, the most fashionable shopping street, which continues up the hill to the Praça de Camões. The Chiado is properly the Rua Almeida Garrett, but it gets its name from a popular sixteenth-century playwright, António Ribeiro Chiado, who has a statue in the act of performing a part, off the Largo do Chiado at the top. Near by, on the other side, is the Brasileira, a café in the high style of the first quarter of the twentieth century, with mirrors, gilt and candelabra. It was the haunt of journalists and writers, of whom the most famous is Fernando Pessoa (1888–1935), whose life-size figure in bronze sitting at a table enables those who wish to be photographed with him. Taken as a child by his stepfather to South Africa, he studied at Durban and spent most of his life as a clerk and translator with small firms. He acquired an almost immediate posthumous fame, being buried near Camões at Belém. This fame has been enhanced by the famous portrait by Almada Negreiros, redolent of what was then called modernism. His birthplace is not far away, a second-storey flat facing the São Carlos opera-house.

The opera and the chase were the favourite occupations of King Joseph, who was content to leave matters of state to Pombal. King Joseph's opera-house was destroyed by fire, and the present São Carlos was built in 1793. The generation of romanticism looked rather to the theatre, in which Garrett excelled, but the second half of the nineteenth century saw an operatic revival, not of the national school, but as the delight of the international set, the *haut monde*. The *fin de siècle* was the age of Portugal's greatest novelist, Eça de Queirós (1845–1900), who, though a 'poor fellow from Povoa de Varzim', fell under the charm of France at Coimbra, became consul in Bristol and Newcastle, and died as consul-general in Paris. His novels turn on the 1870s and 1880s. A brochure shows the many places in Lisbon which figure in his works. He is commemorated by a statue in a small space in the Rua do Alecrim, which shows him covering truth with the diaphanous veil of fantasy, in the shape of a lady who is presumably admiring his genius. His long saga of the Maias is his greatest work; his most charming is *A Cidade e as Serras* in which he contrasts the opulent and unsatisfying life of fashionable Paris with the simplicity of the Minho countryside. He has a great deal to say to us.

The square dedicated to the memory of Camões is at the top of the Chiado. The poet is commemorated by a statue in the centre, erected in 1867, and accompanied by more or less imaginary representations of eight contemporaries. It formed the focus of the Camões tercentenary of 1880, and is the setting for the commemoration of the poet's death on 10 June 1580.

Lisbon was taken from the Muslims with the aid of several thousand crusaders who broke their journey to Palestine in response to the King's appeal. They had gathered in 164 ships at Dartmouth, and the largest contingent was Anglo-Norman. The account by R., identifiable as Raol, has been called the best description of a medieval siege. Raol, perhaps the delegate of St Bernard, accompanied Hervey de Glanvill, leader of the contingent from Suffolk, and senior of the five English constables. Raol says that he built with his own hands a chapel and cemetery for the English dead on the hill facing the castle and went daily to the siege. After the place fell between 20 and 24 October, the crusaders wintered in the Tagus, and continued their voyage in February. On departing, Raol sent a monk named Samuel to make over his chapel and cemetery to the church of Santa Cruz, the King's new foundation in Coimbra. The dead were

3 A typical façade with azulejos

the first English to die in a foreign campaign. The cemetery passed to the Franciscans, whose great convent was the Monte de São Francisco between the Chiado and the Rua do Alecrim. It was dissolved in 1834, and its religious functions passed to the church of the Mártires, built between 1769 and 1784. The former convent became the National Library, moved to the University in the Campo Grande in 1968: another part became the Museum of Modern Art. The church of the Martyrs has a bas-relief showing King Afonso Henriques giving thanks for the conquest.

From the two churches at the top of the Chiado, the road climbs the hill towards São Pedro de Alcântara, with the narrow straight streets of the Bairro Alto on the left and the Trindade and Carmo on the right. The Trindade was a large monastery founded in 1294, and was the first home of the Inquisition. The refectory of the monastery is now the Cervejaria da Trindade, a popular restaurant, which preserves a number of azulejos of the early nineteenth century. One of the oldest and most esteemed restaurants is Tavares, called 'Tavares rico'. At the top is the church of São Roque with the Misericórdia at its side in the small square of Trindade Coelho. The square has a life-sized statue of the ardinha, or newspaper boy, crying his wares.

The church of São Roque was given by John III to the Jesuits, who brought in a number of their relics from Spain: the first Portuguese Jesuit, Simão Rodrigues, who died in 1579, is buried there, as is the Cornish Saint, Francis Tregian, who, having been arrested under Queen Elizabeth, escaped to Spain and Portugal where he lived for twenty years. The present church was built under Philip II in the Jesuit tradition of clearing the nave to give prominence to the pulpit; Tregian is buried near the pulpit and the great Padre Vieira who championed Portuguese independence in the seventeenth century preached his longest sermon from it. It acquired much gilded woodwork in the eighteenth century, and possesses a rich treasury.

One of the lost sights of Lisbon is the 'little English' or Inglesinhos, the students of the catholic college who trooped about the city in their ordinand's garb. The large college was founded by a devout Portuguese in 1622 and continued to function until 1984 when it was finally closed and its archives transferred to England. Most of the Alto in which it stands consists of tenements of some antiquity, with washing hanging about the streets, cage-birds and greengroceries, as well as taverns and *fado* joints. The street of the Grémio Lusitano is supposed to have harboured the first masonic lodge, when secret societies were forbidden.

The building by the side of São Roque is the Misercórdia. The network of Misericórdias is widespread, and is attributed to the piety of Queen Leonor, widow of John II. The Lisbon hospital was at first in 1498 in a palace chapel and later at the Conceição Velha near the waterfront which was destroyed by the Earthquake. After the expulsion of the Jesuits, Pombal gave it their former seminary adjacent to São Roque. It is therefore a modest building compared with some of the provincial Misericórdias founded in the sixteenth century. Closely related to the Lisbon Misericórdia is the lottery. It was begun in the reign of Maria I in 1783, when twenty thousand tickets were printed and 12½ per cent of the takings allocated to the support of the city's hospitals and orphanages. The vendors crying their wares are still a common sight in the streets and the draws take place in the Misericórdia. I have never bought a lottery ticket, but if I did it would be in Lisbon rather than somewhere where the object is to enrich directors at the expense of the optimistic poor.

The road at the side of São Roque takes trams or buses but has only narrow sidewalks for pedestrians. Opposite São Roque is the former British club which had its palmiest days in Edwardian times. Beyond the top of the 'elevador da Glória' is the small garden of São Pedro de Alcântara, and at the top of the hill the square known as Príncipe Real, formerly Rio de Janeiro. It has a pool and seats, and a conifer of Central American origin which provides enough shade to shelter a regiment. The road continues to the Polytechnical School (the former Faculty of Science) and now a university. The site was a Jesuit novitiate which Pombal converted to become the College of Nobles. This was abolished in 1837 and the present building erected after 1844. Beside it two lines of enormous palms, natives of Mexico or Lower California, mark the entry of the Botanical Garden, a quiet haven from the city hubbub. Though small, it is rich in sub-tropical plants, such as the Ficuses who shamelessly flaunt their grotesque roots.

In Lisbon, rain is seasonal, but water is free: such was the theory of King John V in building the Aqueduct of Free Waters, the *Aguas Livres*, to carry water over the Alcântara valley through a channel upheld by thirty-five arches to supply the water-tower at Amoreiras which enjoys splendid views over the city. It was distributed by numerous *chafarizes*, ornamental water-heads or 'fountains', many of great artistic merit. They did not suffice to meet the needs of plumbing as the city grew, and during the Peninsular War visitors complained of Lisbon as malodorous. This was remedied by bringing water from the hills near Santarém in 1869. King John could afford to be more magnanimous than water-companies, which have eliminated bad smells, but produced no *chafarizes*.

The water-tower at Amoreiras doubtless fed the mulberry-trees or *amoreiras* which in turn supplied the royal silk factory. Opposite was the mansion of the Dukes of Palmela, now housing a legal branch of the government. The square known as the Rato is a convergence of roads, one of which leads uphill to the Estrela gardens, a park with trees, a pond, peacocks and seats. Beyond it is the Basilica of the Estrela, the last royal church to be built for Queen Maria I. Its dome, frequently illuminated, is visible from all parts of western Lisbon. Its general style, though deriving from Mafra, replaces exuberance with simplicity in an age which esteemed the classical virtues more than decoration. The Queen died in Brazil in 1816: her tomb is beside the high altar.

Facing the church and adjoining the Estrela garden is the English cemetery, authorised, despite opposition from the Inquisition, by the Anglo-Portuguese Treaty of 1654. Among those who came to Lisbon for reasons of health were the novelist Henry Fielding and the hymn-writer Philip Doddridge. The vicarage, on ample lines, was built toward the end of the same century, and served to house British refugees during the French occupation. It also sheltered many war-time visitors during the tenure of the Rev Fulford Williams in 1940: it is now an international college. The church, dedicated to St George, stands in a quiet grove of trees. On the other side is the still flourishing British Hospital.

Henry Fielding, then the most celebrated novelist of the day, arrived in Lisbon in August 1754 with his family. He was suffering from gout, dropsy and asthma, and had taken a strong dislike to Captain Veale, who had charged £30 for the passages. He was prepared to dislike Lisbon, being overcharged at the coffee-house where he lodged. But when Mr Stubbs, a merchant in grain, found him a quinta at Junqueira ('a *kintor* at Jonquera near Bellisle'), his health improved and he rode out in his chaise, sent home hogsheads of 'Carcavella', and asked for a man, a housekeeper and an amanuensis. He died on 8 October. His grave was unmarked until a French consul put up a sign to point up the philistinism of the English merchants: the Duke of Lafões would have done as much, but for religious scruples. Finally a temporary chaplain erected a monument in 1830.

The Largo da Estrela is the space between the church and the Estrela gardens. From it a steep hill descends to the Largo of São Bento, which faces the former monastery, still often called the palace of São Bento. Founded in 1598 and completed in 1615, it is the Portuguese parliament building, adopted for this purpose after the dissolution of the monasteries in 1834. The chapter-house of the friars then became the house of Peers. The present grand front was built in 1876, and the chamber of deputies was completed by the end of the century. It was then considered the finest building made in the nineteenth century, and is certainly the most imposing, set off by an enormous flight of stairs, which the deputies do not have to climb, since a paved way passes the front. Behind it is the residence of the prime minister. To its right, part of the original monastery used to contain the Torre do Tombo, the public record office, which has been moved to the University City. A former director, an eminent medievalist, used to be greeted formally by the staff lined up every morning to receive him. His predecessors included the chronicler Fernão Lopes, whom Southey thought the greatest of any nation, who worked in the castle of St George. The record office was transferred to São Bento in 1757, and after the dissolution of 1834 vast collections of monastic documents were gathered. Its most eminent director, Herculano, was born in a house near by in 1810.

Eastward from the Rato, the road descends to the Avenida just below the Rotunda, where Pombal, a tamed lion at his feet, surveys rather blankly the Avenue of Liberty, which swirls round his feet to diverge and make way for the Parque Eduardo Sétimo, or Edward VII, whose visit in 1903 it commemorates. In addition to its shady walks it contains the Estufa Fria, or cold greenhouse, where a protection of slats against the strong sun permits the cultivation of a wide variety of exotic plants, particularly ferns. In earlier times the Park had served as a fairground, and the only vestige of this activity is the annual book-fair held at the end of May.

Many of the Lisbon hotels are near the Parque or Pombal or the Avenida. The main museums are on the periphery without being remote. The underground reaches the Praça de Espanha, or Palhavã, the stop for the Gulbenkian collection and headquarters of the Foundation. Calouste Gulbenkian, former mayor of Baghdad, established his collection in his house in the Avenue d'Iéna in Paris and became a war-time refugee in Lisbon, where he died in a hotel in 1955, having set up his Foundation. The park of Palhavã, once used by the children of John V, was bought as its headquarters. In addition to the administration-block which houses exhibitions and conferences, it has the main collection, which remains as the founder formed it, and the museum of modern art, as well as attractive gardens. The collection rivals almost any other in its variety, though, perhaps naturally, it is strongest in the Middle East, antiquity, the medieval Renaissance and the modern artists most appreciated in Paris between 1930 and 1940. It has one good Turner and no Constable. The display, all on one level, is excellent.

The main national art collection, the Janelas Verdes, or Museu de Arte Antiga, is to the west of the city, just above Santos, the first stop from the Cais do Sodré station. It gives its name to the street, Janelas Verdes, or Green Windows, and is the palace built for the Count of Alvor in the seventeenth century, acquired and altered by Pombal. It was opened as a museum in 1884 and has a very miscellaneous collection, including the greatest Portuguese painting, the panels of St Vincent by Nuno Gonçalves. It has also a set of monks by Zurbarán. There is a small garden with a fine jacaranda and views of the river.

The docks below were once the busiest part of the waterfront. In the fourteenth century the royal shipyard was at the Arsenal, next to the Terreiro do Paço. In the time of John II there was a great increase in shipbuilding as can be seen from the numbers of expert carpenters registered. King Manuel's ships were made at the Ribeira das Naus, and the seamen's quarter was the lower end of the present Rua do Alecrim. The present Cais do Sodré, the terminus of the Estoril railway, was the Remolares, the home of the ship's carpenters, later renamed after a companion of Vasco da Gama. In the nineteenth century ocean-going ships came in and were repaired at Santos. Portuguese who left for distant commands often placed their wives in convents, which were numerous in the Santos area. One such was connected to the family of Correa de Sá, the defender of Brazil. Part of it in the Rua das Janelas Verdes is the hotel known as York House. It was acquired by two Scottish sisters who gave it its name, and later by a French lady who decorated the cells and rooms with objects of art and made it a rendez-vous for visiting writers. It has a secluded courtyard with a pepper-tree in which the finches sing in place of the nuns. Further up the hill are the districts of Buenos Aires and the Lapa, favoured by the English residents in the nineteenth century.

On the north-western side of the city the valley of the Alcântara stream is crossed by the Aqueduct and beyond it the park of Monsanto rises to a height of 600 feet with good views of Lisbon. The large park consists of pinewoods which are pleasant for walking and picnicking, though now intersected by busy roads. At its foot is the suburb of Bemfica, widely known for its football-team and also for its zoo, where the elephants ring a bell for their snack and dolphins perform their acrobatic feats. It is gardened and possesses a canine cemetery. The village of Bemfica was once a royal estate which King John I gave to the Dominicans. Their monastery, rebuilt in the six-teenth century, was destroyed by the Earthquake, but the church and cloister survive. They have the tomb of Dr João das Regras whose eloquence convinced the cortes of Coimbra in 1385 to recognise the Master of Avis as the rightful successor to the throne. The chapel of the Castros has the graves of the family, including the great Dom João de Castro, viceroy of India. Bemfica had several stately houses. That of the Mascarenhas family originates with Dom Fernando, master of the horse to John II. His descendant Dom João, second count of Torre and first Marquis of Fronteira, who built the house, was promoted for his part in the wars of the Restoration. Its Sala das Batalhas, or Hall of the Battles, has seventeenth century *azulejos* depicting the battles of Montijo, Ameixial, Montes Claros and the Lines of Estremós. The theme is extended to the gardens, with straight walks amid clipped hedges and statuary. A rectangular tank is backed by large panels of *azulejos*, depicting, amid much else, mounted cava-liers with plumed hats in the fashion of the century. The display of shiny ceramic tiles on the pavilion roofs and the *azulejos*, here accompanied by mythological statues and portrait medallions surrounded by fruit and foliage, mark the peculiarly Portuguese adaptation of the Italianate style.

Another estate at Bemfica belonged to the English merchant and capitalist Gerard de Vismes or Devismes, the fifth son of a Huguenot count settled in England, who arrived in about 1746, prospered under Pombal and endowed the English hospital. He acquired the estate at Bemfica as well as the Quinta of Monserrate near Sintra, both of which he let to William Beckford at different times. The mansion at Bemfica was adorned with paintings and a collection of objects of art and antiquities. Beckford arrived there with a train of servitors, including a band of musicians, in 1787. Devismes himself had already proposed the building of the hospital, but he returned to England in 1792 and it was not inaugurated until the following year. The mansion was built by Oliveira Bernardes and surrounded by a park filled with exotic trees and shrubs. It later passed to the Marquis of Abrantes and was sold in 1847 to the unmar-ried daughter of John VI, Dona Isabel Maria, who resided there until her death in 1876. It now serves as a reform school.

The zoological gardens arose from the estate of the Baron of Quintela whose great fortune passed to the young Count of Farrobo: he built a seat enriched with a theatre, large for 1830 and the first to be lit by gas, with grottoes, caged animals and aviaries. He ran through his fortune, and the Zoological Society acquired its present site in 1904.

The Metropolitan line has a stop at Luz, the site of the military college for the sons of officers, begun at Mafra and installed here in 1859. It occupies the site of a her-mitage given by John III to the sisters of the Order of Christ and destroyed by the Earthquake. The next stop is Carnide, formerly a pleasant village with country houses and quiet lanes. The convent of St Teresa was founded in 1642 for an illegitimate daughter of the Austrian Emperor and passed to a daughter of John IV.

The limit of the city for walking purposes may be set at Alcântara, a thickly popu-lated working-class area with a bridge across the valley traversed higher up by the Aqueduct. It was here that the Spanish troops of the Duke of Alba defeated the Portuguese in 1580 to assure the succession of Philip II. It has become the point of

4a Section of the façade of the Monastery of the Jerónimos

departure for the great modern bridge which joins Lisbon to the south shore in a single lofty span: it was opened in 1966 and named after Dr Salazar. After the revolution
of 1974, it was renamed the 25th of April Bridge and has been enlarged by a railway-
track. This has led to a dense construction at Almada on the south bank. The opening
of a north circular ring-road has done something to alleviate pressure on the streets of
Lisbon itself.

At the time of the Earthquake the royal family was at Belém, and the later royal
palaces have been on the west side of the city. The Necessidades, which now serves as
the Foreign Office, was built in 1745 for the brothers of John V, and escaped the
Earthquake. It has a *chafariz* of 1747, and a private park, the Tapada. Beyond the valley is the Ajuda palace, still in construction when the royal family left for Brazil in
1807. It also has a *tapada* or reserve, intended as a hunting-park for King José, but now
a botanical garden assigned to the Institute of Agronomy. The palace itself replaced
a wooden structure occupied after the disaster. Begun in 1801, it has a large library, a
substitute intended to take the place of the royal collection of the Ribeira.

4b Detail of the façade of the Monastery of the Jerónimos (Antonio Sacchetti)

But the great monuments of sixteenth-century Lisbon are the monastery of the Jerónimos and the Tower at Belém. The influx of Guinea gold brought Portugal into a state of relative affluence after 1450. It increased steadily until Vasco da Gama's epic voyage of 1498, which brought the commerce of the East into the picture. What is remarkable is that Manuel should have been able to undertake many projects at once, without relying on unpaid labour as King Diniz had to do for his castles. The donation to the Jeronymites was already decided when news of Gama's achievement arrived.

5 The Tower at Belém

In 1494 the southern Frenchman Jacques Boytac had been given the task of building the
Jesus church at Setúbal in which he introduced thin and twisted columns to support
stone vaulting: this was the style he applied in the Monastery of the Jerónimos, which
grew into the largest building in Europe, except the great mosque at Cordova. The

technical possibilities of the period are combined with the decoration of the Renaissance and those of the florid Gothic adapted to themes appropriate for a nation of seafarers. The elements were combined without fear of incongruity. Whilst medieval cathedrals had taken decades to complete, this monastery was built between 1502 and 1519, by which time the Renaissance had predominated in the decoration of the main doorway and the cloisters. During the same period the Tower of Belém was erected to guard the entrance to the port (1515–20): it was the work of Diogo de Arruda, a military engineer who responded to the heraldry newly adopted. The theme of the rounded casemates is African: John II had built the fortress of Mina in 1482. The utilitarian nineteenth century blocked the view with encumbrances which were removed in 1940, when the setting was cleared and the splendid gardens laid out. The statue of Afonso de Albuquerque, founder of Goa, surveys the scene from the top of his column.

Belém is also the official residence of the President of the Portuguese Republic. It was the house of the Counts of Aveiras, acquired by John V in 1726. The former riding-school was turned into the Coach Museum in 1905: it contains some of the most extraordinary vehicles ever made. Belém was the scene of the supposed attempt to assassinate King Joseph in 1758, for which the Távoras were barbarously executed by Pombal. He founded the chapel of the Memória to express the king's gratitude for his escape in 1760: Pombal's own remains were reinterred there in 1923. Below it is the house of the Count of Ega, whose possessions were confiscated for his adherence to the French in the period before the Peninsular War. It was awarded to Marshal Beresford, who occupied it as head of the Portuguese army from 1814 to 1820, when it was taken from him and returned to its previous owners. The Colonial Garden, now a park for tropical and exotic plants, was laid out by Henry Newel in 1912, and is one of the most agreeable corners in Lisbon. Among the other attractions of Belém are the Ethnographical and Archaeological Museum in the Jerónimos, and the Naval Museum beside it, as well as the sweet cakes known as *pasteis de Belém*, made at a shop in the main street.

Since the quincentenary of the death of Prince Henry in 1460, Portugal has been celebrating the epic of the Discoveries of the continents until then almost unknown to Europe. The cycle culminated in the commemoration in 1998 of Vasco da Gama's voyage of 1498, marked by an exhibition in Lisbon and the building of the Vasco da Gama bridge across the Tagus, and, in 2000, of the discovery of Brazil by Pedro Álvares Cabral in 1500, for which a flotilla of small ships sailed from Lisbon to Rio de Janeiro. The celebrations were inaugurated in 1960 with the erection of an impressive monument to the men of the fifteenth century at Belém. It takes the form of a tilted plinth with the heroes standing behind the Prince who holds a model caravel and gazes into the unknown. Behind him follow King Afonso V, 'the African', Gama, Cabral, Magellan and others. The monument is 170 feet high, and was conceived when Portugal was still the head of an empire. Politicians have substituted the word 'communities', and this usage has become *de rigueur*. The day that was celebrated as that of the death of Camões, 10 June, is now called the festival of the Communities.

Although Belém was formerly a *concelho*, of which the great historian Alexandre Herculano was mayor, it now forms part of greater Lisbon. The trains from the Cais de Sodré continue to Oeiras, Carcavelos, Parede, São Pedro do Estoril, São João do Estoril, Estoril, Monte Estoril and Cascais, a distance of nearly twenty miles. There followed the opening of the 'Marginal', a road which keeps as close as possible to the shore.

Before becoming Marquis, Pombal was Count of Oeiras, where he and his brothers inherited property. On it he built the most imposing palace, apart from those of the royal house, of his day. It now houses the numerous scientific activities of the Gulbenkian Foundation. The Tagus here flows into the ocean, between the fort of St Julian and a long spit of land. At Carcavelos, the Quinta Nova was formerly part of the Pombal empire. Eight international cables terminate here, and the Quinta was equipped as a training-college by the cable company, which moved its activities to England during the recession of 1930, after which it became the Anglo-Portuguese school. Carcavelos produces a fine wine; the vineyards and pinewoods have been squeezed by the development of the beach and town.

The coast here is a series of resorts, of which the best known is Estoril, where the beach is wider and a casino has been established with gardens and facilities for bathing and idling. The railway line ends at Cascais, formerly a fishing-village with a well-sheltered cove for small boats. Beyond it there is a break in the cliffs at the Boca do Inferno or Hell's Mouth, in which the ocean gargles in spectacular fashion. The open Praia do Guincho remains a wide stretch of sand with only a restaurant or two, until it is enclosed by the hills of Sintra at the Cabo da Roca, known to seamen as the Rock of Lisbon, though a *roca* is a distaff.

The Tower of Belém is the most monumental defence work of the port of Lisbon. It was later supplemented by a series of small forts that guard the coast from Caxias to Cascais. Soon after the Spanish annexation, Philip II commissioned Italian engineers to defend the bar, where the projecting spit from the south bank brings the navigable channel within gunshot of the north side. The large fort of St Julian of the Bar, da Barra, was paired with the circular fort in midstream known as the Bugio. The Bugio is in fact two concentric circles surmounted by a light, and in rough weather surrounded by surf. Several of the other forts are used as summer camps for children. Most were built after the Restoration of independence in 1640, when John IV entrusted the Marquis of Cascais with the defence of the whole area. The forts then came under the command of the citadel of Cascais: most are built low with round sentry-boxes at the corners. They stand at the water's edge at Caxias, Oeiras, Estoril and Cascais, with two outposts to cover the Praia do Guincho.

The city has also expanded northwards to embrace what were country estates in the seventeenth century, and is limited on the east by the elbow that the great river takes coming from almost due north. Although the northern outskirts are accessible by bus, they have been brought into the orbit of central Lisbon by the underground railway.

At the end of the Avenida Fontes Pereira de Melo, in the square bearing his name, Marshal Saldanha has an elaborate monument in which he is accompanied by an allegorical figure of Victory and bronze lions: he stands brandishing one arm, apparently in the direction of his kinsman Pombal. The roads spreading between the park and the broad Avenida da República are the 'Avenidas Novas', residential boulevards lined with trees, pleasant enough without special distinction. Some, like the Avenida Cinco de Outubro, are lined with the jacaranda. The Avenida da República is the broadest of the boulevards, though it can boast only of plane trees. Its houses were built for the wealthy bourgeoisie in the early twentieth century. The Avenida is broken by the Campo Pequeno which has a fantastic piece of building in the Bull-ring, a pseudo-Oriental circus in red brick with turrets of operatic proportions. It is not far from the municipal slaughterhouse built in 1863, though as the bulls are not killed the juxtaposition seems unnecessary.

The Campo Grande, formerly the Alvalade, was a city park in the eighteenth century. The central avenue is now flanked by two belts of trees, and the land to the west, once private mansions, has been converted into the University City, the 'classical university'. The various faculties are housed round a bay above the Campo Grande. The road from the Campo Grande to Lumiar was formerly lined with country houses, of which the grandest was the Quinta de Palmela, begun by the Marquis of Angeja and extended by the first Duke of Palmela. Among the other houses at Lumiar, Queen Maria I occupied the Quinta dos Azulejos with a large collection of *azulejos* of about 1779 from the Rato workshop. Lumiar also had its medieval palace belonging to a son of King Diniz. Beyond Lumiar is Odivelas, once one of the greatest convents, where Queen Philippa died in 1415, as her sons set out on the conquest of Ceuta. It was ruined by the Earthquake, and little is left of King Diniz's foundation of 1295: The area has long been urbanised. On the road to the town is the Senhor Roubado, a small shrine erected to commemorate an act of sacrilege in 1671, though it dates only from 1744: the *azulejos* tell the story of the crime.

Returning to the centre of the city, beyond the Sociedade de Geografia, the Rua das Portas de Santo Antão leads to the *elevador* of Lavra, which climbs up the steep slope on the eastern side of the Avenida. It is not quite so busy as the Glória, but performs the same useful function. It was the first to be built in 1884.

According to tradition, Camões died in a house on the site of No. 139–141 in the Calçada de Santana: the attribution may be apocryphal, but he was buried in the church of Santana and lay there until his bones were transferred to the Jerónimos at Belém in 1880. The former Franciscan monastery of Santana installed by Queen Catarina in 1561 is now part of the medical school. The hill is dominated by the hospital of São José, which replaces the Jesuit house of Santo Antão, vacated on their expulsion in 1759. Not far away is the Military School, in fact the military academy, installed since 1851 in the palace of Bemposta. It was used as a palace by Queen Catherine when she returned from England in 1692, and on her death in 1705 reverted to the crown. Damaged by the earthquake and restored in simple style, it was used by King John VI on his return from Brazil. In 1824 it was the scene of the 'Abrilada', and King John died here in 1826. Dom Miguel and Dom Pedro IV lived there, but when the royal estates were dispersed in 1849 it passed to the army.

One of the finest viewpoints in the city is from the Graça, once the richest monastery in Lisbon, founded by Augustinians in the thirteenth century and rebuilt in the eighteenth. The chapterhouse has the tombs of the Albuquerques, including that of the great Afonso de Albuquerque. After the dissolution of 1834, the convent was transformed into barracks, but the image of the Senhor dos Passos continued to be venerated and was the subject of a procession, the Passos da Graça.

Lisbon east of the Castle and cathedral differs from the west in several respects. The ships of the Discoveries and the Atlantic liners came in to Santos and were built or repaired there or at the yards of Alfeite on the Outra Banda, now the naval headquarters. In contrast, the waterfront east of the Terreiro is more prosaic: the Customs wharf, then the corn dock, the Terreiro do Trigo, and the Cais dos Soldados, or embarkation-place, followed by a commercial and industrial belt.

One of the few remaining buildings of the Discoverers is the Casa dos Bicos on the street of the Cod-fishers, the Bacalhoeiros, which belonged to the family of Afonso de Albuquerque. The exterior, with its Bicos, or diamonds, resembles the Spanish Picos, but the interior has been entirely remodelled. The Bacalhoeiros runs into the Terreiro do Trigo and then the Jardim do Tabaco below the Alfama, and reaches the Santa Apolónia station, which replaces the Rossio as the main terminal. Before the station is the Museu Militar, which, among much else, has more than two hundred and fifty cannon from the days of King Manuel onwards. It is installed in an eighteenth-century palace and is between the military foundry set up for King Joseph in 1762 and the quay of the Soldiers, by the present railway-station.

Not far away is the royal pantheon, the church of St Vincent or São Vicente de Fora, outside the city walls. It was begun for Philip II in 1582 to the design of Terzi, and has a rather uncompromising exterior of two towers enclosing three compartments with niches for figures of saints. It has been made the resting-place for the Braganzas, who have been given matching sarcophagi, though Maria I and Pedro IV lie in their basilica of the Estrela.

Between São Vicente and Santa Engrácia is the Campo de Santa Clara, which is now the Feira da Ladra, or 'Thieves' Fair', an open-air market for bric-à-bric under the shade of trees. I have never found anything, though I have seen a Canadian emerge wreathed in smiles at having found a unique brass tap of early vintage.

Beyond the walls at Xabregas was the site for tourneys, the last of which was held when Prince John reached fifteen in 1552: Camões' pupil, António de Noronha, was held to have outshone the rest. He was killed in North Africa in 1553, and commemorated in the poet's last eclogue composed in India. Queen Leonor, the beneficent widow of John II, retired to her convent of the Madre de Deus, founded in 1509. Its chapel was richly endowed by John III and his wife, and lavishly enhanced with gilded woodwork by John V. Its courtyards were decorated with blue and white tiles, and it has been converted into the Museum for the characteristic Portuguese decorative form, the *azulejo*, taking its place after the Janelas Verdes and the Gulbenkian as the third best museum in Lisbon.

The most famous monuments in the vicinity of Lisbon are Queluz and Sintra. Both are served by trains at regular intervals from the Rossio station: Queluz is eight miles away and Sintra less than twenty. Queluz shares a station with Belas, the seat of the Marquises of Belas, and the scene of a popular pilgrimage to the Senhor da Serra on the last Sunday in August. Belas was once the property of one of the judicial murderers of Inês de Castro, and was confiscated by King Pedro I. It passed to the mother of King Manuel who gave it to the first Marquis: it was visited by John VI, but was then sold and neglected like other former stately homes. It and the neighbouring quintas are eclipsed by the fame of Queluz and Sintra. The palace of Queluz is the most attractive of the royal residences. The estate on the little river Jamor was confiscated by John IV after the Restoration of 1640 and incorporated in the Infantado, the properties intended to support younger sons of the royal house. King Joseph awarded it to his brother Pedro. It was then a country gentleman's residence, which became a palace when Pedro married his niece, the future Queen Maria. It retains its original modest proportions in the rooms of state. The palace stands back behind a forecourt and an arc of one-storeyed dependencies in the road, pink stucco walls and marble pilasters garnished with stone flambeaux. The house itself, designed by M V Oliveira, a pupil of Ludovice, and a Frenchman J B Robillon, was completed by Maria after her husband's death, and was treated as the usual royal residence from 1794. Beckford has left a rather fanciful recollection of its agreeable pleasures before the royal family migrated to Brazil. The throne-room is unpretentious and decorated with mirrors and gilt, and the Hall of the Ambassadors only a little more elaborate. There is a small music-room and a confined council-room, many souvenirs of domesticity and few of great affairs. The gardens are arranged around an animated fountain of Neptune. The stream is diverted into a canal adorned with a hundred yards of blue and white *azulejos* from the Rato factory. Much of the original furnishing was carried off to Brazil, but replaced by John VI. The palace was damaged by a serious fire in 1934, but has now been restored. The adjoining estate serves as an agricultural college, and the stables as a very superior refectory.

The hills of Sintra are a long ridge rising to over 1,600 feet at the Cruz Alta and Pena and plunging into the ocean at the Cabo da Roca, the foreland of continental Europe. In the middle of summer when Lisbon swelters it is cool, fresh and verdant. In the winter its peaks may be swathed in mist and its northern slopes are moist and luxuriant with woods of native and exotic trees. The village which nestles at its foot is on a fertile slope carefully cultivated since Muslim times. Byron thought it perhaps the fairest village on earth and in *Childe Harold* made it a 'glorious Eden'. George Borrow, an agent for the Bible Society who might not have agreed with him about much else, thought it an enchanted land and a Portuguese paradise, and Robert Southey considered it the most blessed nook in the habitable world. They were repeating the words used by Gil Vicente in his *Triumph of Winter*, 'a garden of the terrestrial paradise', and of Camões, who in the *Lusiads* touches it with *saudade*: the departing exile looks with lingering eyes on the dear Tagus and the fresh hills of Sintra.

The train from the Rossio stops in the suburb of Estefania, a walk of ten or twenty minutes on the level from the village and Palace. The road from Estoril climbs the north slope to Ramalhão and the upper village of São Pedro, which commands a fine view of the plain below. The most picturesque approach is by bus or car from Cascais and the bay of Guincho, passing between the serra and the Roca at Azoia, and the small cove of Azenhas do Mar, a sheltered cleft in the rocky coast which is splendid for bathing, providing that the red flag is not flying since the Atlantic rollers can be dangerous. What stands out from São Pedro is the two cones of the Palace in the village square which seem to denote the kitchens of some enormous monastery. On closer approach the palace and its chimneys are seen to be a central block entered from a broad esplanade by a wide flight of steps leading to four ogival arches with a whole series of extensions unfolding behind. The whole passes for Moorish, an illusion fostered by the fact that it faces towards the Moorish castle perched on the crest above and in front.

Sintra owes its cultivation to the Muslim period. It was the westernmost part of the *taifa* of Badajoz, which was almost ceded to Alfonso VI in 1094 and taken with Lisbon by Afonso Henriques in 1147. It is possible that the former governor dwelled on the

6 The Palace at Sintra (José Manuel)

site of the palace, but there is nothing to prove this, and nothing is known of Sintra from the time of the conquest until King Diniz built there. The earliest datable parts of the present palace appear to be from the time of John I in the fifteenth century, after which numerous additions and modifications were made, especially under Manuel. Manueline eclecticism brought the 'Moorish' back into favour. Since the 'free Moors', or *mouros forros*, kept their customs and practices after the conquest there is no reason why the tradition of building and craftsmanship should not have been pre-served. It is reflected in the delicate windows, woodwork ceilings and geometrical single-coloured ceramic tiles called *azulejos* (as if they were all blue, though this was then the exception rather than the rule). The great Salas have painted wooden ceilings: the Hall of the Swans, the Hall of Magpies, which supposedly refers to an indiscretion of King John I, and the Brasões, or Coats of Arms, which shows the bearings of the seventy-two noble families of the reign of King Manuel. The Palace in all its complex-ity and variety is one of the wonders of Portugal.

Outside in the village square the Hotel Central, now a café much frequented at weekends, used to have rooms kept by the memorable Dona Laura. Not far away is the Hotel Lawrence where Byron stayed. The outskirts of the village and the slopes above it are littered with quintas of various ages, sizes and styles. The winding and shady road to the west leads after a long walk to Monserrate, passing the palace of the Marialvas at Seteais. It was built for the Dutch magnate Gildemeister in the eight-eenth century and bought by the fifth Marquis of Marialva, who added the central arch to mark the visit of John VI in 1802. Byron thought incorrectly that the famous or infamous Convention of Sintra, which allowed Junot to leave with his loot after Wellington had defeated him, was concluded here: it was probably signed at the mansion in Lisbon which Junot made his headquarters. William Beckford, who was introduced into the royal circle by Marialva, embroidered his Journals in his travel-books published thirty years later, when he was the forgotten *enfant terrible* of English letters. He had inherited the wealth of his father, a Jamaican planter, at the age of eleven, composed his 'oriental' novel *Vathek* in French at the age of twenty-one, was left a widower with two daughters at twenty-six and, finally, was exiled for a book which, like his imaginary caliph, professed to reject every belief that was not strictly unorthodox. Arriving in Portugal with his servitors in 1787, he was received by Marialva with a kindness he had not found elsewhere. He retained his pseudo-caliphal imagination, but while his novel is now unreadable, his *Journals* are full of observation. He visited Portugal three times, spent his fortune on his Gothic folly at Fonthill which he was obliged to sell, and lived until 1844, passing his later years at Bath, jogging along on a mere £30,000 a year.

The idea of recuperation in Portugal goes back at least to the novelist Henry Fielding. His glimpse of the city is not romantic. But the adjective was applied to Sintra by Pitt's cousin Thomas, who also applied the word to Dom João de Castro, the great sixteenth-century viceroy of India who owned the Penha Verde. Perhaps he meant only extraordinary or sublime. Another romantic who came to love Portugal was Robert Southey, who also rebelled against eighteenth-century education, which esteemed verse in dog-Latin above poetry. Southey took refuge with his uncle, the Reverend Samuel Hill, himself a Lusophile who had taken the chaplaincy at Lisbon on the recommendation of an aunt who had come for her health. The poet Wordsworth may have denounced the Convention of Sintra but Southey (being a good writer of prose) became Poet-Laureate: he composed a massive *History of Brazil*, but his history of Portugal remained unfinished.

Southey expressed the wish that an English painter might come to draw Sintra. J M W Turner was engaged on other things. But a greater writer, Eça de Queirós, saw it in colour when he leaned on the wall at Seteais. He says:

> the great tilled plain below spread like a counterpane in light green and dark green patches with white strips of road winding, and here and there a white house in a clump of trees and always in that well-watered spot a row of polled elms along a brook running between grassy banks. In the distance was the sea, a straight line softened by a bluish diffused mist and above a great round lustrous dome of blue with only a wisp of cloud, forgotten and drifting suspended in the air . . . Seteais was an arch like a heavy frame through which in the rich light of late afternoon there was a marvellous picture, a foreground of lawn dotted with yellow buttercups, then a close row of ancient trees with ivied trunks and, standing out sharply against the light blue of the sky, the dark violet of the Serra crowned by the Pena castle, romantic and solitary on its height with the gloom of the park at its foot and its thin tower lost in the air and its cupolas glinting in the sun as if of gold.

The earliest of the quintas on the road to the west is the Penha Verde of Dom João de Castro. He built the round chapel which bears the date 1542. The Convent of the Capuchos or Santa Cruz was built by his son Dom Alvaro in 1560 to keep a vow of his father. It is a tiny hermitage cut out of the rock with minute cells lined with cork. The altar is a slab of marble and the refectory a stone table. The terms of the vow are not, I think, recorded, but the result can hardly be in greater contrast than that of the promise that set in train the monstrous pile at Mafra, not far away.

The adjacent *quintas* have passed through various hands. The most famous is the house and gardens of Monserrate. If the Cork Convent recalls the memory of the Capuchin monks who carried the saint's love of the natural to its limit, its neighbour is completely different. The original house was acquired by Devismes and rented for a time in 1794 to Beckford. It was later purchased by Francis Cook of Richmond Hill, the master of a textile firm at St Paul's in London whose first marriage was to Emily Lucas, a member of the English community in Lisbon. He had the old house totally reconstructed and replaced by an oriental fantasy worthy of the young Beckford, though with some input from the Prince Regent's Pavilion at Brighton. James Knowles, who had built the Cook edifice at St Paul's, was engaged in 1858 to mould the remains of Devismes and Beckford into an Arabo-Indian medley said to incorporate 1,176 arches containing innumerable arabesques, filigrees and other adornments. The achievement was completed by the landscape gardens, for which Cook brought hundreds of exotic plants under the guidance of Kew and care of his gardener, Francis Burt. Cook's wife died in 1884, and he was then made a baronet and espoused an American adventuress named Tennessee Caflin, who had led a scandalous existence in occultism and liberation and lived until 1923. Her husband's dozen *quintas* were broken up and the Cork Convent passed to the state. There is an active Society of Friends of Monserrate who care for the gardens and property.

The road continues along the skirts of the hills to the village of Colares, prettily situated amongst trees and overlooking vineyards which produce a highly appreciated wine. The South African poet Roy Campbell spent his later years in this area writing versions of his colourful autobiography: he was killed in a road accident in 1957. The rocky coast beyond has several small resorts, including Azenhas do Mar with a crowded cliff-top and a tiny beach. Praia das Maçãs was reached by a tram from Sintra which from 1910 onwards cruised through the countryside to the sea.

The crests above Sintra are occupied by the Moorish castle and the Pena Palace. The 'castle' is a line of four or more turrets joined by a fringe of wall. How much is Moorish and how much is due to the antiquarian enthusiasm of King Fernando II, the consort of Maria II, is now doubtful. The top is at 1,360 feet and has exhilarating views. It is reached by some 500 rock steps. The neighbouring summit is crowned by the Pena Palace and is reached by a road which takes several hair-pin bends to reach a similar height. It is a pleasant walk or ride through the quiet woods. In the village-square before the Palace there are open carriages, each with a pair of horses which are used to the climb. The Pena was surmounted by a monastery, which King Fernando transformed into a palace of considerable size poised on a narrow ridge. It enjoys stupendous views over the estuary of the Tagus and the curving coast to the south. The castle designed by Baron von Eschwege may be described as Rhineland eclectic. Maria II died young, her widower surviving her by thirty years and being briefly considered as a candidate for the vacant Spanish throne after the deposition of Isabella II in 1868. He was an opera-lover, which may throw light on the Wagnerian choice of site for his castle: it attempts to make itself more convincing by incorporating as many elements of the repertoire as possible.

The seaside is full of the holiday-homes of city-dwellers which extend as far as Ericeira. Ericeira is already in the concelho of Mafra. After the republican revolution of October 1910 the young King Manuel II and his mother Dona Amélia spent their last night at Mafra before embarking at Ericeira for exile.

Mafra is the vastest of the undertakings of the opulent King John V, who promised it in gratitude for the birth of his first child. It is outside of the garden area of Sintra, in rough land that affords cover for game, whence its extensive reserve, the Tapada. The site was suitable for a small hermitage, but the present enormous pile rivals the Spanish Escorial, took from 1713 to 1730 to build, and gave employment to thousands of workers. Ludovice made a palace with a great basilica and quarters for two hundred and eight friars, as well as an enormous library. Contemporaries were impressed by its magnificence: Giuseppe Baretti, the Italian critic, thought there were not ten buildings as majestic in the world; Byron found it superb; and Raczynski a model of architecture. Herculano called it a marble folly, and W C Watson, author of *Portuguese Architecture*, writing at the beginning of the twentieth century, thought it impossible to praise as a whole. The library is a magnificent monument to the printed word. It is ninety yards long and ten wide, with carrels for reading and a central dome. The cruciform basilica culminates in the largest baroque dome in Portugal and displays an array of marble, all organised on correct principles and scrupulously executed: John VI added the pair of handsome organs. It was never constantly occupied as a royal residence. John VI came to avoid his troublesome Spanish wife, and during the Peninsular War it fell just within the lines of Torres Vedras: Wellington was able to invite the cream of Lisbon society to the festivities, and to contemplate the French positions when he bestowed the Order of the Bath on Marshal Beresford in 1810, and wandering soldiers found their way into the enemy's positions. It is still perhaps as much to be wondered at as admired.

Mafra is about twenty-five miles north-west of Lisbon. Beyond it, on the old road to the north, is the village of Torres Vedras, made famous by the Lines, a series of hilltop redoubts which stretched to Alhandra near Vila Franca de Xira on the Tagus, thus guarding the whole of the Lisbon Peninsula. The heights were once recognisable by wind-mills, and are crowned by a statue of Hercules placed in 1883 on the Alto do Boneco near Alhandra. Torres Vedras is a small market-town in a wine-growing area that stretches across to Arruda 'dos Vinhos' and Alhandra. The village of Bucelas is well-known for its produce. Torres Vedras was once a place of importance and the residence of kings, the birthplace in 1334 of Leonor, who married the Emperor Frederick III. Not much is left of the 'old towers' that gave it its name, but it has a Gothic *chafariz*, which was built in 1561 by the Infanta Maria and restored in 1831. The church of St Peter has a doorway of the sixteenth century. The monastery of Varatojo was given to the Franciscans by Afonso V in 1478, and after the dissolution became a home. It is again Franciscan and retains its early cloister and church. Further to the north and on the seaward side is Vimeiro, where a stone pyramid marks the battlefield where Wellington defeated the French on 21 August 1808, which, coupled with the risings in the north and in Madrid, forced Junot to abandon Portugal.

Torres Vedras is at the southern end of the Serra de Montejunto, a bare ridge nearly 2,000 feet high which is crossed by the main road to the north: the railways avoid the problem by following the coast (the Western Line) or the Tagus by way of Santarém. The Montejunto was frozen in winter and its ice stored in 'snow-wells' underground to supply the cafés of Lisbon until other means of refrigeration were found in 1880. At its northern end, the small village of Cadaval was elevated into a dukedom by John IV and later passed into the royal family: its dukes appear to have resided elsewhere.

North of Ericeira the coast consists mainly of cliffs broken here and there by sandy stretches where the small rivers reach the ocean. Lourinhã, which Afonso Henriques granted to one of the crusaders after the conquest of Lisbon, is, with Cadaval, almost the end of the district of Lisbon. Its church, battlemented like those of the northern seaboard, and the Misericórdia have their equals elsewhere. In prehistoric times the northern limit of the collective graves seems to have been Paimogo, not far away. Torres Vedras is the centre for the bronze-age cities of Portugal, of which Zambujal, in the parish of Santa Maria, seven miles from the coast, is the best preserved: others are at Vespera, a mile to its south; Penedo and Fornea, near the village of Runa; and Varatojo and Achada, near Torres Vedras. This group belongs to the Alentejo and the south rather than to the north.

The main road and the western railway run inland by Bombarral, passing the site of Roliça, where Wellington had his first clash with the French: the site at Columbeira has a memorial to Lieut Colonel Lake erected by the Worcestershires. A side-road leads to the peninsula of Peniche and the Berlengas, the only immediate off-shore islands of the Portuguese coast. Atouguia was once a port of consequence. It became Atouguia da Baleia, or 'of the Whale', in the sixteenth century. The place itself has a ruined castle, a Gothic church and a *pelourinho* and arched fountain, now dilapidated. Its adjunct Baleal was once an island and is now a quiet resort, remarkable for its rock formations on which the waves continue an age-long bombardment. This display is broken by the port of Peniche, where the sardine is caught and tinned. While the men fish and can, the women wait and make lace on bobbins, and the ocean continues its attack on the dramatic cliffs. The peninsula is five miles round and stops at the cape of Carvoeiro. The battle with the waves is resumed at the rocky cliffs of the Berlengas, some ten miles off-shore and reached by boat from Peniche. They are now uninhabited. The Great Berlenga, about a square mile, is a nature reserve for sea-birds, rabbits and lizards. Its importance for the defence of Lisbon was made plain when Drake and Norris landed their army at Peniche in 1589. The only building on the Berlenga was then a Jeronymite hermitage founded in 1513. The fort of St John was built in 1676, a brick structure on a projecting spur reached from the sea or by an aqueduct serving as a pathway to the land. The second island in the group is much further away and completely unoccupied. The fortifications of Peniche date from the period of the Restoration and later. The town was a British hospital centre during the Peninsular War. There is a private Museum of the War at Gaeiras in a house owned by the Pinto Basto family.

North of Baleal, the rocky coast is broken by the small river Arelho, which links the brackish lagoon of Óbidos with the sea. The lagoon abounds in shellfish, eels and flatfish, and is a haunt of seafowl and other birds. It takes its name from the town of Óbidos, which is carefully preserved as the only place in Portugal to keep its circuit of walls. King Diniz rebuilt the walls, which are probably older: they have been repaired as required. King Diniz gave it to his wife, Isabel of Aragon, on their marriage, and it remained the apanage of the queens until 1833. The church of St Martin was founded in the fourteenth century and the keep has an inscription stating that it was built by King Fernando in 1375. The Misericórdia was due to the charitable Queen Leonor, and the great Renaissance masterpiece is the Tomb of Dom João de Noronha who died in 1526, by Nicholas Chantereine. The *albarrada* (floral) tiles in Santa Maria are of the early eighteenth century, and the painter of Óbidos, Josefa Aiala, is buried in the church of São Pedro.

Óbidos is within walking distance – four miles – of Caldas da Rainha, the 'Queen's hot springs', the queen being Dona Leonor, the founder of the Misericórdias. There are many *caldas*, but this is *the* 'Caldas'. In 1484, going from Óbidos, she found that the warm waters were being used to treat patients and so founded the hospital. The church of the Pópulo was built as its chapel and still has its bell-tower and unusual chancel arch, but has been heavily decorated. The hospital was rebuilt for John V. In the nineteenth century the waters were found to be 'mesosaline, sulphuric, sulphy-drate fluoretated and lithinated' with a radioactivity of 0.08 milligrams. They were therefore beneficial (from mid-May until the end of October) for rheumatism, neur-algia, catarrh, congestion of the liver, convulsive coughs and inflammation of the ovary. The Queen's pine-grove became a park of exotic trees, and tennis-courts, a cro-quet lawn, a boating-pool, a race-track and a cinema were added. Caldas' other activ-ity is ceramics, specialising in realistic figures of fruits and vegetables as well as in caricatures.

At Caldas, the coast road and that which crosses the Montejunto come together and proceed to Alcobaça, the greatest Cistercian monastery in Portugal: it supervised the farming of the area between the Serra dos Candieiros and the sea, with the ports of São Martinho and Nazaré.

12

North from Lisbon

In early times the Castle of St George and the mosque/cathedral were the centre of Lisbon. The eastern side was cast in a secondary part by the epic of the Discoveries and the growth of Atlantic trade. King John V, the Most Faithful, wishing to have a permanent Portuguese cardinal, erected Occidental Lisbon as the see of his Patriarch: in the nineteenth century the trend was continued with the opening of the Avenida and the central station of the Rossio. To the east, there was no Oriental Lisbon: Pombal seems to have thought of the iron foundries as a potential industrial belt, a tendency encouraged in the twentieth century by the emergence of factories along the water-front. This has now been reversed, partly by the establishment of the airport at the Portela de Sacavém and then by the removal of the main railway-terminus to Santa Apolónia. The commemoration of Vasco da Gama's opening of the sea-route to India was the occasion for an exhibition on a large scale and the building of the Vasco da Gama Bridge completed in 1998, with two elegant high spans and a long causeway skimming the water to Montijo on the Outra Banda, giving access to the Alentejo and Algarve and relieving pressure on the crowded first bridge. The opportunity was seized to create a new suburb named Oriente, with a graceful station and a forest of palm-trees planted for the occasion.

The main railway-line follows the north bank of the Tagus to Santarém. The main road to the centre and north diverges beyond Vila Franca de Xira, which until 1966 was the lowest point at which the Tagus was crossed by road. The river here has an extensive water-plain broken up into islets running for nearly twenty miles – the *lezirias* – giving some of the most fertile land in Portugal. They were formerly royal property, but were privatised in favour of a company in 1836. Vila Franca is the centre of cattle-country. The mounted *campino*, in his stocking-cap and waistcoat, controls the herds of cattle with his lance. For the festivities in early July he decks himself in a green cap and red waistcoat. Portuguese bull-fighting is a risky display of horsemanship, punctuated by teams of teasers on foot. The victim, though bewildered, is not killed, but recycled, if that is the word. The Mecca for the sport in Lisbon is the bull-ring at the Campo Pequeno. The ring at Vila Franca is of the same period, though the activity was developed in the late eighteenth and early nineteenth centuries. Bull-runs through the streets take place from time to time, and all those who have suicidal inclinations may take part. The bridge across the flats leading to the pastures and the Alentejo was opened in 1951.

The country-people of the Lisbon area are *saloios*, rustics, in contrast to the citizens, who are *alfaces*, or 'lettuces'. The reason for the epithet is unexplained: perhaps a lettuce is a cabbage with frills. The *saloio* is conventionally either stupid or cunning, according to the sense the speaker wishes to impart. He is a countryman who sends the city its provisions. One does not boast of being a *saloio*.

The town of Alenquer was once the property of the queens of Portugal. It was the birthplace of the humanist scholar Damião de Gois, who died in 1574 and is buried in the church of Santa Maria da Várzea: he lived at the Quinta do Barreiro. The convent of São Francisco, founded in 1222, was the first Franciscan house in Portugal: the church and convent was rebuilt in the sixteenth century, but almost destroyed by the Earthquake.

The city of Santarém is the capital of the Ribatejo, built on a spacious site with ample views over the river. It was a favourite royal residence: John II was swimming in the river when his heir Afonso was killed by falling from his horse while racing along the bank. Over the river, the 'towers of Almeirim', known to Camões and a usual seat of the court of John III, was completely destroyed in the nineteenth century when its stone was used for road-building. Garrett describes the journey to the vale of Santarém in his *Travels in My Country*, making it the 'land of nightingales and honeysuckle', the setting for a romantic story. In the time of Camões, one Francisco de Sousa, who was only half a gentleman, employed a boy to throw stones at the nightingales because they kept him awake. The name Santarém, from St Irene or Peace, was given it in the seventh century. The Romans knew it as Scallabis, and the newspapers still refer to its people as 'Scalabitanos'. It was the Praesidium Julium, from which Caesar and others launched their campaigns to the north but there are no certain remains of the Roman period. It was held by Goths against the Suevic kings, and may owe its cultivation to the Muslims from whom it was taken by Sueiro Mendes, the only place on the Tagus attached to the county of Portugal. Lost under Count Henry, it was regained by Afonso Henriques in a surprise attack before the conquest of Lisbon. The Porta do Sol was part of the Muslim walls, with a view over the river valley which Palgrave, coming with Tennyson, thought one of the great panoramic landscapes of Europe. The old *alcáçova*, or citadel, has disappeared, and the only gate to survive is that of Santiago, near the church of the Alcáçova, founded in 1154 by the Templars, but rebuilt. However, the main defence of Santarém was the river itself, and, further upstream, the castle of Almourol, built by the Templars on an island in midstream.

The most famous native of Santarém is Pedro Álvares Cabral, whose fleet, following the route of Vasco da Gama, sailed to the west and discovered the coast of Brazil in May 1500. Santarém rose to the occasion of the quincentenary in 2000 by honouring his house. He is buried in the church of the Graça with an inscription, which does not mention his feat but records that his widow was a lady-in-waiting of Princess Maria. The church was founded in 1380 for the Augustinians. Its exterior has a fine Gothic doorway surmounted by a large rose-window. The chief tomb is that of Dom Pedro de Meneses, who governed Ceuta for twenty-two years and died in 1437. Cabral lies under a flat stone in one of the apses. The *azulejos* were added in the eighteenth century. Dom Pedro was the second Count of Viana: the third, Dom Duarte de Meneses, who was killed in the Magrib in 1464 while attempting to protect King Afonso V, has an even more splendid tomb nearby in São João de Alporão, converted into a museum. Whether or not his bones were retrieved, his effigy lies under a large canopy with a fore-curtain elaborately carved with Gothic and heraldic themes: it is one of the finest tombs of the fifteenth century. The other medieval specimens in the museum have been brought together from various places.

The church of Marvila, one of the three divisions of Santarém, has a doorway of King Manuel and a simple interior of three naves covered by a wooden roof with vaulting at the high altar and apses. The *azulejos* bear dates showing that they were added in 1617 and 1635. The Jesuit Seminary of about 1676 resembles São Roque in Lisbon in clearing the central space to give prominence to the pulpit. The triumphal arch is enlarged to give the impression of the entrance to a separate building housing the sanctuary with an adornment of Salomonic twisted pillars.

If I have not done justice to Santarém, those who wish for a more formal description of the memorial to Dom Duarte may turn to W C Watson, who says it has:

> a deeply moulded ogee arch subdivided into two hanging arches which spring from a pendant in the middle, while the space between these sub-arches and the ogee above is filled with a canopied carving of the Crucifixion. At about the level of the pendant the open space is crossed by a cusped segmental arch supporting elaborate flowing tracery. The outer sides of the ogee which ends in a large finial are enriched with vine-leaf crockets . . .

Santarém is the site of the regional agricultural fair, and when my luggage was stolen from the train coming from Lisbon, the police were kind and sympathetic. The officer who typed out my complaint in quintuplicate observed sadly: 'Portugal is not what it was; all sorts of people come here nowadays.'

During the Peninsular War, the French, on giving up any attempt to penetrate the Lines of Torres Vedras, fell back on Santarém, where Masséna scoured the countryside for provisions; he held it from 14 November 1810 until 5 March, making spasmodic attempts to stir up Francophile support in Lisbon. While Santarém escaped the worst rigours of the war, the countryside between it and Coimbra was devastated. As the allies followed, there were signs of poverty and ruin everywhere. There was depopulation in central Portugal, but this is hard to measure because of the collapse of local administration and a change of system between the censuses of 1796 and 1822, when A Balbi published his *Essai*: he says that the iron-works at Pedrógão was the only one left working in the country. The villages were rebuilt and (setting aside castles already in ruins) there is a relative lack of older buildings. Probably the roads received little attention until the railway came to resolve the problem of communications. The troubles did not end with the Peninsular War, for in 1833 Santarém was the capital of the Miguelites or traditionalists, while the liberals held the small town of Cartaxo.

The castle of Almourol seated on its island in the river is a reminder of the presence of the Templars, who also owned the village of Constância. The river Zézere, which joins the Tagus, has been dammed to make an artificial lake. The road leads to the vale of the Nabão, the setting for Tomar, one of the most attractive small towns in Portugal, the former headquarters of the Templars. The Templars were brought to Portugal in the time of Queen Tarásia and employed in the defence of Coimbra. Their original castle in Tomar was the octagonal church. As the reconquest proceeded, the Templars were prominent in occupying the Algarve and had their headquarters at the mouth of the Guadiana. King Diniz replaced them with the order of Christ, of which

Prince Henry was governor. Prince Henry devoted their revenues to his discoveries, and King Manuel extended the existing chapel with a great nave to which four large cloisters and one small were added. The main doorway, dated 1515, is by João de Castilho, and is as luxuriant as his contribution to Belém. The door, roof, windows and buttresses are adorned with Renaissance and heraldic themes, including the Greek cross of the Order and a wealth of oceanic references, including cables, sea-weeds and barnacles, culminating in a rectangular window at the back wreathed in maritime symbols, which is the most famous symbol of the Portuguese expansion. The finest of the cloisters, dated 1557, is far more classical, in the Roman style then prevalent, with orthodox columns and plain geometrical decoration.

Near the Convent of Christ is the small church of the Conception, ascribed to Torralva, perhaps the best example of pure classical style in Portugal, where usually less impersonal and more decorated forms were preferred. Watson thought the inside one of the most beautiful interiors anywhere. In the town itself the church of St John had a Gothic portal, and there is a fifteenth-century Synagogue, now restored. The river Nabão has been diverted to make an island with gardens and a modern hotel.

Almeirim, opposite Santarém, was regarded as the Sintra of the winter months by King Manuel. John III summoned cortes to Almeirim in 1544, and young courtiers serving in Africa dreamed of its lofty towers: it did not survive the extinction of the house of Avis, and was finally demolished in 1889. Five miles to its north is Alpiarça, a market town for the neighbouring farms. Near it is the Casa dos Patudos, a house designed by Raul Lino in typical Portuguese style for the politician José Relvas. He assembled a varied collection of paintings and furniture as well as Arraiolos rugs in the first years of the twentieth century and bequeathed it as a museum open to the public.

The Ribatejo is, as its name implies, on both banks of the river. It corresponds to the district of Santarém, which is on the north bank: so too is most of the population, together with the railway to the north and the main highway from Lisbon to Oporto. The opposite bank is level, and the villages stand back from the river – they are few, and strung together by a good road. The land to the east, whether *charneca* or farm-land, is thinly populated. It is not without modest water-courses, but much of the Alentejo side was heath.

Still on the Alentejo bank, the town of Chamusca is the centre of a mixed farming area, which produces wheat, maize and beans and raises cattle and horses. A long bridge links it to the northern bank at Golegã. Its church, the Conceição, has an elab-orate front in the Manueline style, a carved book-plate framed in twisted columns. I have not been there for the horse-fair at St Martin's summer in November, to which Susan Lowndes devotes a page, thinking the assemblage of the gentry, gentlemen-farmers and their people a typical display of democracy in the best sense, illustrating the preference of an easy-going people for naturalness and simplicity. Two generations later, it may have changed. There are more cars than horses. José Saramago, born at the village of Azinhaga and awarded a Nobel prize for literature, admires the church as the finest specimen of the Manueline, but does not feel at home in the flat place whose streets are filled with clouds of dust: for him, the name Golegã is linked to pay-ing taxes and the police-court.

The railway reaches Entroncamento, *The* Junction (like Clapham) where the main line of Coimbra and Oporto takes the smartest modern trains. Another line continues along the course of the river to Constância and Abrantes, still in the Ribatejo. Near Constância the small river Nabão reaches the Tagus from Tomar, and the longer Zêzere, rising in the Serra da Estrela, wanders through the fertile Cova da Beira, making a long artificial lake at Castelo de Bode, the first of the major hydro-electric schemes. Constância was called Punhete, the Fist or Gauntlet, built by the Templars for the defence of their headquarters at Tomar, until Queen Maria II gave it a less defiant name in 1840. It is widely believed that Camões had a house on the river here. He does not mention it by name and the claim has not been substantiated. However, in the middle of the river is the island on which the Templars built their castle of Almourol, the most picturesque ruin on the river. It served to ensure communications with Évora.

The railway crosses the Tagus and runs through the Alentejo for a short distance before reaching Abrantes, where it again divides, the Beira Baixa line turning north towards the Estrela and the border city of Guarda, while another route goes south of the river. It was formerly an international line of some importance, which explains why the station at Torre de Vargens is adorned with a profusion of Portuguese azulejos. A convenient autorail ascends the heights of the Upper Alentejo and stops at Beirã, where a bus takes the steep and winding road up to the heights of Marvão.

Abrantes, which Camões called 'fresh', stands on an eminence commanding the Tagus. Several princes, including Dom Jorge, the son of John II, and the children of King Manuel, were born there. Its former palace was attached to the castle, where King John I assembled his forces before marching to Aljubarrota in 1385. Its governors were later Almeidas, who were accorded the title of Counts of Abrantes: Dom Lopo died in 1484 and his tomb is in the regional museum named after him. A younger brother, Dom Francisco, was the first viceroy of India, and perhaps the patron of the poet's grandfather, who perished in Indian waters. Camões' mother was a Sá or Sá de Macedo of Santarém, but she gave birth to Camões in Lisbon. The importance of Abrantes lay in its strong position at a place where the river became navigable after passing through the gorge of Ródão. It was rebuilt or strengthened for Philip II in 1580 and recovered its military importance in 1798, when the Marquis of Alorna raised his regiment there and replaced the old palace with barracks. He became a partisan of the French. In 1807 Junot and his army marched across northern Spain and occupied it, a feat for which Junot was made Duc d'Abrantès, his wife being the incorrigible scribbler known as the duchess d'Abrantès. It was a ploy intended to confuse since the Portuguese counts of Abrantes had been promoted to the rank of marquis. He was appointed by the Prince Regent to head the Council of Regency when the royal family withdrew to Brazil in November 1807. The Marquis of Abrantes was then lured with other members of the nobility to France, supposedly to treat with Napoleon, but in fact so that General Junot could issue his orders under the bogus style of duke of Abrantes: there were no dukedoms in Portugal except in the royal house.

The former palace was transmogrified in 1792 for military purposes, but the church of Santa Maria do Castelo remains as the regional Museum, named after Dom Lopo de Almeida whose fine tomb it contains with others of his family, and azulejos, images and carvings. The principal church is St John's, founded by the saintly Queen Isabel in 1300 but restored and enlarged in the time of Philip II. The church of the Misericórdia is attached to the hospital founded by John III's younger brother

Fernando. The entrance by the side door is dated 1548. The *talha dourada* was added in the eighteenth century, when the board-room was enhanced with fine wood-work.

To the north-east of Abrantes, off the road to the village of Mouriscas, is the little chapel of Our Lady of the Woods: it has a fine seventeenth-century *azulejo* figure of the Virgin with the prayer that she may convert the English. Its appearance in so remote a spot has caused surprise, but a coat of arms on the ceiling unites Coutinho with Napier: Coutinhos were governors of Abrantes and a Napier came to Portugal from Scotland to fight in the wars of Independence: his son Francis married Maria Coutinho. Beyond Abrantes the Ribatejo ceases and the river is no longer the placid and open stream that flows through central Portugal but a deep channel contained in the gorge of Ródão, marking for some distance the frontier between Portugal and Spain.

Portugal is much given to local festivities. Oporto celebrates St John's day on 24 June, and Viana do Castelo makes the Agonia on 18 August a regional home-coming. In smaller places the village or town is decorated, and there is a procession to or from the church, a concert in the bandstand, sometimes a competition between local bands, dancing and junketing, and finally a firework display. The festivities may take the form of a pilgrimage to some sanctuary, often on a high point, with picnick-ing and perhaps a fair. Susan Lowndes, writing in 1949, praised the standard of com-munal enjoyment, which she compared with life as it was in England when England was still merry. The little whitewashed church was decorated with branches, banners and paper flowers; so was the square outside it with the ubiquitous and inevitable bandstand. The village children were dressed as angels, and shrines gay with flowers were carried by robed church-wardens, walking on streets strewn with rushes and scented herbs. The events were announced by posters and a programme was printed. These occasions have declined as the state has taken over education and provided entertainment for all and sundry.

Between Tomar and Ourém at the Cova de Iria, the town and sanctuary of Fátima has grown up where on 13 May 1917 three children saw a vision of the Virgin Mary, who promised further signs. The sanctuary now covers a large area, with houses, lodg-ings, shops and a railway station. It attracts large numbers of pilgrims, particularly on the thirteenth day of each month from May to October.

The devotion of Fátima is something apart from the pleasant relaxation of rural Portugal. Those who wish to see country people as they are might visit the fair at Santana every Sunday morning. There are several Santanas, but this one is some-where between Santarém and Rio Maior on the confines of Estremadura and Ribatejo in the middle of nowhere, or rather of mixed farming and vineyards interspersed with pinewoods. A space of some ten acres by the roadside has been concreted beside a level park for perhaps three hundred cars, though not enough for the occasion. High awnings cover row upon row of coats, trousers, shirts, caps and their female equiva-lents. There are fruit and vegetables, produce, tools, kitchen utensils, garden equip-ment, electricals and electronicals, chickens, ducklings, quails, a fishmonger, cafés and bars, and everything imaginable, except (I think) books and pictures. It is crowded with families who have driven from far and near. The clothing has names like Balmoral and Savile Row but is made in Portugal. My friends need a grey corduroy coat and a narrow trowel with a long haft: both are absent but will be present next Sunday. I am an 'ancient ally' and am greeted with a handshake, but do not have to purchase anything.

Ourém was once the seat of the counts, of whom the first was João Afonso Teles de Meneses, favourite of Pedro I, and the second the Galician Andeiro. It was sacked by the French in 1810. It stands on a steep hill and is entered by narrow gates. The ruined castle has been restored, and the church contains only the tomb of the fifteenth-century count, grandson of King John I. For both Masséna in 1809 and for the Spaniards in 1385 the invasion-route lay through central Portugal. John I's resounding victory on 14 August 1385 was won at Aljubarrota by his Constable Nun'Alvares Pereira who built the chapel at St George, with a figure of the saint slaying the dragon, and outside a niche with a jug of water for passers-by to relieve their thirst. But the great monument is the Monastery of Santa Maria da Vitória or Batalha, some ten miles to the north on the road to Leiria, one of the most splendid buildings in Europe. On the right of the noble nave is the Founders' Chapel for the tombs of John and Philippa and four of their sons, built between 1387 and 1434. King Duarte added the octagonal chancel, continued and ornamented by King Manuel, but never completed and known as the 'Unfinished Chapels'. The royal cloister formed part of the original plan with two dozen ogival arches, but was embellished by the architects of King Manuel with latticed screens. The use of limestone permits carved tracery of all kinds. The chapter-house is remarkable for its size, uninterrupted by supports: it has the tomb of the Portuguese Unknown Soldier.

Not far away is an earlier monument of national significance, the Cistercian abbey of Alcobaça, the grandest of all Cistercian buildings. The first King, Afonso Henriques, had annexed a large area south of Coimbra, then half-abandoned, and granted it to the new reformers, who cultivated land and devotion, rather than the power which had fascinated the Cluniacs. They began to build Alcobaça in 1178, following the disposition of Clairvaux, a central nave reaching the maximum height with no unnecessary adornment, and a refectory of similar proportions ending in a rounded chancel with a pulpit. The austerity of the original intention has been modified by the addition of a baroque façade with Benedictine figures and by the tombs of King Pedro and Inês de Castro with their extraordinary vision of reward and punishment as drawn in c. 1360. The 'cloister of silence' is ascribed to the reign of King Diniz. The abbot of Alcobaça came to control thirteen townships and three sea-ports. The area is best-known for its orchards. The small port of São Martinho, a sheltered circular inlet, is a favourite holiday resort. The shore from here northward is a succession of sand-dunes, broken only occasionally by a rocky foreland.

The city of Leiria, clustered round its castle perched on a hill-top, is associated with King Diniz, the farmer, poet, castle-builder and husband of a saint. He planted the shore with pine-woods to protect the fields from invasion by the sandy beaches. The songs of the king refer both to the greenness of the pines and his ships, and thus foretell the maritime expansion realised a century after his death. The Pinhal d'El-Rei still has its own system of arboriculture. In Portugal, the pine, *Pinheiro*, may be wild, *bravo*, or tame, *manso*, and that chosen for silviculture is the fast-growing and straight, if drabber, *Pinus pilaster*, rather than the slower and more picturesque stone pine. Cups are attached to the stem to collect the resin. The sand is 'fixed' with dune-land plants in preparation to take the saplings.

The castle on its prominent peak has been rebuilt to King Diniz's specification. It included the open gallery above the walls, a feature of Muslim architecture, in welcome relief from the surly battlements of earlier times. In the twelfth century it was

7 The Cistercian Abbey of Alcobaça (João Paulo)

one of a ring of castles that defended the approaches to Coimbra; Soure, Penela, Miranda do Corvo, Gois and Arganil. Leiria was the most southerly and exposed, being overrun as late as 1135. The conquest of Lisbon made it secure, and Diniz and St Isabel were free to contemplate the orchards of Alcobaça from its height. Leiria was

8 The Castle at Leiria (António Sacchetti)

one of the three new dioceses created in 1545. Its cathedral was designed in 1551, at a time when the decorative gusto of the Manueline period was no longer feasible.

Leiria has its place in the parliamentary history of Portugal, for it was at the Cortes of Leiria of 1254 that King Afonso III summoned for the first time representatives of the *concelhos*, the existing townships, so that commoners were admitted to the counsels of the nobles and ecclesiastics. The step had been taken already in Leon, and was a proof of the emergence of commerce and of the need for agreement about the nature and value of the coin. Leiria's own contribution was a modest textile-industry and the timber sent to Lisbon for ship-building. It has been credited with the first book printed in Portugal, now ascribed to Chaves: the early printers were Jews, whose numbers increased at the time of the expulsion from Spain in 1492. The first Hebrew type was brought from Italy to Spain, and from Spain to Portugal, where there was greater tolerance. An early office was that of Samuel d'Ortas in Leiria, but the priority is hypothetical. A much later industry was that of glass-making at Marinha Grande, between Leiria and the coast. It was begun by John Beare in 1748, bought out by William Stephens with capital found by Pombal in 1769, and continued until the deaths of Stephens in 1802 and his brother in 1826, when it reverted to the state. Beare's original interest was in the supply of wood, which also provides a second industry with resin.

The fishery for Alcobaça and Leiria was Nazaré, just south of the dunes and pines of the Pinhal d'El-Rei. The cove is protected by a promontory; the upper town, the Sítio, has a church much frequented for its festivities in September, where Afonso Henriques' governor is supposed to have been saved by a timely prayer from falling over the cliff while hunting. The beach is wide and the large boats with their pointed prows were formerly drawn up by man and woman-power, or by oxen which waited their turn on the shore. The boats are drifters working in companies, and the whole community, men, women and children, used to wear rough wool dyed in tartans, the men with shirts and trousers, and the women with full skirts and a black fringed shawl. While the oxen stood by, the women attended to the nets, saw to their children and knitted on the beach. But the supposed antiquity of the place, which pleases visitors, is mythical. The first reference to the fishery is of 1643, and the concentration at Nazaré follows the decline of Pederneira, which had supplied the monks of Alcobaça.

North of Leiria, the coastal road and the western railway are separated from the shore by the pinewoods and reach the mouth of the Mondego at Figueira da Foz, while the main road from Lisbon and the main Lisbon-Oporto line go inland by Pombal to Coimbra. Pombal is still in the district of Leiria and the province of Estremadura. Its castle, founded by the Templars in 1171, was rebuilt in the time of King Manuel before being abandoned. The town was the place of exile of the famous Marquis, who was immediately dismissed on the death of King Joseph in May 1777: he was still wealthy, and spent his exile in defending himself against his many enemies.

Soure is already in Beira. It is a broad and fertile basin, which was devastated in the campaigns of 1116 and lay empty for nearly seven years, when Queen Tarásia entrusted two priests, one of whom became St Martin of Soure, with the task of resettling it. Its *veiga* (plain) now consists of rice-paddies. Penela on the next road to the east, now a village, was a hill-top fortified in 1080, destroyed in the same campaign and equipped with an imposing fortress, the strongest of the defences of Coimbra. Further to the east, Miranda do Corvo was a forward defence, now half-enclosed by the Serra de Lousã. The river Mondego is the longest to flow entirely through Portuguese territory. It rises on the southern flank of the Serra de Estrela, curves round the northern end and traverses a high plateau before winding through a series of gorges at Penacova and Lorvão, to reach the valley of Coimbra and the sea at Figueira da Foz. In the middle ages Coimbra was a port, but its river became only a thin stream between sandbanks in summer: it is now controlled and stabilised.

Coimbra, like Lisbon and Oporto, stands on an eminence overlooking its river. If Lisbon represents authority and Oporto commerce, Coimbra is the Lusitanian Athens, the seat of the university, finally installed by John III who gave it his palace in 1537, and the sole centre of higher studies until the republic of 1910. Pombal spent a month there in 1772 to impose his reforms – the extirpation of all traces of the Jesuits and the introduction of modern studies. He shut down its only rival, the Jesuit University of Évora and Coimbra remained the place at which theologians, lawyers and administrators, doctors and scientists, were trained. It spoke the most correct Portuguese and its students in their gowns composed poems as they strolled by the river or in the Botanical Garden. Nowadays there are universities everywhere, and it likes to think of itself, as I may of Cambridge, as the least bad of what is available.

In Roman times Coimbra was called Aeminium, and has a vast *cryptoporticus* which may be seen under the Museu Machado de Castro. The comfortable and aristocratic settlement was Conimbriga to the south. After the Germanic invasions, its bishop migrated with his flock to the security of the hill-top, bringing the name with them. Under the Muslims it was the main stronghold in the west, and the valley of the lower Mondego was the most fruitful area of Portugal. It was taken by the Christians after a long siege in 1064, the first large city to be occupied by the non-urban conquerors from the north. Portuguese has absorbed a wide range of Arabic words, for officials, domestic ware, cultivated plants and commerce. After the conquest, it was governed from 1064 to 1092 by Sisnand Davides, a native of Tentúgal, who rebuilt the community with Arabic-speaking Christians from the south. Later, his work was partially undone by the intransigence of the French clergy imposed by Cluny. The counties of Portugal and Coimbra were united only when the Emperor Alfonso VI bestowed them on his daughter Tarásia on her marriage to Count Henry. Their son Afonso Henriques made it his principal seat, founding the great church of Santa Cruz, where he is buried. The building has now been restored to its former glory, though its cloister and dependencies remain occupied by the Post Office and market, and it still nurses a café in its bosom.

The ancient city gate, the Arco de Almedina, somewhat strengthened after the conquest, stands in the main thoroughfare. The climb up to the old cathedral, the Sé Velha, is by a stone stairway, with a tangle of medieval alleys and streets. The cathedral itself stands on a platform, the site of the former mosque. It was erected between 1160 and 1180, and is imposing in its austerity, a rectangular block, crowned with battlements and a round Romanesque doorway. The chancel is rounded and flanked by semi-circular chapels, and the crossing is covered by a dome. The cloister and north portal were added in later styles. The altar, of gilded wood, dates from 1498 to 1508. By the side of the cathedral, the Rua do Deão was inhabited by Camões' Coimbra family. The Palace of Sub-ripas, an ancient town-house with sixteenth-century additions, houses the Institute of Archaeology. The Tower of Anta at the end of the street is also medieval, but owes its name to António Nobre, the poet esteemed for his *Só*, full of *saudade*, Anto being a diminutive of António. The Rua de Quebra-costas, Breakback Street, has 76 steps, with nine pauses.

Although it is possible to get to the cathedral by car, the cobbled lane continues upwards to the main University square. At the Porta Férrea, a bedel in his dark uniform shows the way to the Via Latina, the broad stairs of John III's palace, now very appropriate for graduation photographs; the Sala dos Capelos, with portraits of former rectors in their magnificence; and the splendid Old Library of John V; not to mention the view of the Mondego valley. There are plenty of students in term-time, though they no longer wear the traditional *capa e batina* or gown and cassock. The bedel may point out the *calouros* or freshmen, but no longer the *tricanas*, the country girls who rode in on donkeys from the villages with cabbages, beans and peas, and loitered on the way to chat.

The Museu Machado de Castro is an elegant building, the former bishop's palace, which stands over the Roman cryptoporticus. The large and rather unpoetic buildings before and beside it house the various faculties and the modern library in the style of 1930. Much as one may sigh for traditions, most of the old religious colleges are at the other side of the town, and the present arrangement permits a greater density of students (if that is the right collective term) without the use of bicycles, which would be useless. The practice was for the young men to dwell in 'repúblicas', usually on a provincial basis, where they joined in hiring a cook. Some of these still exist, but the students are probably better provided for in modern residences: in my time, the pensão of Dona Adélia had two rich students, who sat in their black academic dress at a table apart: they were outnumbered by a professor of mathematics, a young doctor, a visiting judge, an American Arabist and ourselves.

9 The University Library at Coimbra (Nuno Calvet)

Beside the Faculty of Letters is the Iron Gate leading into a square. In the corner is the Old Library by Laprade, the gift of the opulent John V, dating from 1714 to 1728. Its three lofty rooms are covered from floor to ceiling with book-cases decorated in gold, scarlet and green, and culminating in a full-length portrait of the donor. It forms the most magnificent display the printed word could aspire to find. When Unamuno, who was rector of the parallel institution at Salamanca, was told of the telephone, he is said to have asked if it would improve anything he had to say. The answer is no, but the quiet carrels provided by the architects of John V give a pleasant feeling of being in reading-distance of other spirits no longer with us. The university clock-tower, which is visible for miles and is known as the Cabra or Goat, was added in the eighteenth century.

Also on the hill is the New Cathedral, the Sé Nova, built for the Jesuits in 1598. Its exterior is flat, but relieved by curved decorations in the mannerist style. Descending the hill, the visitor comes to the Botanical Garden, designed by William Elsden for Pombal and the rector Francisco de Lemos, who resisted the great man's plea for economy and long outlived him. It is a beautiful spot, where the quiet of the plants is barely disturbed by doves coming down to drink at the fountain on summer evenings, or the murmur of students conning their texts.

Outside the Botanical Garden is the aqueduct of twenty-one arches built c. 1568, probably on a Roman predecessor. The easy way down – that taken by the public transport – is by the Rua Alexandre Herculano and the Praça da República, the entrance to the park of Santa Cruz, much frequented by fire-flies and glow-worms, and so by the Avenida to Santa Cruz. After King John III brought the university from Lisbon, it was intended that the Rua da Sofia should be a high street lined with colleges of various Orders. It is now a shopping street, but there remain the College of the Carmo, founded in 1541, on the right; the Treasury of Santo Domingos of 1556, but unfinished; the Graça, the Augustinians, founded in 1548; São Pedro, founded in 1540; and St Thomas, the large Dominican college of which the cloister was founded in 1556, the rest being replaced by the law courts, the Palácio da Justiça.

The tangle of streets between Sofia and the river has atmosphere but not architecture, and the thoroughfare cut through parallel to the river has neither. The railway station, Coimbra A (Coimbra B being a mile away with the main line) was once an open-air market under a grove of olives, and water-carriers supplied the city from jars carried in the panniers of their mules. From the station, trains used to run along the water-front blowing their whistles on the way to the village of Lousã. The water-front is lined with trees, and the railway has brought hotels to face the river, with a pleasant walk to the small park at the end. The main shopping street, Coimbra's Baixa, runs from Santa Cruz to the bridge, where there is a statue of J J de Aguiar, who dissolved the monasteries in 1834.

Beyond the Mondego, is the suburb of Santa Clara. The old monastery of Santa Clara a Velha was founded by St Isabel, the widow of King Diniz, who retired there for her declining years. It was subject to flooding when the river was in spate, and though attempts were made to make the altars higher, the church was finally abandoned. The new convent, Santa Clara a Nova, or Santa Isabel, was built in the seventeenth century, but contains the Gothic tomb which St Isabel had had made in about 1330. It has a recumbent figure of the queen in her nun's garb on an elaborately carved chest mounted on crouching lions.

Not far away is the Quinta das Lágrimas where it is supposed that Inês de Castro was murdered by the ministers of Afonso IV in January 1355. A fresh spring emerges from the rock to weep convincingly at the spot. Prince Pedro, to whom Inês had borne several children, was undoubtedly absent, and his father Afonso IV was at Montemór on the other side of Coimbra. But the story that her little children were also assassinated is a myth perpetuated by Camões. The splendour of the tombs at Alcobaça, like the legend that King Pedro crowned her after her death, having been legally married to her, is misleading: he found solace. The fiction owes its origins to the ambitions of the sons. The moral of the story is in the lengths to which the imagination of those in power will go and their limitations: if the king's advisers had been more cunning, they might have spared the unlucky Inês and removed her offspring.

Now engulfed by the growth of Coimbra the village of Celas has a Cistercian convent dating from 1219, and related to the first 'General Studies' or university founded by King Diniz. Part of the cloister remains: it was rebuilt by John III. It has a sixteenth-century doorway and vaulting. It is now a charitable home, and its paintings are in the Museum in Coimbra.

Further up the narrow valley of the Mondego is the monastery of Lorvão, which formed part of the church of St Martin in the sixth century, was protected by the Count of Coimbra in the ninth, and supplied the army of Fernando I in the siege of Coimbra in 1064. It stands on a peak reached by a causeway, and most of what exists is of the eighteenth century. A favourite excursion from Coimbra is to the hill village of Lousã, which had the first Portuguese paper-mill. The vale of the Arouce is guarded by a tiny castle, intended rather as a watch-tower since intruders were unlikely to choose this route. Penacova, where the railway crosses the Mondego, has a conical hill eight hundred feet high, and is best known for its romantic views and clear air: it has a home for sick children.

The advantages of Coimbra come from the lower valley of the Mondego which flows serene and gently down, as Camões says, to meet the sea at Figueira da Foz. The ridge that faces the city levels out and the stream passes between rice-paddies on the south bank and maize-fields on the north, neither of which the poet would have seen. The best road follows the north side and just off it is São Marcos, once the property of the Silvas, chief justices in the fifteenth and sixteenth centuries, who built a Jeronymite monastery. A fire in 1860 left the church intact. It contains the finest collection of sixteenth-century tombs in Portugal. The oldest of the five is of Dom Fernão Teles who lies in his armour under a stone curtain upheld by savage knights. The others are by Nicholas Chantereine who carved the pulpit at Santa Cruz, the tomb at Óbidos and other works. The chapel of the Magi with its retable of the Deposition is the most grandiose piece of Renaissance sculpture in Portugal, dating from 1522. The ivory-like texture of the stone permits the exceptional delicacy of the work: it was quarried at Ançã two miles to the northeast. São Marcos is now the property of the University, which uses it for functions.

The village of Tentúgal, where Sisnand Davides was born, has a Misericórdia and a Gothic church. The principal town of the Mondego valley was Montemor, called o Velho, the Old, to distinguish it from its namesake in the Alentejo. It was the birthplace of Jorge de Montemayor, who wrote the famous Diana in Spanish, and also of Fernão Mendes Pinto, whose Peregrination is a vivid account of his experiences in the Far East and Japan in the 1550s. Its walls stand on a rise overlooking the plain and contain the ruins of the palace and the early church of Santa Maria, restored in the six-teenth century. The town itself has two churches: that of the Anjos was built by Diogo de Azambuja, who governed Safi in Morocco and founded the castle of Mina in 1482: his tomb dates from 1518. The flats between the town and the river have been subject to flooding and, though they lend themselves to rice-farming, are also a breeding-ground for mosquitoes.

The Mondego meets the sea at Figueira da Foz, an important port, shipping centre and seaside resort. It has spacious sands and numerous hotels stretching northward to include the village of Buarcos as far as Cape Carvoeiro with its prominent light-house. It is the most popular beach with the Portuguese and is crowded during the summer months. The summer ocean is intensely blue and the sunsets are spectacular. The road from the south crosses the estuary and the wide beach at Lavos is quite secluded. It was here that Wellington landed his army in August 1808. Madrid had rebelled against the French in May, and northern Portugal had quickly responded. Finding the north already liberated, Wellington chose this as the best place to land for his rapid advance towards Lisbon, which he freed with the engagements at Vimeiro and Roliça.

Figueira is not an ancient place. In medieval times Coimbra was a port, supplied with fish by the villages of Buarcos and Quiaios, and defended by the fortress of Montemor, but Figueira was exposed to attack by sea. It was only in the eighteenth century that Pombal gave his support to ship-building. It contributed tall ships to the annual cod-fleet which fished the Grand Banks of Newfoundland and dried the catch to make the staple *bacalhau*. This activity has diminished since the onset of national-ism of the sea. The port area had been turned into an attractive promenade. It has no medieval monasteries or great houses, but a good museum. It was the birth-place of Fernandes Tomás, the leading spirit in the revolution of 1820. To the north, Figueira is sheltered by the Serra da Boa Viagem, with viewpoints over the estuary of the Mondego. Its pinewoods are recovering from the effect of a forest fire.

The Roman and modern road from Coimbra to Oporto runs due north, taking the railway with it. But at Pampilhosa the line divides, that to the east being the main way to 'Europe', with a long slice of Spain standing between. Seven miles on is the spa of Luso. It has a number of hotels and its waters can be bought almost everywhere: they are efficacious for hypertension and arterio-sclerosis, and, for those who do not have those problems, for 'diverse irregularities of the metabolism'. Luso stands at six hun-dred feet, but it is at the end of the Serra do Bussaco, a long ridge made famous by the battle in which the Anglo-Portuguese armies held off Masséna's attempts to scale the heights on 27 September 1810. Wellington and Beresford had spent the night at the little monastery of the Discalced Carmelites, and the victory is commemorated at an obelisk and a small museum. The forest of Bussaco was originally an area reserved for the meditation of the monks, where laymen were forbidden by papal authority to cut wood and women to enter. The monks introduced a variety of trees, including the 'cedars' from Mexico, but the papal injunction was flouted in 1888 when an Italian stage-designer devised a Manueline palace for King Carlos, which was later turned into a luxurious hotel. The cypresses reach a hundred and twenty feet with a girth in proportion and add grandeur to the native forest, itself luxuriant. The palace-hotel is not so much a royal folly as a splendid anachronism, as exotic in time as King Fernando's hill-top palace at Sintra is in place.

The flatter lands to the north of Luso and those to the east are now well-known centres of wine-production, the Bairrada and Dão. Dão is the river that flows by Santa Comba to enter the Mondego, while the Bairrada is a collection of villages, which pool their produce at Mealhada and Anadia. Most of the older cottages are not white-washed as in the south, but mud-coloured with roofs of red pantiles. Along the coast, the pines of Leiria give way to the series of lagoons about Aveiro, sometimes referred to as the Portuguese Venice, though it is much more Portuguese than Venetian, with its glistening salt-pans, and its few and useful waterways, more reminiscent of a Dutch town placed in the south. The *ria* of Aveiro is a saline lagoon separated from the ocean by a sandy shoal. It is some twenty-five miles long from Ovar in the north almost to Mira in the south. It has only one outlet to the ocean at the level of Aveiro, where it is at its broadest. The water in front of the city is divided into rectangular fields in which the salt is piled in pyramids. The Canal of the Pyramids is a straight thorough-fare between the pans which becomes the City Canal, dividing the town in two. The railway station is a long stride from the city. Near it is the church of the Barrocas, by Laprade who designed the library at Coimbra, to house a shrine of St John brought there from outside: it dates from about 1710 and thus predates the famous library. Laprade had made a tomb for the Bishop of Miranda, who was rector of the University of Coimbra and died at his house near Ilhavó in 1699. It is possible that Laprade was one of the first to speak the language of the baroque in Portugal.

The great monument in Aveiro is the Dominican convent of Jesus, now used as a museum. It was built in the fifteenth century, and inhabited by the Infanta Joana sister of John II. The high altar is a gamut of gilded woodwork, and the princess, who was beatified in 1693, lies in a marble chest more intricate than funerary. Her portrait painted by Nuno Gonçalves or his circle lends her a kind of melancholy splendour. The museum is rich in religious paintings and vestments. Other churches of Aveiro are São Domingos, which serves as cathedral, much damaged, but with an eighteenth-century façade, the Misericórdia, designed by Terzi in 1585, but plastered with later *azulejos*, and the seventeenth-century Carmo.

The tall ships were made and mended at Gafanha, opposite the city. They partici-pated in the annual cod-fishing expedition to the Newfoundland Banks, and dried and salted their catch in long trays by the wharf. The great schooner Dom Fernando, the pride of the seas in the middle of the nineteenth century, was rebuilt in Aveiro for the Exposition of 1998 as a floating maritime museum.

A typical occupation of the *ria* is that of the *moliceiro* who uses a flat-bottomed boat with a single sail to harvest *moliço*, water-weed widely used as fertiliser. At the south-ern end of the lagoon Ilhavó makes ships and provides seamen both for the high seas and for the fisheries of the coast. It has a museum of maritime activities. Ilhavó is also the ceramic centre of the Vista Alegre porcelain industry, the oldest and most famous in Portugal. It takes its name from the Quinta da Vista Alegre which had belonged to the Bishop of Miranda and was owned by the Pinto Basto family, who obtained the right to assume the title of Royal Factory with a monopoly of porcelain production in 1826: early specimens are much prized. At the opposite end of the lagoon, to the north, is Ovar, once simply Var, which has given a name to the fishwives of Lisbon, Varinas. It is also cattle-country and produces milk and cheese. Like many Portuguese places, it has its own speciality, which is *pão de ló*, a kind of sponge cake. That of Aveiro is *ovos moles*, or soft eggs, the yolks beaten in sugar, formerly a conventual delicacy.

Beyond Ovar there is a small lagoon at Esmoriz, close enough to the sea to provide a home for water-fowl. The coastal plain broadens and both road and rail come close to the sand-dunes with their characteristic but unobtrusive flora. At Espinho the beach is broad enough to match Figueira. The town dates from about 1840 and has been laid out in strict grid-pattern with streets numbered instead of commemorating forgotten politicians. The main road is lined with palm-trees and hotels. The beach is continuous with Granja, built about a generation later, and with slightly greater pretensions. These are now suburbs of Gaia and Oporto, and the railway turns inland to cross the great river by the dramatic bridge of Dona Maria Pia. The Romans took a more direct route, avoiding the marshes and the numerous small rivers that feed the lagoon. The same route was followed in reverse in the Middle Ages by those who set out from the Minho to reconquer Viseu, Coimbra and ultimately Lisbon.

The area south of the Douro was known as the Land of St Mary, not very precisely defined, but including the domains of the monastery of Grijó, some ten miles south of Gaia and the castle of Feira, now much restored, twenty miles further on. Grijó is simply the Ecclesiola, or 'little church', from which one Sueiro Fromariques established a protectorate far and wide before being killed in 1103 near Santarém, being taken by surprise while pitching tent by a party of Muslims from Badajoz. The monastery was finally discontinued in 1770. The chief monument of the Terra de Santa Maria is the castle of Vila da Feira, placed on a steep hill to dominate the coastal plain. It was held for Afonso Henriques by Ermígio Moniz, brother to Egas Moniz, the royal tutor, and entrusted by Afonso V to Fernão Pereira who gave it its Gothic appearance, with conical turrets and parapets. The *vila* at its foot was known as Santa Maria of 'the Feria' or fair, held by the governor of the castle by royal licence.

At Albergaria-a-Velha, 'the old hostel', Queen Tarásia founded in 1120 a shelter for those travelling the road to Coimbra. It had only four beds, and nothing is now left of it, but its date entitles it to be considered as the birthplace of the Portuguese tourist industry.

Although the Romanised inhabitants lived in some state at Conimbriga and its fortress, Aeminium, there were few stations on the road to the Douro – Talabriga, near Branca, and Lancobriga, at Fiães, near Vila da Feira. How important these places were remains unknown, but so far no sign of mosaics has appeared between the Mondego and the Douro. The same may be said of Roman statuary, which is represented at Coimbra, but absent between it and the Douro. Silver was extracted near Sever on the river Vouga, but in general the native *civitates* stayed without much sign of influence from the conquerors, this being the remotest part of the province of Lusitania.

A little further inland, the city of Viseu has on its outskirts the large Roman camp known as the Cave of Viriatus. It is a thick clay wall surrounding an octagon of thirty hectares, a cantonment large enough to hold a considerable army. It has yielded only a *denarius* of 40 BC. This suggests that it was near a native *civitas*, but was only an early Roman centre in that one or more roads met there. Whether it has anything to do with the Lusitanian hero is uncertain. His name is often associated with the Serra da Estrela, but no traces of him or of the Romans exist there.

The road from Coimbra to Viseu passes Bussaco and crosses the hills into the valley of the Dão, widely known for its wines. Santa Comba Dão, once the property of the bishops of Coimbra, was the birthplace of Dr Salazar, whose father was a farm-manager and mother a teacher. It has a plaque showing that the widow Queen Catherine of England stayed there in 1692. The road forks, that to the left passing parallel with the Serra de Caramulo, to Tondela and Viseu. The Serra is snow-capped in winter and has two sanatoria, which enjoy the purity of its air at two and a half thousand feet and look across the fertile vale of Besteiros to the Serra da Estrela. The Besteiros, once crossbowmen, now dress vines and grow oranges and apples.

Viseu is the capital of Beira Alta, standing on a rise of fifteen hundred feet, a provincial market-town with a notable cathedral and a museum which displays the works of its great painter, Vasco Fernandes, known as Grão Vasco. Its high plain contains the valleys of the Dão and Mondego: the ridge of the Estrela is some twenty miles away. The centre of Viseu is the cathedral square which Robert Smith called one of the finest ensembles in Portugal of the seventeenth-century style, the former episcopal palace on the left, now the museum, the chapter-house on the right, a granite crucifix in the centre, and the Manueline front devised by a Spanish architect in 1635. The fourth side of the square is occupied by the Misericórdia, a beautiful baroque exterior dating from 1775. The cathedral is in fact a medley, for the two towers that contain the front are Romanesque, with later pinnacles and a clock. The fine interior preserves the vaulting of 1503. The façade collapsed in 1635, which accounts for the rather incongruous doorway. The museum has several galleries of paintings, ancient and modern, including Columbano and others of the nineteenth century, but its greatest exhibits are the works of Vasco Fernandes, the sixteenth century religious painter who was employed by many churches of the region. His masterpiece is the majestic portrait of St Peter seated on his throne. Viseu was walled in the fifteenth century but only fragments remain, one being the Porta do Soar, adjacent to the house of the Melos.

The city is separated from the Cova de Viriato by the small river Paiva, which served as a moat for the vast encampment which covers an area not much less than the city itself. The name Viseu is not recorded until 572, when it was a church of St Martin with a bishop and eight subsidiary churches. It seems to have been linked by a route which crossed the Estrela and made for Mérida by Idanha and was connected by a route through the valley of the Vouga to meet the coast road at Cabeço de Vouga. No signs of the Muslim occupation appear to have survived, but in about 917 it was the border from which King Ramiro II of Leon, as prince, defended the frontier. Half a century later, it was under Muslim rule, which probably did not extend much to the north of Lafões, the Arabic for 'two brothers', perhaps hills. In 1027 King Alfonso V of Leon was killed by a bolt from the walls, while attempting to besiege Viseu, and it was finally taken by Fernando I in 1058, serving as a base for his conquest of Coimbra in 1064, when his forces were supplied by the monastery of Vacariça, near Luso, once governing a large area. When Coimbra had been taken, it was soon exposed to the attacks of the Almoravids. The Muslims then sent their raiders in from the weak frontier of Salamanca, obliging the Christians to fortify a chain of places to defend the Beira or Side, from which the province takes its name. Afonso Henriques in due course restored the dioceses of Viseu and Lamego whose bishops accompanied him in the siege of Lisbon. It was sacked by the Castilians in the time of King Fernando. John I restored its walls, and after the conquest of Ceuta created the dukedom of Viseu for Prince Henry the Navigator. The royal palace was demolished in the sixteenth century. Its Spanish bishop Ortiz de Villegas enriched its cathedral, and in the nineteenth century the bishop of Viseu, Alves Martins, was the leader of a political party. But the main railway lines to Europe and to the north passed it by and Viseu is close to the heart of Portugal rather than its pulse.

In modern times Viseu is easily reached by road and it does not matter if motorways by-pass the main towns. But in the days of railways, the international line followed the valley of the Mondego, and a narrow-gauge branch-line from Santa Comba to Viseu was added only in 1880. Viseu was also reached from Espinho and Oporto by the Vale de Vouga line, passing through bucolic country without much preoccupation about revenue from passenger-load. In 1941, the war-time years, when there was no coal, the trains were fuelled by wood, and large cords stood on the stations to replenish the tenders. Sparks came through the windows and burned holes in the lace covers. But there was a restaurant service: on buying the ticket, you ordered a meal, and at a given halt a large tin box was placed on the table: it contained steak and eggs and everything needed for a hot meal, which was certainly necessary as trains fed on wood have little regard for the time-table.

The road from Viseu skirts the end of the Caramulo and reaches the Vouga at São Pedro do Sul. The river rises far away in the Serra da Lapa and has run nearly half of its eighty-mile course. Although it has no large town, its basin is one of the most thickly populated parts of rural Portugal. The northern slopes of the Caramulo are noticeably gentler and the Serra de Arada to the north reaches 3,400 feet. The geology is probably complicated, but made more so by the fact that each village seems to give its name to the same Serra, the Arada becoming São Macário on the east and the Gralheira on the west. The Sul which gives its name to São Pedro is not the point of the compass but a stream flowing down from São Macário. São Pedro has hot springs which break through a crack in the granite to treat a wide range of ailments. In the town the former Misericórdia is now the town-hall, and Susan Lowndes was at pains to get the key in order to see its eighteenth-century church, which she found splendid, magnificent and charming, but she failed to get into the Misericórdia though she admired its quite lovely façade. I have to admit that I did not make the effort, but I did take the north road to Castro Daire and Lamego in a temperamental old car, despite warnings that the road was very high. It was, but I have a memory of its wildness and of an old man praying beside the road, and of my wife's relief when we completed the journey. Four miles beyond is the more modest resort of Vouzela, which has a thirteenth-century Romanesque church. The Arabic 'two brothers' or Lafões was an area rather than a single point, the two hills of Lafão and Castelo being the end of the Caramulo. The hot springs of São Pedro were the Caldas de Lafões, and several villages added 'de Lafões' to their name. The hill-sides are cultivated in terraces like those of the port-wine country and the valleys provide pasture for cattle. In the Gralheira there is an Albergaria das Cabras, and goats were almost as numerous as sheep: kid is a delicacy in the whole area. The lowlands produce *vitela de Lafões*, or Lafões' veal. In earlier times, the standard-bearer of King Afonso V was an Almeida who bred his cavalry horses at the Quinta dos Cavaleiros in Vouzela, now a hospital. As in the Minho, vines are trained in arbours and the district makes its own *vinho verde*.

At São João de Serra, otherwise the Gralheira, a road passes through the mountains to the vale of Cambra, ringed by mountains and watered by the river Caima, still relatively isolated. The river has been dammed for irrigation purposes. The church at Roge, with a large carved sixteenth- or seventeenth-century cross, is a good example of the same period. The village of Macieira, made the seat of the *concelho* in 1514, was the home of a Dona Constança Afonso, whose brother killed a son of King Sancho I in a duel at Grijó in 1245. The river springs from the rock in a spectacular, if seasonal, waterfall at Frecha de Misarela. The whole area was populated in pre-Roman times. Oliveira dos Azeméis was a stop on the main road from Coimbra to Oporto, the *azeméis* being the beasts of the posting-system. It has a mansion of the Corte Real family built in 1697, and a garden and chapel with extensive views from the tower. The 'new inn', Albergaria a Nova, is in the parish of Branca, a likely site for Talabriga, the native town taken by Brutus in 136 BC. It seems probable that the marshes and lagoon of Aveiro were once much larger and that they have been silted up by the Vouga and other streams. The ancient road would thus run above sea-level and would have been fairly densely populated when Caesar required the mountaineers of the Estrela to move to flatter areas.

An area which is both remote and accessible is that between the basin of the Vouga and the Douro. For those who like mountain driving, the aim should be to reach the vast and isolated monastery of Arouca. It is the church in the diocese of Lamego called Arevoca in 572, perhaps then a hermitage of St Martin. Livy mentions the opposition of the Arevaci in c. 150 BC but they may then have been in another place (or another people). It is supposed to have been destroyed by the Muslims: if so, it owed its revival and expansion to Dona Toda Viegas, 1096–1158. Like other wealthy widows, she doubtless intended to create a patrimony for her son, who was governor of the 'terra of Arouca' from 1117 and died in 1144. It later passed to Queen Mafalda, daughter of Sancho I, from 1220 until her death in 1256. It was damaged by fire in 1550 and again in the eighteenth century: what now stands is a reconstruction of the eighteenth century with fine choir-stalls and chapter house, and a twentieth-century refurbishment. The modern village is small, but a centre of festivity for the harvest-thanksgiving. It may well be wondered how royal ladies reached so wild a place: the answer is by litter, which the novelist Camilo Castelo Branco saw as doomed to disappear after centuries of service in 1850. There are several approaches to Arouca, from São Pedro do Sul, from the vale of Cambra and from the valley of the Douro. The first two were formerly marked as dangerous, but the rise from Castelo de Paiva is more gradual and sweeping. During the Peninsular War, Arouca was a redoubt which resisted the French. One of the nuns was a sister of Beresford's aide William Warre, and when they visited her and suggested she should leave, she replied that she felt safer where she was.

Castelo de Paiva, from which Arouca is reached, is likely to be remembered for the catastrophe of 2001, when its bridge collapsed in time of spate and the travellers in a fully occupied coach were drowned. The 'castle' is a nineteenth-century assumption: it was formerly the Concelho of Paiva, with perhaps an ancient *castro*. The Paiva, a stream flowing northwards into the Douro, is impassable, going through a deep trench at Alvarenga. The centre of the township is Sobrado, with a modern town-hall and *misericordia*. After the narrows of Alvarenga the road follows the Paiva to Castro Daire, under the shadow of the Serra de Montemuro. This range reaches over 4,000 feet and has only a few small villages, such as Bigorne, Pico de Talegre, perhaps more populous in prehistoric times than today. It is sheep country. It still has wolves which, when they attack sheepfolds in a hard winter, the press describes by the conventional epithet of 'corpulent', which is precisely what they are not. The flocks were formerly nomadic, following the Peninsular practice of being moved in search of fresh grass by designated tracks, the sheep-walks. The geographer Amorim Girão describes their approach in a cloud which might have stirred the heart of Don Quixote, and their stampede to cross the Paiva at the Ponte de Pedrinha, a mile or so from the town. Castro Daire is half-way from Viseu to Lamego, passing between the Montemuro and the Serra de Leomil.

Lamego, on the southern fringe of the port-wine district, is on the main road between Viseu and Vila Real which crosses the Douro a few miles to the north at Régua. The road up from the river has many twists and turns, and Lamego stands in more open country at about a thousand feet. Its high point is its castle on the site of a pre-Roman castro above the Balsemão stream. The keep remains, but what is left of the walls suggests that it was not very large. The most remarkable feature of the citadel is a large Gothic cistern. Sacheverell Sitwell, coming from Viseu, thought nothing could be more beautiful, or more happy and laughing, than the last few miles to Lamego: it is one of the prettiest towns in the whole of Portugal. He admired its numerous baroque buildings, and did not forget to mention its wines and hams, which provide Oporto and other places with charcuterie. Outside the walls is the church of Almocave, probably the Arabic word for cemetery, adjacent to the citadel, a small Romanesque church of the twelfth century, well preserved, with a rectangular tower added later. At the southern end of the citadel is the cathedral, originally a Romanesque building with an austere-looking tower to which a trim Renaissance façade was applied between 1508 and 1515, and a cloister soon after. In the eighteenth century, essential rebuilding of the nave took place and the ceiling was painted by Nasoni. In front of the cathedral is a triangular public garden, and facing this the former bishop's palace, now the Museum.

The chapel of the Sacrament has a fine baroque silver altar-frontal of 1758 to 1768. The museum contains paintings by Grão Vasco as well as others from the cathedral, and tapestries, furniture and some carriages, quite different from those preserved at Belém, and the litter used by eighteenth-century bishops. The main boulevard of Lamego is the Avenida which leads up to the Sanctuary of the Remédios, an ancient hermitage on a hill replaced in 1750 by a large baroque church, approached by a monumental granite double staircase or Via Sacra for pilgrims coming to the sanctuary, which resembles the setting for Bom Jesus at Braga. There are nine landings with pillars and balustrades, and stone figures of prophets and kings in a style reminiscent of the Aleijadinho at Ouro Preto in Brazil. The church stands in a space surrounded by more statues of prophets and Old Testament Kings: the two towers were added only between 1880 and 1905. Its festivities are in the first half of September.

There is no evidence that Lamego was a Roman city. It appears as a diocese in the church of St Martin of Dume in 572. There was probably a road which crossed the Douro near Régua, and another which followed the north bank of the river and then crossed to the south, eventually reaching Mérida. In the Middle Ages, the barons of the middle Douro held it and lost it again, and it was finally occupied by Fernando I only in 1057, seven years before the conquest of Coimbra. All this area was in the domain of Egas Moniz, the leader of the barons of the Douro valley and tutor of Afonso Henriques, who played a chief part in bringing his young charge to the throne in place of Queen Tarásia and her Galician count in 1128.

It is likely that the area was abandoned by the Muslims when Fernando took Lamego: it now has a number of small churches and monasteries dating from the eleventh and twelfth centuries, though few castles, which were placed further south and to the east. These places required some exertion to reach. Cárquere, perhaps a pre-Roman *civitas*, has a church said to have been founded by Egas Moniz when the boy Afonso was miraculously cured of an illness: it was later partially extended and has the tombs of the senhores of Resende; Resende has the Casa de Soenga, a grand house built in 1779, with gardens and statues and views over the river; São Martinho dos Mouros is a Romanesque church of the twelfth century in almost its original condition, combining the simplicity and strength the times required. Not far away, Eça de Queirós placed his last novel, which he did not live to see in print, *A Cidade e as serras*. The church at Barros is another Romanesque monument, of the thirteenth century, with a later bell-tower.

South of Lamego, off the main road, is Tarouca, once a fort and centre of a *terra* belonging to Egas Moniz and the seat of the Meneses, counts of Tarouca and governors of Tangier. It is now a village, with a Romanesque church with a Manueline tomb, perhaps intended for the first count, and a Misericórdia, also of the sixteenth century. Ucanha, a village on the Varosa stream, given by Afonso Henriques to the widow of Egas Moniz, has an ancient bridge with five spans and a massive toll-tower, built in 1465. It belonged to the convent of Sarzedas, a Cistercian house founded by Teresa Afonso, governess of the king's children: its façade was remodelled in baroque style in the eighteenth century but the convent fell into disuse. The monastery of São João de Tarouca, said to have been begun in 1124, has the tomb of Dom Pedro, the genealogist and first Count of Barcelos, son of King Diniz, who retired to the village of Lalim. It was abandoned; when its pictures were removed to Lisbon, there were local protests and they had to be returned and restored to their former neglect. Armamar, which can be reached from Lamego or Régua, is remote enough to have escaped unwelcome attention, and has a thirteenth-century Romanesque church. Tabuaço, once the centre of several *concelhos*, includes the Romanesque hermitage of São Pedro das Aguas, perched on a precipitous ravine above the river Távora.

13

Oporto

The city of Oporto is the undisputed capital of the north, second only to Lisbon and metropolis for the province of the Minho, the source of Portuguese nationhood and the most populous rural region. It is about half the size of Lisbon, but has enveloped the surrounding townships without obliterating them. It is the port of entry and interchange for the teeming countryside to the north and for the valley of the Douro. One may still be aroused in the middle of the city by the crowing of cocks, even if the creaking of wains has given way to traffic-jams. It and its territory have given the name Portugal, and the word attached itself to the wines of the middle Douro. The true centre of the producing area is sixty miles away. The large barrels or pipes were formerly brought down the river on the characteristic *rabelos*, barges with a single sail, broad in the beam and of shallow draught, and deposited at the 'lodges' – *lojas* – of Vila Nova de Gaia on the south bank of the river. They have been replaced by other modes of transport, but a few are moored outside the *lojas*, with the names of the companies inscribed on their sails, rather as Vasco da Gama's sails were embroidered with scenes of Portuguese history, if the *Lusiads* is to be believed. They are brought out for an annual race.

Oporto – the Port – is built, like Lisbon, on the north bank of a great river, and its traditional centre, the cathedral, stands on a high bluff overlooking the stream two hundred feet below. There is no inland sea, but the river is nipped between the cathedral hill, formerly called Windy Hill, the Pena Ventosa, and another height surmounted by the Convent of the Pilar. The oldest part of the city lies below the cathedral where the river widens. The sea is four miles away at Foz, where a sandspit reduces the clearance to a hundred yards or so. The entrance may be dangerous, and only smaller ships reach the wharves to load wine and unload a variety of imports. For liners and freighters, a large mole has been built at Leixões on the ocean. The old walled city was an oblong including the cathedral and about a mile of water-front. It went no deeper than the present Praça da Liberdade, now the main central thoroughfare. The crowding together on uneven ground goes some way to explain the architecture of old Oporto. The houses had narrow frontages on the steep cobbled streets, and were built close to a line in three, four or five storeys, with broad overhanging eaves and wide balconies of no great depth. These are adorned with railings worked in a variety of patterns by the guild of ironsmiths. There was no royal palace and little space for leisure or monuments, though the well-to-do owned *quintas* in the

10 View of Oporto with 'rabelos' (João Paulo)

vicinity. It was a burgh dominated by the bishop and the bourgeoisie. Queen Tarásia had granted Oporto to its French bishop Hugh in 1120, probably in return for his help in having Rome recognise her queenhood.

It was already a commercial centre in 1147, when its bishop received the crusaders from England and the Low Countries and negotiated with them for the conquest of Lisbon. In order to evade episcopal taxation, the merchants shipped their goods on the opposite bank at Gaia. There followed a prolonged struggle in which the citizens held their own against the bishop and the nobility of the region. They benefited by their support for John I and the house of Avis, for it was in Oporto that John married Philippa of Lancaster and that their famous son Prince Henry was born in 1394. The city then had probably only 5,000 inhabitants. It began to spread in the seventeenth century, by which time it was controlled by a group of interrelated families. It did not suffer from the great Earthquake of 1755 or from the imposition of a single style of architecture, but the Almadas, father and son, judge and governor in the late eighteenth century and related to Pombal, set out to provide it with monumental buildings, such as the hospital of Santo António and the University, to which the British consul, John Whitehead, added the elegant Factory House, or club for the more prosperous British merchants. Although Oporto was briefly occupied by the French in April 1809, Soult was soon driven out by Wellington and Beresford, the most notable catastrophe being the collapse of the bridge of boats across the Douro, in which many lives were lost.

Oporto had been the first to rebel against the French occupation in 1808, when Bishop Castro presided over a Supreme Junta, thus proclaiming the city's love of independence. It was not molested after the precipitate flight of Soult, but in 1820 the liberal revolution was proclaimed in Oporto and quickly spread to Lisbon. The two groups had different ideas, but those of Oporto prevailed. The revolution did not long survive the death of its leading light, but in 1832 Oporto again showed its preference for liberal institutions when the ex-Emperor of Brazil, Dom Pedro, landed with a makeshift army to claim the throne from his brother, Dom Miguel. The Miguelites evacuated the city, but they could count on the great majority of the countryside and besieged Dom Pedro for almost a year. The siege was less destructive to the city's fabric than such prolonged assaults usually are, for the port remained open and the Miguelites lacked control of the sea. The issue was settled elsewhere, but Oporto's reputation as the citadel of liberalism was confirmed. Dom Pedro is commemorated by an equestrian statue inaugurated in 1866 in the Praça da Liberdade. This was formerly the 'new square' outside the city walls. From it the main avenue, the Avenida dos Aliados, flanked by banks, cafés and the Post Office, runs northward amongst parterres to the city hall, or Concelho da Cidade, a massive building surmounted by a tower and carillion, built in 1920 in the municipal style favoured in Flanders and the north.

As befits a commercial city, Oporto has probably more shops to the acre than any other place in the Iberian Peninsula. In the nineteenth century it spread its wings in all three available directions. The fashionable shopping area was the Boavista, and various attempts were made to superimpose a system of straight boulevards. The Boavista was used by carriages and wagons on the way to the seaside at Foz or Matosinhos. With the introduction of public transport systems the need for long straight thoroughfares increased. Mule-drawn cars were replaced by electric trams – the eléctricos – at the end of the century. The Rotunda of Boa Vista dates from 1915 to 1917, but the shady boulevard has been engulfed by the spread of the city northwards. The fashionable street is Santa Caterina, which runs almost parallel with the Avenida dos Aliados. It is closed to vehicles. This makes access difficult to Oporto's most typical hotel, the Grande Hotel do Porto, though the porter can easily remove the bollards. There is an elegant early twentieth-century café, the Majestic, various tea-shops and a large emporium (called in Portuguese um shopping), and at Christmas the whole scene is lit up and attracts many street-sellers, a band of Andean minstrels with an amplifier and dumb mimes (who do not need one). A little below it is the Bolhão, the general vegetable, fruit and produce market, a bustling hive of activity that still remains in the heart of the city and affords the nearest thing to an overview of Portuguese domestic life. It is a solid, two-storeyed structure of stone and iron of monumental proportions occupying a whole block. In general, the pace of Oporto is a brisk walk, as of people who have business to attend to. It is said that Braga prays, Coimbra sings and studies, Lisbon idles and Oporto works. The men like to appear neatly dressed like bank-clerks, or at least as if they had just come from a bank. In the shops they are attentive: it is their business to be. One wonders how people live in the picturesque but tumbledown tenements, narrow wells with rickety stairs lit only by skylights and enlivened only by thin cats, pots of flowers and singing-birds – there is a Papageno who sells goldfinches in cages at week-ends near the railway station. Oporto may be drab, but it is not monotonous.

Oporto is best seen from the high esplanade in front of the cathedral or the tower of the highest church, the Clérigos, or from the great iron bridges that span the Douro, masterpieces of the utilitarian art of the nineteenth century. Until the railway age, which in Portugal dawned in 1856, it was quite usual to travel to Lisbon by ship in a couple of days. It is now done in three hours by rail. At first the line ended at Gaia, and the traveller got out without crossing the river. The cliff on which the cathedral stands was too high for the level at Gaia and the station at Gaia too high for a crossing at river-level. The conundrum was resolved by Eiffel who designed a monstrous steel span which carried the line at a height to the east of the cliff, reaching the station at Campanhã. It was begun in January 1876 and finished at the end of October 1877. The trains still cross in stately fashion suspended in mid-air to survey the valley below. The bridge was named after Dona Maria Pia, queen to King Luis. Then in 1880 a road bridge combining two levels was planned, to be completed in October 1886. Its lower level linked the wharfs of Gaia to the Oporto water-front, and its upper level ran from the upper part of Gaia into the centre of Oporto. It was built by a Belgian company and named after Dom Luis. It was at first subject to a toll, lifted in 1920. Meanwhile, a tunnel was built to connect Campanhã to a large new station at São Bento, once the site of the Benedictine monastery, built in the palatial style then in favour and adorned with enormous blue and white azulejos depicting scenes from Portuguese history and the evolution of transport. It was opened in 1890 and operates a shuttle to Campanhã and local services, while the main line from Lisbon continues to the Minho and to the frontier at Valença. The two iron masterpieces remain the chief links between Oporto and the rest of Portugal south of the Douro, though they have been supplemented by the road bridge at Arrábida, further down the river, which makes it possible to reach the north without going into the heart of the city.

The ancient centre of the city is the Sé, one of the five great cathedrals of medieval Portugal. It is remarkable for its elevated position and massive scale initiated by the French bishop Hugh. The open square in front has an equestrian statue of Vimara Peres erected in 1968 and a Manueline pillory. The 'city tower' at one corner is a modern structure to house the archives. The adjoining bishop's palace was added in the eighteenth century. It is grand, if different; the portico, also of the eighteenth century, jars against the austerity of the great building. The modern tendency has been to reject later ornamentation and restore the grandeur of the original pile. The cloister is a Gothic addition of the fourteenth century. The hill may have been an ancient *castro* but there are no traces of this or of the Roman ferry station, the *portus*. Recent excavations show that it was indeed the 'new castle' built by the Sueves on the north bank, where King Rechiarius was murdered by the Goths in 456. The name Portocale appears on the coins of Leovigild who overthrew the Suevic kingdom in 585, and those of four of his successors, but after the Muslim invasions of 711 the place disappears from view until Vimara Peres occupied the territory in 868. The port played an essential part in the southward movement of the Christians until Bishop Pedro Pitões negotiated with the passing Anglo-Norman crusaders for the conquest of Lisbon in 1147. But Oporto had no royal seat and constant rebuilding in a cramped space militated against conservation.

Below the cathedral is the Jesuit church or college, known as the Grilos after the mother church in Lisbon. It was built in about 1560 with a severe façade, and taught theology until the extinction of the Society by Pombal in 1769. After the victory of the liberals, its building became a barracks, but the chapel with a baroque altarpiece was turned into a museum of sacred art.

The cathedral quarter was the Cima da Vila or 'up-hill', the lower part being the water-front west of Dom Luis' bridge. Its centre was the custom-house or Alfândega, a fine specimen of fourteenth-century building. It is called the Casa do Infante in the belief that Oporto's most famous son Prince Henry was born here and so is carefully preserved. Henry was probably born in a palace constructed for Afonso IV against the wishes of the bishop and later demolished. His name has been given to a square, the Praça do Infante, with a statue erected in 1899. Both his parents, King John I and Queen Philippa, are honoured by squares in Oporto, and the convent of Santa Clara is supposed to have been built in accordance with a vow made before Philippa's death in 1415. The convent has been secularised, but the chapel remains with a fine Renaissance doorway and a richly gilded baroque interior. Carved woodwork, often chestnut, is preserved in choir-stalls, pulpits and other parts of churches, and already in the sixteenth century it might be coated with gesso and gilded. But it was the gold of Brazil that permitted the luxuriant decoration of high altars, organ-cases and roof-ing. Gold was thought the most extraordinary of colours and the 'church of gold' the supreme ideal of a pious bourgeoisie. The church of St Francis which adjoins the Stock Exchange or Bolsa has a modest exterior, but the interior is a profusion of gilded wood-carving, or *talha dourada*, in which the Portuguese came to excel.

It was not until well into the eighteenth century that Oporto's growing prosperity was translated into architecture. Under the Spanish domination Philip II had granted the city an appeal-court for the north, obviating the need to take cases to distant Lisbon. After the Restoration, the pressing need was to defend Lisbon, and the Braganzas did not visit the north, though two illegitimate scions were bishops of Braga. The most influential figure was Niccolo Nasoni, a citizen of Oporto from 1725. His best-known work is the Torre dos Clérigos, built between 1731 and 1749 for a guild of priests. It is a church with a single oval nave, entered by a double staircase and a small portal set in a baroque façade and surmounted by a slender tower that narrows in stages to a bell-chamber: its high and original profile has made it the badge of the city. He also designed the bishop's palace and private houses, including the Museum of Decorative Arts, built for a wealthy canon and occupied by the nineteenth-century poet Guerra Junqueiro. Nasoni's tower is in granite, but he usually respects the Portuguese preference for white spaces with a granite edging and frames.

The area beyond Nasoni's Tower was developed by João de Almada e Melo and his son Francisco. Stirred by what was being done in Lisbon, Almada sought to renovate the water-front, not apparently much changed since John I opened his Rua Nova. His aims were shared by John Whitehead (1726–1802), the long-standing British consul. The result was the redevelopment of the area in eighteenth century style, and Whitehead's English Factory (in the Portuguese sense of a trading centre) was fur-nished in the best English style (the 'English Factory' in Lisbon never had a building of its own, assembling rather in the house of the consul). For a time the merchants congregated in the 'Street of the English' where they are depicted by J J Forrester, who saw them standing in the street in knots to do their business. Whitehead obtained plans for the projected hospital of Santo António from his contemporary, John Carr of York. They were for a Palladian edifice of enormous size. The massive classical façade was completed, but the design had to be reduced to a rather simpler scale: apparently

Carr reckoned on brick, while the intention was to use stone throughout. Another majestic classical quadrangle close to the hospital was the Faculty of Science. Portugal had no university except Coimbra, but in 1762 Oporto set up a school for training naval-officers, the Royal Nautical School. By 1802 it taught mathematics, commerce and modern languages and became a Royal Academy, which in 1837 added physical and chemical sciences to become a Polytechnic Academy. It became a university, as did Lisbon, in 1910.

Another building of the time of the Almadas is the art gallery and Museum named after the sculptor Soares dos Reis (1847–89), whose 'Wild-flower' and 'Exile' are often reproduced. The museum brings together several earlier collections, including that of the English resident and collector Thomas Allen. It is strong in local painters of the nineteenth century and in ceramics. The building was the house of the brothers Carranca, nicknamed so: a 'carranca' is a scowl or frown. It was the principal house in Oporto when Soult occupied the city and used it as his headquarters: he is said to have left abruptly in the middle of his dinner, which was consumed by Wellington.

The first English traders to settle in Oporto were agents for merchants dealing in dried cod, wine and general commodities. The rise in their fortunes is due to the seventeenth-century treaties, which revived or confirmed ancient privileges. Oporto wine gradually prevailed over 'Lisbon wine' and its position was sealed by the Methuen treaty of 1701, which guaranteed a preference in duties on Portuguese wines. Oporto wine was fortified and rendered 'generous' by the addition of brandy. The English merchants travelled up the valley of the Douro and began to acquire vineyards. To compete with their influence Pombal launched his Real Companhia in 1756, which defined rather arbitrarily the area from which authentic port-wine could be produced. The region has now been somewhat extended, but the principle still holds good – what is authorised and inspected is alone authentic port. Pombal, who had been minister in London, knew that fears lest the English market be sated or saturated were groundless.

After the brief French occupation in 1808, when Bishop Castro formed his Supreme Junta, Consul Warre provided an information service of French troop movements, and his son was Beresford's aide in restoring the Portuguese army. Warre was the oldest name in the port-wine trade and celebrated its third centenary in 1970. The British community in Oporto continued to flourish in the nineteenth century. In 1900 Charles Sellars published his *Oporto, old and new*, a gallery of bewhiskered Victorian worthies. The most noteworthy was Joseph James Forrester, who arrived from Yorkshire in 1831, settled at Gaia, made a survey of the river Douro, was a good artist and pioneer photographer, was made Baron Forrester by King Luis in 1855 and perished in a boating accident at the dangerous rapids, the Cachão de Valério, in the river he loved in 1861. It is said that he was sunk by the weight of his gold-belt, while the ladies of the party, which included Dona Antónia Ferreira, the matriarch of the industry, floated in their crinolines. Some of the English intermarried with the Portuenses, but the community as a whole acquired a reputation for insularity and even arrogance. The novelist Júlio Diniz, whose mother was English, draws an interesting picture in his *Uma família inglesa*, subtitled 'Scenes from Oporto life'. Mr Richard Whitestone, the man of business, lingers over his breakfast and his *Times*, while his daughter, the brave Jenny, engineers the promotion of his devoted and loyal Portuguese clerk to director, so that her rather indolent English brother may marry the clerk's daughter. Needless to say, this takes some time and the novel runs to two volumes. It is content to ignore the sort of religious problem that might have occurred. In 1890, Lord Salisbury's African Ultimatum shook both the Portuguese government and the British community of Oporto. The Ultimatum led to an attempt at a republican revolution in Oporto in 1891: it was unsuccessful, but played some part in bringing down the monarchy in 1910. The incident led to the removal of another long-serving consul, Oswald Crawfurd, who had produced three books on Portugal, but it was his opinion that Portugal should not have colonies in Africa (which he had never visited). For many years he passed his summers in England, where he was director of a firm of publishers, leaving his vice-consul to mind the shop.

The Oporto monument to the Peninsular War at Boavista may not be a great work of art, but it is an enormous display of baroque energy. It was initiated in 1908 and quite dwarfs the Lisbon monument of the same period. The satirist Ramalho Ortigão, who was born in Oporto, remarked that the people of Oporto had two dislikes, authority and Lisbon. Be that as it may, Oporto does not like to be outdone. In 1808 it expelled the French invaders and Bishop Castro set up his Supreme Junta without awaiting orders from the royal family in Brazil. In 1820 it made the first liberal revolution which obliged John VI to return, and in 1832 John's son Pedro, the ex-Emperor of Brazil, implanted liberalism. The great siege confirmed the city's claim to be *invicta*, the unconquered city. The central square is not only the Praça da Liberdade but has Dom Pedro's statue and a plaque showing his heart being given to the city: it is, not inappropriately, the heart of Oporto. It is still the centre of movement since numerous buses and trolleys converge and turn there. The building on its south side looks stately and classical enough and was intended to be part of a convent, but was transformed into shops and offices, where the dandies of the day strolled: it is known as the Cardosas, after the heiresses of a tobacco monopolist.

In Portugal the victory of liberalism is closely associated with the romantic movement in literature. Both the poet and dramatist, J B Almeida, best known as Almeida Garrett, who revitalised the Portuguese theatre, and Alexandre Herculano, who rewrote Portuguese medieval history and strove to invigorate municipal life, lived in Oporto and served in Dom Pedro's army. Garrett's name is bestowed on the square in front of the São Bento station and his statue is in front of the City Hall. Herculano, who gathered together the documents of the suppressed monasteries, was underlibrarian of the Oporto Municipal Public Library, the finest collection outside of Coimbra and Lisbon, housed in the quiet Jardim de São Lázaro, the former convent of St António. Both settled in Lisbon, but the cultural interests of Oporto were upheld by Passos Manuel, prime minister and leader of what would now be called the left-of-centre liberals in the 1840s. Oporto was the only city outside Lisbon to have an opera-house. It was instituted by Almada and destroyed by fire in 1908: the present theatre of St John was constructed on the site between 1912 and 1918. St John is the patron saint of Oporto, and his feast on 23 and 24 June is celebrated in the streets, where troops of young people brandish stalks of garlic at one another's heads (now usually replaced by plastic), and end the day with dances and a firework display. The symbolic plant is the herb basil, and pots of sweet basil, *mangerona*, are sold everywhere to decorate the house.

The literary eminence of Oporto begun by Garrett and Herculano was continued by the novelist Júlio Diniz (1839–71), who was not born in the city but was trained as a doctor there and filled his sentimental stories with settings in and about Oporto.

The enfant terrible of Portuguese literature was Camilo Castelo Branco (1825–90), who was born in Lisbon, but spent most of his tormented literary life in Oporto, drawing on legends and memories of the Wars of the Two Brothers. He is not easy to translate, for his work is imbued with himself and his times. The most famous Portuguese novelist, Eça de Queirós, was born in the fishing-town of Póvoa de Varzim, where his father was a magistrate, but he detached himself from Oporto, if not from the Douro, and made an international career as a consul. Guerra Junqueiro, who was regarded as the greatest poet of his day but now sounds rhetorical, was only one of a galaxy of writers at the end of the century. António Nobre (1867–1900), whose fame rests on the monosyllable *Só* (*Alone*), the title he put to his book of poems, was born in Oporto, but settled in Coimbra.

Oporto had its own newspapers, including the *Primeiro de Janeiro* or 'first of January', commemorating the revolt of 1891, and a periodical, the *Tripeiro*. The *tripeiro* is the conventional name for the inhabitant of Oporto, corresponding to the 'lettuce' for Lisbon. There seems to be no reason why the people of Oporto should be tripe-eaters. In any case, there are plenty of places to eat in Oporto, less conspicuous than in Lisbon, for there are more rainy days and less tendency to eat out of doors. They range from the Escondidinho, the 'little hide-away', tucked away at the top end of the Rua das Flores, to a floorful of small restaurants in the 'shopping' in Santa Catarina, which also has the café Majestic and other eating-houses, tea-shops and bars. The Abadia is a former conventual refectory like the Lisbon Trindade. The Brasileira is a large refurbished café. These are near the heart of the city. But many prefer to go home for lunch, thus adding to the traffic jams, and on days out to eat at the Foz or Matosinhos or Leça.

The anatomy of central Oporto would not be complete without a reference to the Palácio da Bolsa or stock exchange, which stands in the square of Prince Henry, adjoining the golden church of St Francis and occupying the site of the former Franciscan convent. It was built by the Commercial Association some twenty years after the suppression of the monasteries. Its massive façade incorporates a recessed arcade with four columns and pediment raised far above the ground, and its most surprising feature inside is its Arab hall, in a lavish pseudo-Oriental style that would have appealed to Sir Francis Cook of Montserrate. But the wealthy merchants lived outside the ancient *vila*. Forrester and other English residents settled at Gaia, near their wine lodges. Others built mansions on the western avenue beyond the area favoured by the Almadas and towards the Foz. When they departed their active life, they were buried in the new cemetery of Agramonte opened in 1855, where many leading families had tombs and chapels reminiscent of the famous Recoletos in Buenos Aires. Not far away in the Rua da Boa Nova is the small British cemetery used by protestant members of the community since the later eighteenth century.

There are few parks other than small gardens in the city limits. The lack was partly resolved by the creation in 1865 of the gardens of the Palácio de Cristal on the model of the London Crystal Palace. It occupies a fine site on the escarpment overlooking the river. The building was sacrificed to make way for a concrete shell capable of providing for thousands at sporting events, but the gardens remain. Several fine houses were built on the wooded escarpment on the north bank of the river, which is crossed by the bridge of Arrábida, half-way to the Foz. The Foz was a favourite seaside resort, with a fort, bathing-beaches and hotels: it is cooler than the city in summer and in the winter heavy seas pound on the shore.

Further inland, on the Avenida Gomes da Costa is Oporto's most original museum, the Serralves, a severe clean-cut house in the French style of the 1920s, used as a gallery for modern or contemporary art and set in a spacious park of trimly clipped shrubs. Not all contemporary art is the vulgar and meaningless fodder of dealers, and the Serralves Foundation is a brave attempt to sift the grain from the chaff. It provides an elegant setting unlike the pseudo-factories of Paris, London and Lisbon.

What is reputedly the oldest building of the city is the small church of St Martin of Cedofeita, some way north of the Santo António hospital. It was perhaps originally a hermitage, which has been carefully restored to its 1220 state, a single Romanesque nave with granite vaulting and a separate chapel for the high altar. The doorway of a triple archivault resting on groups of carved capitals recalls the churches at Lourosa and Rates.

Vila Nova de Gaia is famous for the thousands of casks of wine stored in its 'lodges'. They are easily accessible by foot across the Dom Luis bridge. The lodges are not subterraneous caves but large dark sheds in which the casks and bottles are marshalled in neat array ready for engagement. In this vinous Valhalla and paradise of cooperage visitors are welcomed and regaled. But Gaia is a township on its own, not a mere dormitory suburb of Oporto. Its chief monument is the Convent of the Serra do Pilar perched on a cliff overlooking the river, and made famous as the point on the south bank held by the Liberals. The church and cloister are both round, in the style of the cloister of the Emperor Charles V at Granada, and unique in Portugal. They were built for the Augustinians in 1576 and 1583. The sculptors Soares dos Reis and Teixeira Lopes (1866–1924) worked in Gaia and their houses and studios are shown to visitors.

The city of Oporto, including part of Gaia, is recognised by UNESCO as part of the world's heritage, a distinction due largely to the planners known by the improbable acronym of CRUARB. It establishes a 'protected zone' including most of the water-front and the streets as far north as the Avenida and the City Hall and as far south as the wharfs of Gaia. Within this is the smaller 'historic city', which comprises the medieval burgh, the eighteenth-century extension and only the Pilar on the south bank. It resumes the work of urbanisation started by the Almadas, though with an important difference. The poorer medieval habitations were cleared away by Almada and his contemporaries to make way for better forms of building couched in the classical style. Much of the older property was allowed to become squalid in the twentieth century. The present object is rather one of preservation, to conserve the general appearance of the older parts of the city and to cleanse and modify what already exists with respect to the requirements of decent living. Oporto remains true to its name, a commercial centre rather than a political principality or an industrial complex. Its history and its relation with the Atlantic ports of England and Flanders make it the southern end of the north, rather than the northern tip of the south. It is thus more open to the rest of Europe than Lisbon, with its universal and imperial past, and as such preserves a European rather than an exotic façade; a compound of traditional styles that is to be preserved against the excessive obtrusion of some technological supermarket.

14

North of Oporto

Beyond the Foz, the Atlantic coast has a string of sandy beaches. Next to Leixões, the ocean port for Oporto, comes the fishing-town of Matosinhos, which has a baroque church and a Franciscan convent. The small river Leça gives its name to Leça da Palmeira and a few miles inland Leça do Balio. The coast continues to Vila do Conde, passing a prominent obelisk rising above the sands to commemorate the place at Mindelo where Dom Pedro and his liberal army landed in 1832 from the Azores to take Oporto where they were besieged. The dunes and pools are now a bird-sanctuary at which avian visitors are ringed. Leça do Balio was the former headquarters of the Knights of St John, the Hospitallers, who moved south to Crato in 1312. It may have been a church with a defensive tower against the Vikings. The present building dates from c. 1350 to 1374, the work of the *balio* Frei Vasques Pimentel. It consists of three naves in regular rectangular plan with a lower triple chancel with stone vaulting. Both church and tower are battlemented. It governed many places in the fourteenth century, and King Fernando's irregular marriage to Leonor Teles was celebrated here in 1372.

The whole area north of Oporto was the Terra dos Maias, the powerful family which liked to trace its origins to King Ramiro II in 917. It covered some sixteen parishes from the sea to the present airport of Pedras Rubras and beyond. It now has no centre, the Alto da Maia being overspread by later development. The church of Aguas Santas dates from the twelfth century, and passed to the Knights of St John and then to Malta. Its baroque trappings have been removed and its original appearance restored. The old roads to Braga by way of Famalicão, and Guimarães by Santo Tirso, have been interwoven with the excellent new system of toll-ways which whisks vehicles through the pine-clad rolling hillsides, avoiding long stretches of ribbon development, but, as everywhere, making errors difficult to rectify and remote places hard to find. Residents who have taken computerisation in their stride slip through the toll-ways and a gadget on the windscreen identifies them so that invisible wizardry sends them a monthly bill for their accumulated mileages. Buses are able to enjoy the same privilege, but the casual visitor must take his ticket (or in Portuguese 'retire his title') and pay at the other end of the motorway.

The town of Santo Tirso stands on the river Ave that flows between Braga and Guimarães to meet the sea at Vila do Conde. It was or was near the birthplace of St Rosendo (916–77), cousin to King Ramiro, enormously wealthy in land, founder of Celanova, the great monastery of Ourense. In 1096 the patron of Santo Tirso was

Sueiro Mendes, the stout governor of Santarém and uncle-in-law to Queen Tarásia. He fell from grace. The Benedictines built a fine new monastery in baroque style. They were expelled in 1834, and the abbey was acquired by a native son who had made a fortune in Brazil and was made Viscount of São Bento. It is now handsomely refurbished as a museum, principally of local archaeology, and an exhibition centre. The slope above it is neatly gardened. The town had one industry, a textile mill. It is now growing and acquiring new shops and occupations. The old families who built substantial houses in the nineteenth century are prominent in the professions, medicine and law, and farm their estates producing wine, corn, fruit and honey. They are much intermarried and foregather weekly and on festive occasions. They travel frequently: the older generation learned French and visited Paris: the younger know English and are internationally-minded. Like other Portuguese, they are sensitive to foreign opinion, hospitable, and appreciate good manners and their food. On top of the nearest mountain, Monte Córdova, there is a large modern basilica with fine views over the valleys and a centre for pilgrimages of local devotion. Near its base is Roriz, a small Romanesque church with a decorated doorway and a separate bell-tower; nothing is left of the cloister, which in 1223 was inhabited by Augustinian monks.

To the northwest a longish mile before reaching Vila Nova de Familicão is Santiago de Antas, another Romanesque church, slightly larger if not quite so attractive as Roriz. Famalicão is a market and industrial town on the northern railway and road to Braga. A league (i.e. five km) to the west is São Miguel de Seide, for twenty-five years the home of the most Portuguese of novelists, Camilo Castelo Branco, whose career from failed seminarist to imprisonment for adultery and ennoblement as viscount was every bit as chaotic as the stream of novels that poured from his pen to stave off poverty. Threatened with blindness, he shot himself on 1 June 1890. The house is set in a meadow and was restored after a fire in 1915. The lower floor is a coach house and dependencies, and a flight of steps leads up to the barely furnished living-quarters, with some of the varied books which the writer turned to account for his tales of the old north.

The motorway reaches Braga, the capital of Roman Gallaecia, and religious capital of Portugal. The Suevic kings made their seat at Dume outside the walls, where St Martin founded his church in c. 550: it is now only an archaeological site, but his successor, St Fructuosus, is related to the unique classical church of Montélios on a Byzantine plan of a central square with four projecting arms, going back to the seventh century. The barbarian kings avoided walled cities, and Roman and modern Braga is a couple of miles away. The Roman walls existed until modern times, but only parts now remain. After the Muslim invasion, the bishop withdrew to Lugo in Galicia, and the diocese was much diminished, being restored by the efforts of Bishop Pedro (1071–91). The existing building was probably begun by the French archbishop St Gerald (d 1108) in Cluniac fashion, but took many years to complete. Count Henry and Queen Tarásia, the parents of Portugal's first king, are buried in tombs made by Archbishop Diogo de Sousa who had the Renaissance chapel built. Prince Afonso, the eldest child of Philippa of Lancaster and John I, who died at ten in 1400, also has his tomb here. The 'chapel of glory' has the fine tomb of Archbishop Pereira (c. 1330), ancestor of the Holy Constable, and initiator of the episcopal palace. Braga benefited by the influx of gold from Brazil and from two royal archbishops, the brother and son

of King John V, who ruled the diocese from 1741 to 1789. Braga added two magnificent baroque organs decorated with gilded carving which extends to the lofts and
choirstalls, united by a hump-backed bridge and balustrade. Organ-music was
intended to stir the soul, and the baroque seemed a kind of music in gilt.

The zone round the cathedral has been closed to vehicles, which flow through
underground passes and come to rest in a large car park-beneath the main square. The
city has several specimens of secular baroque. Near the cathedral is the city hall, Paços
do Concelho, an elegant two-storeyed palace in which the taste for adornment is
restrained. The same can hardly be said of the Palacete do Raio (or house of the
Mexican) where the doors and windows are of moulded granite surmounted by a
balustrade and garnished with blue and white azulejos. Both are attributed to Suares
da Silva (c. 1755–69), as is the archiepiscopal palace, built for Archbishop José de
Bragança and turned into the Public Library in 1842.

Most of the other monuments are near the city centre. From the arcaded square
with its splashing fountains the broad Central Avenue runs eastward to cross the small
river Este and climb a winding road to Bom Jesus do Monte, a sanctuary on a spur
1,200 feet high. It is more directly approached by the stairway, which ascends by
stages each adorned with statues on religious themes. The pattern of white panels
edged by grey granite makes it visible from afar. It was begun in 1784 and completed
in 1811. The funicular was added in 1882. The hill or mountain is wooded, and the
shrine surrounded by gardens, with a large hotel and restaurant, particularly attractive in the evening as the sun sets over the city below. The shrine is a favourite place
for weddings. After the ceremony the custom is for the whole party to line up under
the trees to be photographed individually with the bride and groom. From the next
spur, the Sameiro, a similar, if more celibate, view is enjoyed by the diocesan seminary, which is handsomely gardened. It is also a much-frequented sanctuary of local
fame. Beyond the hill, at Falperra, is one of the best baroque church façades, attributed to Suares da Silva in c. 1751. It was at a high point, some 1,500 feet, on a road
infested with highwaymen and so gave rise to the hermitage and later church of
St Mary Magdalene.

A few miles to the east a by-road leads to Briteiros, the most extensive of the pre-
Roman *citânias*. It contains a triple circuit of walls with circular and rectangular
dwellings partly arranged in streets and continued to be inhabited in Roman times.
The archaeologist Martins Sarmento placed many of his findings, including the Pedra
Formosa with its intricate knotted design, in the museum in Guimarães. Its situation
on the Monte São Romão overlooking the valley of the Ave is beautiful and evocative.
Within sight is the smaller citania of Sabroso, a scattering of huts within a single
defensive wall. A third such site is at Sanfins near Paços de Ferreira.

A few miles from Bom Jesus, on the road from Braga to Chaves, is the small but
typical castle of Lanhoso, on a bald hill-top above the river Câvado. It was occupied in
Suevic times and was Queen Tarásia's refuge when invaded by the bishop of Santiago
and her half-sister Queen Urraca. The road up passes stones that may have been from
ward-houses. The miniature castle on two floors is of that period, and a short film is
shown inside telling its story: I like to think of it as the heart of Portugal.

The city regarded as the cradle of the nation and birthplace of the first king of
Portugal is Guimarães, only fifteen miles to the south-east. The name Guimara/Vimara
comes from the restorer of the territory of Portugal, but what he claimed is not recorded.

11 The Sanctuary of Bom Jesús near Braga (José Manuel)

Asturian counts were few and dominated vast areas. A sort of frontier existed on the Douro in 835. In the following century, Dona Mumadona, who had perhaps nursed Ramiro II, ruled the monastery of Guimarães, was favoured by the king, and founded the castle for her son to defend. Guimarães became the wealthiest monastery in the territory, and the castle the main seat of its counts. The castle, now unoccupied, has been given prominence and, with the later castle of the dukes of Braganza, has a symbolic importance. Alfonso VI bestowed it on his daughter Tarásia on her marriage to Count Henry: their son was baptised in the small church of São Miguel by the castle. The palace of the dukes has been restored in Flemish style. These monuments stand in a gardened park at the north end of the long narrow strip that was the medieval walled town. Dona Mumadona's convent was replaced by the Colegiada and church of Oliveira which now house the museum, one of the richest in the Portuguese provinces. The Colegiada boasts of having had the only Portuguese pope, Pedro Hispano or John XXI (1276), as prior. The stone baldachin outside commemorates the victory at the Salado against the last attempt at an African invasion in 1340. The archaeological museum named after Martins Sarmento houses the spoils of the great *citânias*.

The streets of the old quarter were formerly dedicated to the various guilds which flourished in the fourteenth and fifteenth centuries; some arcades remain, with specimens of enclosed balconies projecting above the street. The guilds brought the House of Avis to power in 1383, and the marriage of Queen Philippa's daughter Isabel to Duke Philip 'the Good' sealed Portuguese relations with Flanders, displayed in the much restored ducal palace.

Guimarães shares the new University of the Minho with Braga. The people of the Minho are industrious, but not industrialised: there is no belt of heavy manufacture. The textile mills of the nineteenth century were spaced out in the small towns, not always to the profit of the numerous water-courses. Portuguese workers prefer to join small-scale undertakings in which they do not surrender their identity. The ancient linen-industry survived until the twentieth century, the moist climate of the Minho being favourable to flax, but this excellent textile is now expensive and hard to come by.

The concelho of Paços de Ferreira is close to the *citânia* of Sanfins, not the best known but one of the most evocative of the iron-age townships, which must have depended on grazing its sheep on the surrounding slopes. The name Ferreira implies an early iron-foundry. In the twelfth century it had the large monastery of São Pedro, of which only the church remains. It is a single high nave with a rare polygonal aisle. The township has now become the 'furniture capital' of Portugal, where innumerable 'repros' are produced. Its street has lines of showrooms and its centre has acquired a modern monument which the Iron Age might have admired.

Such places fall within the catchment area of the capitalists of Oporto. The traditional eastern limit of the Minho was the Serra do Marão, a dramatic height which parts the sea-board from the interior. The river which gives the province its name is far away to the north. The main road from Oporto to the north follows the coast to Vila do Conde at the mouth of the Ave. It was already 'villa de Comite' in 953. In 1206 King Sancho gave it to Maria Pais, the 'Ribeirinha', in return for his 'conversations' with her. Its one enormous monument is the convent of Santa Clara. The façade is due to the corregedor of Oporto, Almada, who built the bridge over the Ave. Behind it is the church of Santa Clara, founded by a son of King Diniz; his tomb is in the Founder's chapel. After a long period of abandonment, it was restored in 1928. The convent itself is now a correctional school. Like other estuaries, that of the Ave was once used for shipbuilding, which was ended by the silting of the river-bed. On the south side of the river is Azurara, a fishery brought into existence to evade the dues collected for Santa Clara: its battlemented church was built in the fifteenth century, and given a Manueline doorway.

Its fishery was transferred two miles to the north to Povoa de Varzim, where Almada built a mole, permitting ocean-going boats to find shelter. The fishermen have their own types of boats adapted to the depth of water and types of fish they seek. Povoa is the birthplace of Eça de Queirós, whose father was a magistrate there. The road follows the coast to the mouth of the Cávado, crossed by a bridge between Fão and Esposende. The estuary is almost closed by a long spit, occupied by the small seaside resort of Ofir. Fão is from *fanum*, a Roman shrine, and Ophir may evoke far-away quinqueremes. The 'cavalos' (horses) of Fão are rocks that rise from the sea. The sands fringed with green pines are very tranquil for a vacation. The Cávado takes a long rest in its Lago before being directed by a light-house into the sea. Esposende once had salt-pans belonging to the monastery of Guimarães. In former times the river was crossed at the small city of Barcelos, half-way to Braga. Its nobility is ancient: it was the first county in Portugal, created by King Sancho I. The title was long held by the eldest son of King Diniz, Count Pedro, the genealogist. It passed to the dukes of Braganza, who built their palace and the Gothic bridge in the fourteenth century. The ducal palace is in ruins, but the ground floor serves as an archaeological museum. The massive granite mansion of the Pinheiros dates from 1448. Before it is a lawn with a fine pillory, and the ancient church, the *matriz*, begun in the thirteenth century with an entrance and rose-window with Gothic developments and Renaissance additions. The riverside is walled and crowned with a colonnade. It leads to a gardened space, the Passeio dos Assentes. The array of architecture was enriched in c. 1708 by the church of the Senhor da Cruz, a Greek cross set around a cylinder with a low cupola adorned with tiles. It uses the favourite Portuguese contrast of white walls edged with dark granite. In addition to its noble houses and churches, Barcelos has fine gardens and open spaces, the largest being the Campo da Feira, with a weekly market. Barcelos is the centre of the earthenware industry and large numbers of pots and dishes of all kinds are displayed. The usual style is a brown slip adorned with creamish lines or foliage. Their intrinsic worth is in recalling the charming little city where they are made.

The countryside to the east and north of Barcelos is rich in deciduous trees, fields of maize, fruit and vines, and is dotted with country houses, in marked contrast to the Alentejo where isolated dwellings are rare, or even to the centre, such as Alcobaça, where a great monastery supervised the cultivation of an extensive area. There are various examples of small Romanesque monastery churches, though many have been altered or replaced. Just outside Barcelos is the house of the Azevedos, a stout square tower of the twelfth century. Four miles on the road to the north side of the river is Manhente, with a small Romanesque church, defended by a robust square tower: an inscription on the doorway records the date 1025. Vilar de Frades, five miles from Barcelos on the other side of the river, is an ancient Benedictine monastery with a Romanesque doorway and a single vaulted nave added in the sixteenth century. Nearby, among the fields, is the now isolated church of Santa Eulália of Arnoso, with

stone carved portals regarded as a masterpiece of early Romanesque. I have failed to
find it. Some distance away, with local aid, I reached the once great monastery of
Pombeiro, tucked away in a valley near Felgueiras: it is supposed to date from 853,
and was refounded in the eleventh century. Queen Tarásia's supporter Gomes Nunes,
count of Tuy, was its protector and lies here.

The northernmost district is that of Viana, now called 'do Castelo' to distinguish it
from Viana in the Alentejo, but formerly Viana da Foz do Lima. Its river, which rises
in Spanish Galicia, runs the gauntlet at the frontier and flows placidly across to meet
the sea at a broad estuary. Viana was formerly a busy port and shipyard, but the river
is no longer navigable, though the men of Viana took advantage of its being the first
in Portuguese territory and closest to the north. Among its sons were Gonçalo Velho,
sent by Prince Henry to settle the Azores, and João Alvares Fagundes, who in 1521
attempted to settle Newfoundland. Its hinterland was the teeming Lima valley, the
Riba-Lima. Viana is the smallest in area of the *distritos*, less than a third of Braganza,
which it exceeds in population. It has only two small towns, Ponte de Lima and Ponte
da Barca. Viana was a fishing-village when it was chartered by King Afonso III in 1253.
According to a saying, the lords of Barca bade the men of Ponte to tell the fellows of
Viana to send up fish. This changed after the discovery of America: Pedro Tourinho
was captain of Porto Seguro in Brazil, and Correa, the famous Caramurú, head of an
Indian tribe.

The view of Viana and its estuary, one of the finest in Portugal, is from the mountain of Santa Luzia, which has an excellent hotel. Vehicles make a long detour, but
there is a funicular and the descent through pine-woods is steep but easy. The centre
of old Viana is the town-hall, dating from the time of King Manuel, a battlemented
block over an arcade of three ogival arches. In front of it is the *pelourinho*, a fountain
mounted on concentric steps. The Misericórdia, begun in 1520, is built around open
arcades on three levels and decorated with sculptures in a style of its own. The
Misericórdia church dates from the seventeenth century and has an elaborate baroque
interior. The main church, the Matriz, has two stout Gothic towers with a Manueline
frame to its portico surmounted by a rose-window. Another fifteenth-century building is the house of the navigator João Velho with two dissimilar arches. The patron of
the city is the Senhora da Agonia, whose church is to the west near the fort or Castle,
built in the sixteenth century. The festivity of the Agonia, between 18 and 20 August,
is a regional home-coming, celebrated with dancing and fireworks.

To the east of the Campo da Agonia stood the large Dominican monastery, of which
only the church of Santa Cruz remains. It has a composite façade of the Renaissance,
and was built or extended by Archbishop Bartolomeu dos Mártires, who died in 1590:
it has his tomb. The square in front has the large house built in 1720 for a wealthy
canon: it now houses the public library and the regional museum with collections of
ceramics, furniture and a display of traditional village dress. The most imposing of the
noble houses is the palace of the Counts of Carreira, which dates from the sixteenth
century but was modernised in 1704 in a simple and attractive composition.

From Viana the road and railway follow the coast northwards past the seaside
resorts of Afife, Âncora and Moledo to the mouth of the Minho at Caminha. Moledo
has a curving sandy beach and faces the only island off the coast, the Ínsua, once fortified but now uninhabited. On the Spanish side is the dark cone of Santa Tecla.
Caminha stands between the Minho and the small stream of Coura. In the fifteenth

century it had ten towers and four gates. It is now entered by a narrow passage under the determined-looking clock-tower, flanked by the peaceful Misericórdia with a Renaissance doorway of 1551 and the town-hall. No less picturesque is the fountain or *chafariz*, which matches the one at Viana. The Casa dos Pitas dates from 1490, and has varied windows surmounted by a line of merlons. The main church is of the same period and was finished in 1556. It has a single bell-tower and is otherwise in conformity with the Romanesque tradition, a portal under a rose-window giving access to a high central nave.

From Caminha the rail and road continue to Lanelhas, which has the Casa da Torre, the fortified mansion of the Bacelar family, and the village of Vila Nova de Cerveira, once a place of importance and strongly fortified: it defied Soult's attempt to land in 1809. Nine miles to the north-east is Valença do Minho, the principal fortress of the area, where bridges carry road and rail traffic over to the ancient Galician city of Tuy. Valença stands on a height overlooking the river and is an elaborate system of defences in the style perfected by Vauban. The fortress contains a picturesque government *pousada* named after São Teotónio. The rest is full of shops selling cloth, rugs, ceramics and all manner of curios. It is much frequented by Spanish ladies who flock to carry off by fair means what former generations could not plunder.

Valença has grown in size and has acquired a broad thoroughfare with banks and cafés. Along the roads are modern houses with garages, adorned with flowers and exuding a comfortable calm. Before the riverside forts, there were *torres*, squat granite cubes with only slits for windows. When the Norsemen attacked, the owner would pack his possessions and lock up, sending his family to the hills. One such is the Torre de São Julião, the manor of the medieval Silvas, now carefully transformed into a modern house among fields and vineyards overlooking the valley below.

At the village of Boivão, a road by the church, narrow and cobbled, climbs up the steep hillsides to the Princess's Castle, a bizarre natural rock-formation. On a fine day in April, one gazes over vast spaces in both countries, the hillsides patched with golden gorse in flower, with little sign of houses or even shepherds, but a welcome stand of clear piped water.

The frontier extends along the Minho, which carries a substantial body of water throughout the year, to Monção, Melgaço and São Gregório, the most northerly point of Portugal. Although the train has disappeared into Spain, there are ample buses which serve the numerous villages and isolated dwellings in a variegated landscape. The typical wine of the Minho is *vinho verde*, which, being slightly tart, breaks down the fat that accompanies cooking in oil. There are also many vestiges of an earlier Portugal. At Ganfei, two miles from Valença, are signs of what was a large Benedictine house in the eighteenth century. Some distance from Friestas is the church of São Fins, a good example of a Romanesque abbey church. Lapela is the keep of a once considerable fortress by the river-bank. Monção was a polygonal fortress of the Vauban type: it resisted a siege for four months in the War of Independence (1658–59). To the east and a little upstream is the thermal establishment in its park: it treats rheumatism and other ailments. Four miles outside Monção is the palace of Brejoeira, built by a Minhoto plutocrat between 1804 and 1828 on royal lines as if to emulate the Ajuda palace in Lisbon.

Above Monção the Minho narrows. The little river Mouro runs between the villages, and has a plaque commemorating the fact that on 1 November 1386, King John I met

John of Gaunt, 'time-honoured Lancaster', a meeting full of portent since it led to the King's marriage to Queen Philippa.

The last town in northern Portugal is Melgaço, now best known as a summer resort. It boasts a ring of walls of which only part survives. They include the keep and the castle gate. An inscription says that the walls were completed in 1263: it was taken after a long siege by King John I. It has a modest Romanesque church, but the best monuments are at Orada, only a mile away, of the time of Afonso Henriques, and at Paderne, three miles to the south, founded as a nunnery in the eleventh century and later passed to the Augustinians. Above the frontier post at São Gregório, the Minho becomes solely Spanish and pursues its course to Lugo. In Portugal, the road enters the Peneda-Gerez National Park.

A road south from Monção passes through Arcos de Valdevez to meet the Lima at Ponte da Barca, which can also be reached by roads that follow the river from Viana do Castelo. In 1900 plans were approved for a railway from Viana up the Ribeira Lima to the frontier. It does not exist; perhaps priority had to be given to hydro-electric schemes to dam the rivers Homem and Câvado which provide power and light and create artificial lakes. There are roads on both sides of the river and bridges at Ponte de Lima and Ponte da Barca. The landscape remains bucolic and unspoiled. On leaving Viana by the north bank, there is a viaduct in tribute to the railway that never was, and at Cardielos, the Romanesque church of São Claudio de Nogueira. There are noble houses, but no great estates. The land is cultivated in small plots which sufficed to keep a yoke of long-horned oxen slowly busy. Possibly the best-known country mansion in Portugal is Bertiandos, a fortified tower with extended additions in the seventeenth and eighteenth centuries. The entrance to the upper floor is by a flight of stairs, and both sides have open colonnades. In the lawn that separates the buildings from the main road stands a Roman milestone in distant memory of other passers by. The castle belonged to the Pereiras, the family of the Holy Constable.

Two miles beyond is the small town of Ponte de Lima on the south bank. The river is broad and shallow, and the bridge skims over in 24 arches, of which the first five are Roman and the rest medieval. The Lima was sung by Camões' contemporary Bernardes, and the town has been thought one of the most beautiful in Portugal, rather for its charm than for any single feature. It was first chartered by Queen Tarásia in 1125, perhaps to stay any further invasion from the north. Its *concelho* is said to have fifty *solares*, noble houses, a few within the old walls, but mostly built by the defenders on the north side: the south being more ecclesiastic. Only two of its ten towers remain. Two *alamedas* of plane-trees shade the riverside walks and the gleaming sand of the *areal* which the river has disowned. The main church, St Maria dos Anjos, is the familiar type with a single tower, a doorway with a pointed arch and a rose-window. The principal mansion is the palace of the Count of Aurora, an eighteenth-century house built for Dom José de Braganza, the princely archbishop of Braga.

The villages of the Lima and Viana itself are famous for the richness and intricacy of their needlework. *Minhotas* formerly displayed their wealth in gold chains, ear-rings and other adornments, worn for weddings and festive occasions. This finery was accompanied by embroidered skirts and bodices, using baize, preferably scarlet, and linen. The patterns were worked in cotton, white or coloured, enhanced with metal thread and sparkles, and combining floral sprays, hearts and intricate designs employing several different stitches. These, or versions of them, are adopted for small girls and for folk-loric activities.

Above Ponte de Lima, the mountains begin to close in and the road turns between hills. The large Romanesque church at Bravães was part of a Benedictine monastery of the eleventh century and later passed to the Augustinians and the Order of Christ. On the north side of the river is the larger Benedictine monastery of Refojos, a medieval refuge transformed by an elegant baroque reconstruction.

The first recorded lord of Bravães was Pedro Vasques, Queen Tarásia's majordomo, and probably governor of the castle of Pena da Rainha, now lost, near Luzio. His daughter married a Valadares, of a smaller domain at Castro Laboreiro near Melgaço. Much of the Minho was then divided into *terras*, held by dominant families. The upper Minho was the *terra de Nóbrega* whose castle, now a ruin, was three miles south-east of Ponte da Barca. King Manuel made the crossing at Barca the seat of the *concelho*. It had a ferry, the *barca*, but the king was persuaded to build the bridge of ten arches by the matriarch Dona Maria Lopes da Costa, who left one hundred and twenty descendants by her two marriages and lived to be a hundred and ten, if the sources are correct. The main church is of the period, though modified by the desire of the local families each to have its own chapel. The bridge was restored by the active Almada of Oporto, and the market and town hall are also Pombaline.

North of Ponte da Barca, on a bend in the short river Vez, is Arcos de Valdevez, the scene of an encounter between Afonso Henriques and his cousin Alfonso VII of Leon and Castile in 1140, when the frontier between the Minho and the Lima was still unre-solved. The town is a collection of narrow streets with a pleasant front on the river, which has a weir and a leafy island.

The mountains above it are the Serra Amarela, or Yellow Hills. They have never been auriferous. But the frontier mountains rise higher to form the Serra of Soajo and Penedo. The roads from Valdevez and Ponte da Barca converge and reach the frontier at Lindoso. The river Lima becomes the Spanish Limia. Both take their name from the pre-Roman Limici, who had a *forum* which Spain places at the source, the lake of Antelo, now reclaimed, but the Portuguese are inclined to find elsewhere. The first famous Limicus was Bishop Hydatius (d c 469), the chronicler of the Sueves, whose see was at Chaves, which is certainly in Portugal. From Ponte da Barca the river flows through a narrow trench and the border is at the castle of Lindoso, now in the Portuguese National Park of Peneda and Gerez, a nature reserve of great size with every facility for camping and tramping. It can be entered from Melgaço in the north, from Valdevez or Ponte da Barca, or from Gerez. It has benefited from the electrifica-tion schemes which have created artificial lakes, *albufeiras*, on the tributaries of the Lima, the Homem and the Câvado, which add aquatic activities to the enjoyment of the mountains with their deer, wild boar and ponies.

The mountain villages are sharply distinct from the white and red cottages of the valley. Their cabins are dark and their plots of cultivable soil confined. The corn is kept in rectangular roofed barns raised from the ground, *espigueiros*. The dress was of coarse brown wool, with gaiters and sandals. The village of Suajo was the centre. It was replaced by Valdevez in 1852.

The eleventh-century counts of Portugal intermarried with those of Celanova, in Spanish Ourense. A younger brother of the Galician count governed Ponte de Lima and married a daughter of Queen Tarásia. Another brother Gomes Nunes, count of

Tuy, was an adherent of Tarásia, but a vassal of Alfonso VII, a situation which cost him his title as the two countries parted company. Peneda, at the north end of the Park, is a sanctuary and place of pilgrimage. Until recently it was connected with Soajo only by a rough track. The Serra Amarela reaches 4,000 feet, is roadless and covered in snow in winter. The trails are now well marked and the whole area relatively accessible.

Lindoso, the centre of the Park, with a cluster of traditional barns on stone perches, is reached from Ponte da Barca, and has hydroelectric installations dating from early in the twentieth century. It had a ruined frontier castle ascribed to the reign of King Diniz, who is supposed to have given it its poetical name. The Park is more often entered from Gerez, where the Roman road from Braga to Astorga crosses the mountains at the Portela do Homem: the river Homem flows down to join the Câvado north of Braga. Before the frontier, the vale of Albergaria is a forested bowl watered by the Homem and surrounded by the rugged heights of the Serra de Gerez of which the most striking is Pe de Cabril (3,700 feet). Another high pass, the Portela de Leonte, takes the road down to Gerez, a resort with hot springs, the Caldas, beneficial for disorders of the liver. There are hotels of various categories; I was able to find one without the nuisance of television, but that was long ago. The liverish may take their choice and there are plenty of shops. The ring of mountains above has a wide variety of vegetation, and the fauna includes the eagle and wolf, but no longer apparently the wild goat. Among the rocky heights the Pedra Bela is a fantasy of erosion. The upper valley of the Câvado, which saw the hasty retreat of Marshal Soult in 1809, is now a series of reservoirs, from Pradela to Salamonde, the largest, and Caniçada.

In the twelfth century the centre of the foothills was the Terra de Bouro, the 'burg', or former barbarian settlement in the Roman empire, like Burgos. It ceased to exist in 1922. But if the Bouro is only a shadow of its former self, the twelfth-century monastery of Santa Maria do Bouro remains. It was sold for £130 in 1940, and Susan Lowndes noted its fallen splendour, a faded pink and white seventeenth-century façade with niches for the statues of five kings, a ruined granite staircase, and a range of store-rooms a hundred yards long, with a huge marble table, granite sinks and ovens, a very large cloister and a charming chapter-house, bereft of its *azulejos*, lead roofing and ironwork, sold for scrap.

Further down the Câvado is Amares, a small town with an ancient stone bridge across the river. Five miles to the north-west was the Casa da Tapada, where the poet Sá de Miranda (1490–1558) lived in exile, vituperating against the corruption of trade with the East and embracing the poetry of the Renaissance, paving the way for the young Camões, who perhaps portrayed him in the *Lusiads* as the Old Man of the Restelo. He is buried in the church of Carrazedo, a suitable place to bid farewell to the Minho, where he dwelt by his fountain surrounded by friends, neighbours and books.

15

Interior Portugal

The high road to the east from Oporto strikes out for a very different Portugal which the writer Miguel Torga (1907–95), who was born there, called a 'marvellous kingdom'. It is not a kingdom, and has no name but that bestowed on it from outside, Trás-os-Montes, 'beyond the mountains'. The range in question is the Serra do Marão, rising to 4,250 feet. The pass at the Espinho commands a vast panorama. Those who dwell beyond are their own masters: 'Para cá do Marão, mandam os que cá estão'. It is a large land-locked province whose capital Bragança is far away near the border with Spain. It is quite different from the teeming maritime Minho which wears its heart on its sleeve (at least the seamstresses of Viana do). The rivers of the Minho go directly to the sea, whilst those of Trás-os-Montes rise near the Spanish border in the north and first find their way to the Douro. The largest of these is the Tâmega, already a broad stream when it flows under the great Roman bridge at Chaves, which is certainly in Trás-os-Montes, but passes through Basto and Amarante in the Minho, and pours into the Douro some twenty-five miles east of Oporto. The historical border of the province seems not to have been fixed. It comprises the two districts of Bragança and Vila Real. More recently the city of Oporto has been made the centre of the Douro Litoral, which includes both sides of the river, and Vila Real has become the capital of the Alto Douro, and includes Lamego south of the river.

On leaving Oporto, the road, whether it knows it or not, traverses the Douro Litoral. The first river to cross is the Sousa, a small stream flowing through a wide valley. Its name has been carried all over the world. In the eleventh and twelfth centuries the only family that could match the Maias were the Sousas who acquired many estates. The Paço de Sousa stands a little off the main road near Paredes, and was an ancient hermitage when the Sousas made it their Benedictine monastery under Egas Moniz, the tutor of Afonso Henriques: he is buried in the church, which exceeds the usual Romanesque building of the time. Egas' successor as *mordomo-mór* was Gonçalo Mendes, 'o Sousão' (1157–67). Their castle was at Aguiar de Sousa, and the present town of Penafiel was previously Arrifana de Sousa. Penafiel is three miles south of Bustelo, an ancient monastery much enlarged in the eighteenth century. Five miles away, Meinedo was occupied by the bishop of Oporto in the sixth century, but is now a modest church of the thirteenth. The vicinity has a dolmen at Santa Marta, ruined Roman baths at São Vicente, still a spa, the well preserved church at Boelhe, and the monastic church of Travanca, founded in the eleventh century and endowed by Queen Tarásia, with a massive external defence tower: this is already in the *concelho* of Amarante.

Amarante is an attractive town on a cliff overhanging a double curve in the river Tâmega. Its main street sweeps down to the bridge, which was originally Roman, though much different from the long series of arches that crosses the river far away at Chaves. It lasted until 1220, when it was replaced by St Gonçalo. The present crossing, erected between 1781 and 1790, in three high spans, takes advantage of a narrow gullet in the river, which, as in 2001, can rapidly rise and flood the waterside houses. St Gonçalo is supposed to have been a great traveller and is the protector of seafarers. His tomb is in the Dominican convent of São Gonçalo, founded in 1540. It has a colourful cupola which stands out above the houses, and a portico as complex as a baroque high altar, with niches for St Dominic and others, forming a distinctive composition. The interior has numerous baroque details, extending to the tomb of the saint, who rests his head on tasselled red stone pillows. This is not inappropriate since his bridge-building extends to matrimony and he is thought to take an interest in the affairs of lovers. His feast at the first weekend in June is celebrated with dancing. Symbolic cakes are exchanged for the occasion, though the pastry-shops of Amarante attract clients from afar at any time of the year.

From Amarante it is a short drive to the Marão and its summit at the *pousada* of São Gonçalo, the direct way to Trás-os-Montes (in winter occasionally blocked by snow). A less dramatic road leads to Peso da Régua and the wine-country of the Upper Douro. The railway, having wandered inland round Penafiel and Amarante, rejoins the river and follows it to Régua, sixty miles from Oporto, though the crow may fly it in less. Régua is the seat of the Casa do Douro, which regulates the production of the wine. The great vineyards begin at Barqueiros and stretch almost to the Cachão de Valério where Joseph Forrester, the wine merchant, was drowned. The river glides down through banks that are steep, if not quite so precipitous. The area demarcated by Pombal's Company is a fringe mainly on the north side, which widens to admit the lower valley of the Corgo. The schisty hills are bare-headed but their slopes are covered with man-made terraces (*socalcos*). The summer heat brings on the grapes, which are harvested in September by crews of pickers, *rogas*, who bring their families like hop-pickers in Kent, to share the work and the rejoicing and festivities. Formerly wide-horned oxen brought the barrels on lumbering carts to be loaded on the *rabelos*, sailing-craft with a single sheet that carried three lines of barrels, two below and one on top. In the eighteenth century, the growers held their wine-fair in February at Régua, and the shippers came from Oporto to buy. The shippers gradually acquired estates and settled amidst the gardens. In the nineteenth century, the matriarch of the owners was Dona Antónia Ferreira who survived the accident in which Forrester was drowned.

The main road has a spectacular drop to the highlands of Vila Real. The 'Royal town' was named by Sancho I and was given a charter by King Diniz in 1289. Before that the chief place was Constantim, on which Henry and Tarásia bestowed a charter in 1096. But in Roman times the principal settlement was Chaves, which distorts the very Latin name of Aquae Flaviae. It lay on the route from Braga to Astorga, and its great Roman bridge bears the names of the ten tribes that contributed to build it under the direction of the Seventh Legion. Trás-os-Montes was crossed by a main

12 The vineyards of the Douro (João Paulo)

road, and the workings of the gold mines at Jales may still be seen. There are many vestiges of Rome, though no important building or temple. The well-known group of sacrificial tanks at Panóias relates to some antique cult though their patron bore a Latin name. The ten romanised tribes who appear at Chaves do not include the Brigantes, a people that has given its name to the present capital of Bragança. Much of the province was thus known to the Romans and well controlled, but still tribal and with no single native capital. The Brigantes also gave their name to a celticised people who occupied Roman Britain between York and the Wall. The British Brigantes also had no known centre but a series of small towns or villages, where they existed in independence and founded iron, though policed by numerous military posts on the roads. The people of Trás-os-Montes are considered dour and independent, though this is not incompatible with warmth of heart. The most famous son of Trás-os-Montes is Fernão de Magalhães or Magellan, who in 1519 set out to be the first to circumnavigate the world. He was killed in the Philippines but his name survives in the 'Magellanic clouds' which he observed and which turned out to be a prelude to human knowledge of other galaxies. At the court of Henry and Tarásia, the big man from Bragança was the 'Bragançáo', who contributed to the defence of Coimbra. He liked to consider himself the descendant of Dom Alão, perhaps a legendary Alan. The loyalty of the house was secured by a marriage to one of Tarásia's daughters.

Vila Real is now familiar because its wine is sold in flasks with the picture of the palace of Mateus, the work of Nasoni, two miles to the east. The city stands on a high plateau. It began at the point where the Corgo and Cabril meet, where there are parts of the old wall: from the Paços do Concelho and Misericórdia a broad tree-lined avenue marks the modern centre. It has an old military tradition; King John I made Dom Pedro Meneses the first governor of Ceuta. His heirs continued to hold the African outpost, being promoted to the new rank of Marquês in 1451. They sided with Spain at the Restoration of 1640 and were duly disgraced: the palace of the Marqueses of Vila Real was an empty shell in 1900. Vila Real also claims Diogo Cão, the discoverer of the Congo in 1482: one of a group of fifteenth-century houses is shown as his birthplace. In 1762 the town successfully opposed O'Reilly and his Spanish force, and during the Peninsular War was held by General Silveira, later Count of Amarante, who began the handsome Paços do Concelho, originally intended as a hospital and his residence in 1817. The second Count was the first to proclaim the traditionalist Dom Miguel as king in 1823. In 1919 Vila Real was briefly occupied by the royalists of Paiva Couceiro. Its most recent hero was Carvalho Araujo, killed while commanding a minesweeper against German attack in 1918.

The main church of Vila Real was a Dominican monastery authorised by John I (being on royal land) in 1421. It was dissolved in 1834 and destroyed by fire. The church itself is of the traditional Romanesque-Gothic type, and was given a gilded high altar in the eighteenth century. The Capela Nova, the New Chapel, is a small baroque building on a corner site, and is also called the Clérigos, recalling the great church of Oporto by Nasoni. The clerics of Vila Real were given a classical façade with an ornamental portico and a soaring curved upper storey with three statues, St Peter being in the middle on the crest of a baroque wave.

The finest secular mansion in the neighbourhood of Vila Real is the palace and gardens of the Casa de Mateus, to the east of the city. The mansion was built for Botelho Mourão and finished by his successor Sousa Botelho, ambassador to France, where he produced his lavish edition of the *Lusiads,* illustrated by Fragonard, Gérard and others: he died in Paris in 1825, having got through his fortune. The house stands behind a rectangular pool, a recent addition, and has a balustraded stairway leading to the main entrance, the central body being recessed between two projecting wings. Nasoni adorned the extensive gardens with balustrades and statuary. The chapel is dated 1750. The taps, surprisingly, do not run with rosé wine; it is produced by the Sogrape company which makes profitable use of a coloured photograph of the famous house.

It is a far cry from Mateus to the rock-sanctuary of Panóias, some five miles down the road to the village of Constantim. The 'sanctuary' is a series of altars with a Latin inscription that shows that they were used for blood-sacrifices to some unmentionable deities when one Calpurnius Rufinus dedicated a temple there. The next village, São Martinho de Antas, was the birthplace of Miguel Torga in 1907. The *Antas* are mega-liths or dolmens of awesome if no longer venerable antiquity. Small prehistoric sites are numbered in dozens, but away from the coast the great *citânias* fade away, though there are still *castros.* Of the two roads north from Vila Real, one follows the Corgo by Vila Pouca de Aguiar to Chaves while the other crosses the mountains to Murça and ultimately Bragança. The Roman road to Murça passes across a high plain where stony villages shelter poor shepherds and their flocks. It descends to Murça, which owes its fame to its prehistoric pig, a granite boar mounted on a plinth, which appears on the labels of its wine.

Between the roads is a Roman mining-centre. Três Minas, now abandoned, has extensive workings, and is a small village with an isolated Romanesque church. Jales, on a high plain seven miles from Vila Pouca, is worked at a depth beyond the reach of the Romans. The broad shoulders of the Marão are protracted northwards by the Serra do Alvão, which divides the valley of the Tâmega from the Corgo. The poet Teixeira de Pascoais, whose mystical and metaphysical reveries were dreamed from his window overlooking the Tâmega at Gatão, faced the heights where the idyllic Minho turned into the granite asceticism of the Serra and the elegiac drama of Trás-os-Montes. Celorico de Basto and Aguiar de Pena, above Vila Pouca, were held by the heirs of a Gueda the Old who perhaps descended from the region of Chaves. Both castles are ruined. Mondim de Basto is a centre for the afforestation of the Serra. Vila Pouca occu-pies a *veiga* or plain of some size. A short way to its north is the spa of Pedras Salgadas with hotels, a park and a group of springs which produce the best known sparkling bottled water in Portugal. It stands at nearly two thousand feet, is cool in summer, and, according to the learned Professor Charles Lepierre, a boon to the liverish. There follows Vidago, an even larger spa with a Grand Hotel dating from 1878 and a Palace Hotel opened in 1910. The *fin de siècle* atmosphere is enhanced by the leafy setting, in which the less afflicted can play a round of golf. Ten miles further north is Chaves, almost on the frontier with Spain.

Chaves stands on a high plain, its *veiga,* crossed by the Tâmega, already broad and fast-flowing, which in turn is crossed by the famous Roman bridge of eighteen arches (six of them now submerged). It has two inscriptions, one showing that it was finished under Trajan in c. 104 AD, and the other naming the peoples who contributed to its construction. It was then called Aquae Flaviae, the name adopted for its chief and most spacious hotel, which also has a small thermal establishment, a facility prized by footsore legionaries on their long march from Astorga to Braga. Chaves has nothing to do with the modern Portuguese word for keys, but is a version of *flavias,* light brown or Flavian. The neat little railway-station has been closed, and we are again dependent on the roads, even if we do not have to march them. When the Sueves settled round Braga and Oporto, Bishop Hydatius wrote his brief annals in Chaves, where he negotiated between the new settlers and the older inhabitants. But Chaves was a fortress rather than a diocese. It has a castle, of which the lofty keep in the style of King Diniz and part of the bulwark remain. In the eighteenth century, a new fort on artillery-proof lines was built to the north, and its hospital of St John became a school of military surgery. The fortress known as São Francisco was built around the time of the Restoration and the struggle for independence (1644–67). The 'defenders of Chaves' are the militia who defied the judgement of their superiors and insisted on defending it against the French in 1808.

Chaves is now a pleasing and peaceful small city. The square by the castle has the Paços do Concelho, built in the nineteenth century as the residence of the Perdizes family. The church of the Misericórdia has a baroque façade with recessed apertures separated by Salomonic columns in late seventeenth-century style. The main church or *matriz* is a Romanesque temple with a vaulted chapel and a sixteenth-century north door. The former house of the dukes of Braganza was turned into barracks and houses a military museum.

The suburb across the river beyond the Roman bridge is called Madalena from its eighteenth-century octagonal church. On the opposite side of the thoroughfare, once much trodden by pilgrims on their way to Santiago, is a large public garden donated to the city by the banker Sotomayor. Chaves' main claim to literary fame, after Bishop Hydatius, is that of having produced the first book known to have been printed in Portugal, in 1489: it is the 'treatise of confession', perhaps printed by an itinerant *converso*: only a single copy is known.

The country round Chaves is an extensive high plain watered by the Tâmega, which is tamed by weirs and about a thousand feet above sea-level. It is divided into small-holdings and market-gardens and is idyllic during most of the year. The traditional pairs of oxen have been replaced by tractors, and the traditional crop of rye by wheat. But rye-bread celebrates festivities and takes its name – broa – from the Roman borona.

The road north of Chaves passes through a thinly populated area to reach the Galician town of Verín and its fortress of Monterrey. The pre-Roman peoples on the two sides of the frontier were akin, and the frontier, now open, suggests that the two countries were separated by a tract of deer-forest used by both. West of Chaves the road climbs up to the Serra de Barroso and the new 'lake-district' of the upper Minho. The Barroso is the most Portuguese of cattle, and the village of Boticas is in another veiga where sheep graze in green fields with stone dykes that recall places in Wales: its light wine is bottled and stored underground as 'dead men's wine' (*vinho dos mortos*) awaiting the recall to life. Its water is also bottled at Carvalhelhos.

Bragança is due east of Chaves by bus, which follows a winding road through low hills and green valleys for some sixty miles. Susan Lowndes thought it one of the great drives of the world, and was entranced by the high pastures, the groves of chestnuts, and the slopes covered with oaks and hornbeam, with occasional severe villages built of granite blocks. There are now fewer oxen with their fox-skin caps to keep off the flies and fewer men on horseback, but more buses and cars taking villagers to Vinhais or Bragança for the shops and diversions. Vinhais was once a *castro* and then a medieval castle, of which only the gate, a tunnel, is left. It was demolished to make way for the large eighteenth-century convent of São Francisco. Most of the township is spread along the main road. Its houses include the mansion of the Counts of Vinhais and a Misericórdia. Some two miles on is Castro de Avelãs, a unique church in that its round apse is constructed of brick, unlike the Portuguese Romanesque. It served a Benedictine monastery probably protected by the great man of Bragança, the Bragançáo.

Bragança was dominated by its castle, which stands aloft above the street that led up to its walls. Its neighbour across the frontier is Puebla de Sanabria, also a castle on the summit of a hill surrounded by its dependants. Perhaps the Bragançáo preferred the rulers of Guimarães to his immediate neighbours. Bragança, remote and snow-bound in winter, was formerly another world from Lisbon with frontiers not far away to the north and east. It has solved the problem of expansion by building an entirely new suburb without greatly altering its own appearance. Bragança is a series of rib-bons; one leads from the railway station to the Post Office, the next continues to the main church, where it divides into two ribbons that join at the church of St Vincent, and so up the castle hill to the old walled town. The castle is well preserved, as they say of the old, meaning that they are not quite as they were. At the barbican gate is a statue of the second duke, Dom Fernando, rather larger than life, as befits the succes-sor to the Bragançóes. The space around the keep is lined with trees. The most remarkable structure is the Domus Municipalis, of the twelfth or thirteenth century. The lower floor, of stone blocks, is enclosed and probably served as a cistern. The upper floor is pentagonal and lit by open arches on all sides, probably serving as the meeting-place for the deliberations of the council: it is unique.

Although Bragança is the seat of a bishop, its *matriz* is the sixteenth-century Jesuit church, taken over after their expulsion by Pombal in 1759. Opposite is the eighteenth-century house of the Calainhos, once owned by a cavalry-general and a passable model for the town house of a prominent provincial family. The Paços do Concelho is in the former residence of General Sepúlveda, a distinguished figure in the war against Napoleon. The Misericórdia is an early one, dating from 1518. The former episcopal palace is now the provincial museum, named after the Abade de Baçal, who was its director from 1925 to 1935, and devoted himself to the history of Trás-os-Montes, to which he contributed eleven volumes of *Memórias*. In his old age he continued to walk from the village of Baçal, which he served for half a century, to the city.

North of Bragança an area of some 2,000 acres adjoining the frontier has been des-ignated as the Montesinho Nature Reserve in order to preserve its wildlife and trad-itional customs. The Serra reaches almost 5,000 feet and affords grazing and potato-fields. The population is sparse, and there are few roads. The wildlife includes the wolf, deer, boar and smaller carnivores, and much of the area is heath, cistus and broom, with its own flowers. There are facilities for accommodation and camping. The whole region preserves vestiges of age-old collective traditions, with communal flocks and herds, forge, mill and press. The village most studied is Rio de Onor, which was described by the late Jorge Dias in 1953. It is in fact two villages, one in Portugal and one in Spain, with the same name and divided by the Açor stream. The inhab-itants speak both languages, as well as the dialect. They have their own festivities and songs, to the sound of bagpipes and drum. They were highly organised, with their own 'majordomos', two mayors elected annually on a basis of strict equality of house-holds. There were women majordomos for the church, and one to ring the bell for council-meetings. Infringements were fined, and the majordomos kept a tally of debts incurred, which were paid in wine and drunk by the council: meetings were frequent. There were villagers who had emigrated to Cuba or the United States to work, but they returned to resume their place in this little self-contained world, which turned to Bragança only for the cure for such intrusions as the potato-beetle.

The north-west frontier now follows the little river Maçãs, which the road from Bragança to Zamora crosses. The border is then an almost roadless wilderness until it reaches the Douro and the city of Miranda (do Douro). The river continues to be the frontier for some sixty miles until it turns westwards and becomes entirely Portuguese. At Miranda the Douro is already a substantial river flowing through a gorge between precipitous flanks of brownish rock. The city, with a cathedral built when it first had a bishop in 1545, a date when the court of John III and Queen Catarina was itself bilingual, is well-known for its dialect *mirandês*, a hybrid of Portuguese and old Leonese, the language of a medieval empire which remained unstandardised until Castilian was imposed on it. A century later, after the Restoration, relations were less cordial, and according to legend the Portuguese were led in the war of 1711 by a mysterious Boy, who vanished after giving them victory. He was the child Jesus, who with a toy sword and paper hat was venerated in the church. The bishop was removed to Bragança in 1782, and after the Peninsular War Miranda was scarcely more than a large village. It was revived by the damming of the Douro and by the requirements of tourism.

Its Museum brings together the folk traditions and crafts of the area. The men of Duas Igrejas, a village close by, preserve the dance of the *pauliteiros*, a kind of sword-dance with short sticks to the sound of the pipes and drum. It is done in white skirts with fancy stockings and hats adorned with flowers for St Barbara whose feast is in the middle of August. It belongs to the world of Folk Dance Festivals and has been per-formed at the Albert Hall.

The core of Torga's 'marvellous kingdom' is a plateau not quite so elevated as the Spanish *meseta*, nor yet so mountainous as Beira to its south. It is crossed by several small rivers which flow southwards into the Douro, and its serras, Bornes, Nogueira, Mogadouro, are the bare summits that separate them. The population is not scattered as in the Minho, but clustered in villages, often under the shelter of a castle, now ruined. Apart from the highway to Chaves and Bragança there were few roads until modern times, and travel was by horse, donkey or litter, and transport by ox-cart until the light railway up the Tua valley was built in 1880. When Camilo went from Vila Real to Oporto, he joined a friend in his litter and passed the time telling stories. Camilo regarded the arrival of steam with some apprehension. He need not have wor-ried: there is only the international line up the Douro, which now ends at the frontier, the light shuttle up the Tua to Bragança and the once pretty stations on the Chaves line, today closed. There are however good roads which wind and dive between the slopes or follow the valleys unless some gorge or ravine obliges them to find their own way. The change was wrought by the Highways Board, reformed in 1933. In 1910 Aubrey Bell described Murça as a street of white-washed granite houses adorned with a profusion of flowers: even its Pig had been painted in red and green. The village of Franco was paved part in rock, part in straw: its inn was hard to find and had no window-frames or panes, but weather-beaten wooden shutters and doors. The hostess had to be summoned from the fields to 'arrange' scrambled eggs, an immense rye loaf and a basket of green figs, which he thought well worth the two hours' wait. The villages were surrounded by olives, stands of sweet chestnuts and wide tracts of rye, and there were immense flocks of black sheep on the hillsides. The rye was cut in July, in hot weather by moonlight, and, long after the last ox-cart had sung its way home, the still air carried the three notes of the Angelus from some distant tower.

Susan Lowndes, writing in 1949, when Bell was still alive but in British Columbia, noted that after Murça the really splendid country began, with two or three solidly built villages strung out over twenty miles. She exclaimed: 'What vast sweeps of country. And what colours!' Mirandela was so attractive with the wide river valley and splendid medieval bridge of seventeen arches, the open streets and lovely houses and churches, that it would be a pleasant place from which to explore those unvisited little towns which lay off the main road. The road was first-class all the way to Bragança, which she found a smiling, gay town in richly cultivated country, very unlike the usual foreign conception of the place as surrounded by gloomy mountains and desolate scenery. She thought the road between Vinhais and Chaves one of the great drives of the world. The British Naval Intelligencer, writing seven years before, thought it 'narrow, winding and dangerous'. Perhaps he was thinking of a battleship: the regular bus services inspire no such thought.

Mirandela, standing in a valley of the Tua, is a centre producing corn, oil, wine and fruit, especially peaches. The palace of the Távoras, the family savagely persecuted by Pombal in 1759, now serves as the Paços do Concelho. All that remains of its fortifications is the Porta de Santo António. Most of the smaller townships fall within twenty miles. The circle might begin due north at Torre de Dona Chama, 'Lady Flame'. A Dona Chamoa is recorded in 1050; so was Chamoa Gomes, who bore a son to King Afonso Henriques. The town was chartered by King Diniz and has its own Pig, like Murça. Further round to the north-east, on the main road to Bragança, is Macedo de Cavaleiros, under the shelter of the Serra de Bornes, a round-topped ridge, which, like its northern prolongation, the Nogueira, reaches 4,000 feet. Still further round, south-east of Mirandela, is Alfandega da Fé, the 'inn of the faith'. It stands on the fertile vale of Vilariça, with an artificial lake, and a reputation for its olives and almonds: its groves formerly produced silk, but there is now no trace of the industry. Its name may refer to some ancient trade-route: Zamora was the last place on the Douro to be held by the Muslims, who may have bought their supplies here.

South of Mirandela is Vila Flor, a name said to have been bestowed on it by the poetical King Diniz, who chartered it in 1268, separating it from Moncorvo. Its cultural centre or museum was once the house of the Aguilar family and is ancient, and the house of the Lemos is a neat *solar* of the eighteenth century. The Fonte Romana is a spring covered by a brick cupola resting on four pillars and columns. Moncorvo is the first point in Portugal at which the Douro was bridged, and King Diniz's intention was probably to link together the frontier fortresses. The castle has disappeared, but the main church leaves the impression that it was intended for a larger place. Its exterior is dwarfed by an unattractive central tower. Hopes that an industry would emerge from the presence of iron-ore deposits under the Serra de Reboredo have been dashed. Outside Susan's twenty-mile limit, the prize for original place-names goes to Freixo da Espada à Cinta or 'Ash Sword-in-Belt', overlooking the Douro and Spain beyond. Freixo is a not uncommon place-name for the days when the ash was in demand for lances. The place is dominated by a lofty seven-sided tower. Nothing remains of the rest of the fortifications, but the church is of the Manueline style, unusual in the north.

Returning to the twenty-mile circuit, a little to the west of Vila Flor is Carrazedo de Anciães, in reality two places. Anciães, the older, has the ruins of a large castle. It once chose its own governor, but having forfeited the right, fell into decline, and in 1732 the judge moved the seat of the *concelho* three miles away to Carrazedo, destroying its precious *pelourinho*. It has its place in pre-history, for the first painted rock-shelter was noted at Ribalonga: it was described in 1734 but lost and rediscovered in 1930. A similar site exists near Alijó on the main Vila Real-Bragança road. To the north-west is Valpaços, which was on the Roman road from Chaves and stands on the edge of the Terra Fria, the cold uplands, and the Terra Quente, the 'warm-lands', where the valleys prevail. The Romans mined intensively and crossed the Rabagão at Possaços on the road from Valpaços to Dona Chama. There are plenty of traces of their passage, but none of a centre in rural Trás-os-Montes. The archaeology of the region is much less well known than that of the south and the coast, and may yet have surprises in store. Perhaps it was depopulated by Roman forced labour for the mines. The milestone from Valpaços notes the emperor Macrinus, who gives the date 217 AD, after which the production of gold declined. The chronicler Hydatius, bishop of Chaves in the fifth century, does not mention the region to his south. The missionaries of St Martin were active in Braga and the valley of the Douro, and followed the rivers and the Roman road to Chaves and Bragança. The Muslim conquest of 711 exposed the area to attack from Zamora, upstream on the Douro, which they held after the frontier had moved south. Nothing is heard of Trás-os-Montes until the Bragançóes put it together again.

Beira Baixa is the part of the Beiras between the Serra da Estrela and the river Tagus. It includes the wool-towns of Covilhã and Fundão on the southern flank of the mountain range and the Cova da Beira, a long and fruitful weald through which the river Zêzere winds to enter the Tagus near Constância. It also includes the city of Guarda, perched on a spur of the Estrela and overlooking from a considerable height the main railway and road-link with Europe. The sub-province corresponds approximately to the district of Castelo Branco. Its area is roughly equal to Portalegre or Santarém, that is, smaller than Évora or Beja, but more populated than either, though the border with Spain is only sparsely occupied. Castelo Branco itself stands on a plateau. Susan Lowndes says the city has one supremely interesting thing, the great formal garden, the extraordinary Jardim Episcopal created by Bishop Mendonça in the eighteenth century. Sitwell notes that there is nothing to see except a garden, but it is one of the most elaborate and formal of old gardens in Portugal. Even the *Guia de Portugal* thought that the city could be seen in a day, adding that Landmann, whose views of Portugal are the most agreeable memento of the Peninsular War, thought it one of the handsomest towns in the province.

Castelo Branco was not a Roman city, even though the adjective 'albicastrenses' has been invented for its inhabitants. In later Roman times the capital was at Egitania, now Idanha, which had a squadron of cavalry probably intended to police the mining-area to the north. It had become a Roman municipality in the time of Augustus, and had a temple of Venus, baths, a bridge and other sites. It would have lain on one or more roads leading north to Monsanto and Belmonte in the mining area. The principal

remains are the walls, arch and basilica. It was a diocese in the church of St Martin of
Dume in the later sixth century and produced the only Gothic coins (apart from
Mérida) for Roderic, the 'last of the Goths', at the time of the Muslim invasion of 711.
Roderic had probably been *dux* of Lusitania and, on his death in battle and the fall of
Mérida, the Christian resistance ended. The destruction of the society of Romanised
landowners may have taken place only in the ninth century, after the collapse of the
long rebellion and reluctant submission of ibn Marwan. Idanha is now divided from
Castelo Branco by the flooding of the river Ponsul. The modern place, 'a Nova', is
some distance from the Roman Egitania.

The submission to the Christian reconquest and the military Orders began in the
reign of Afonso Henriques. The choice of Castelo Branco was owing to its command
of a vast area of country on both sides of the Tagus. Under the Knights, the 'White
Castle' governed two communities, that to the north, the more indigenous, with the
same rights as Elvas, while Vila Franca de Cardosa received from Sancho I the customs of Covilhã. Whatever the significance of the division, it seems to have endured.
Even in the twentieth century, when writers noted the sense of activity and business
in the capital of a large area, it seemed that the upper classes lived withdrawn in families 'in dark and as it were proud independence of one another, from obscure rival-
ries now beyond recall'. King Diniz and Queen Isabel visited it in 1285, extended the
walls and increased the number of gates from four to seven. The absence of convents
except for the Graça is unusual. So too the cathedral, for at first Castelo Branco was
the winter resort of the bishops of Guarda. The bishop's palace was built as a seminary by Dom Nuno de Noronha, rector of the university of Coimbra and bishop of
Guarda. He was a man of wealth and ostentation and set out to overtake the decisions of the Council of Trent. The garden began in the Italian style with clipped
hedges and fountains and was developed into a divine staircase like Bom Jesus at
Braga, flanked with statues of Old Testament kings and prophets, reminiscent of the
Brazilian Minas of the Aleijadinho. It is not quite the only thing Castelo Branco has
to show, for the Civil Government is in the former palace of the Viscounts of
Portalegre dating from 1743 and containing the provincial museum, with paintings
and tapestries, and the old town has a cross of St John, Manueline, though his chapel
has been demolished.

North-east of Castelo Branco, the roads make for the former Spanish frontier, now
open. The excellent highways owe much to 'Europe' and many villages record the
debt. Idanha suffers from touristic enhancement and there is a modern folklore promoted to attract visitors. Monfortinho, very near the border, is a spa which treats
practically all the ills of suffering humanity. Those who do not wish to flaunt their
own good health may find a very good and moderate hotel just out of sight. The
Spanish mountains, the Gata, are protected for their wild life. The European lynx has
long been extinct in Portugal, but did not ever require a passport. The wild boar
occurs on both sides, and its parts are pickled or bottled for the connoisseur to take
away. Hunters have their gun-club not far away: its dining-terrace overlooks a flood-
lit pitch for *caçadores* (hunters) to pot pigeons, clay or otherwise, round the clock. The
Spanish side is packed with *cotos* or reserves, where the ground flattens into vast olive
plantations and tobacco-fields with their perforated brick drying-sheds. Coria, a small
Roman city in Spanish Estremadura, played an unrecognised part in the defence of
Portugal, since it is midway between Seville and Coimbra, which the Muslim horse,

bred in the fields of the Guadalquivir, could not reach when fended off by the strong escarpment of Coria: its fortified bluff and fine Roman bridge are still to be seen.

The next Portuguese village is Penha Garcia, straggling down a steep mountainside and boasting of tales of the perils of contraband by intrepid riders in the dark carrying packages of Portuguese coffee to exchange for Spanish tobacco (nowadays the guards cross over in joint pursuit of drug traffickers). There is also a fossil trail, supposedly frequented by forgotten animals of a remote past which have conveniently left their bones behind. 'The Old Forge' offers coffee and a demonstration of the art of making horseshoes and even the more delicate bootees worn by oxen. Monsanto is one of the 'most typical villages' in Portugal. Many of its houses sprout in the spaces between enormous boulders. The novelist Fernando Namora worked for two years there and it is the setting for his scenes from a doctor's life: it now has its own rush-hour.

Penamacor has a ruined castle with a single tower like a gaunt warning finger a few miles from the frontier. For a few weeks in 1584 it was the capital of a kingdom. After the Battle of the Three Kings in Morocco, an adventurer claimed to be the last right-ful king, Sebastian, appointing his own court and bishop of Guarda. King Philip II was not amused: the powerful rarely relish mockery of themselves except by licensed jesters. A company of regulars came to catch the king, a dark young man from Alcobaça, who was exhibited in Lisbon and showed no resemblance to the late pale prince. He was sent to the galleys but escaped to France. His 'bishop of Guarda' was executed: perhaps he had devised this method of tapping ecclesiastical revenue. No trace of the royal abode is to be seen.

The road runs north by the Guadunha, only half as high as the Estrela but well above Helvellyn or Snowdon. It is crossed near Alpedrinha, whose first claim to fame is as the birthplace of a cardinal, Dom Jorge da Costa, who accumulated the arch-bishoprics of Braga and Lisbon and the sees of Évora, Oporto, Viseu, the Algarve and Ceuta. He owed his hat to Sixtus IV, lived to be a hundred and has a sepulchre of splendour in Santa Maria del Populo. Before setting down this tale of local boy mak-ing good, it seemed best to check: the source is the *Miscellany* of Garcia de Resende, who added that he made his brothers archbishops. In the middle ages, it was not unusual to leave dioceses unoccupied while the crown collected their income. But this seems not to have been the case here. Born in 1406 plain Jorge Martins, the hero began his dazzling career only at fifty when made tutor to Afonso V's sister: he became bishop of Évora in 1463 and archbishop of Lisbon in 1464, changed his name to Costa and was made cardinal in 1474. Prince John did not like him and threatened him, so he left for Rome and never returned. He was given Oporto in 1501 and acquired Braga on the death of his brother in 1503, but gave it up in 1505 without ever having set foot there: he would then have been ninety-nine.

To the north rises the enormous flank or thigh of the Estrela, dotted with the white buildings of the shepherds and weavers of Covilhã. The higher levels are the largest grazing area in Portugal, but are snow-bound in winter, when the sheep are folded until the spring grass appears. The woollen industry is centred on Covilhã and Fundão, once the home of weavers and fullers. When the Jews were expelled from Spain in 1492, several families bought residence-permits to settle here. Although Covilhã was the seat of the *concelho*, taxes were collected at Fundão, which became independent only in 1747, when John V made it a *vila*. Pombal set up a royal woollen-mill in the building used now as the town-hall. But after the liberal 'revolution' of

1820, the industry was privatised and quickly ruined. It remains the administrative headquarters for the fertile Cova da Beira, and as a mining-centre enjoyed a period of fortuitous prosperity during the wolfram boom of 1942. Its centre is a small square with a *pelourinho*. The houses rise to three floors and give it a city-like appearance quite different from traditional towns of the interior.

The Cova da Beira, the trench or pit, is the weald of the river Zêzere which rises under the Torre, the highest point in the range, with a tower which just reaches 6,560 feet. Weather permitting, the slopes are used for skiing, with accommodation at the former sanatorium of Penhas da Saude. A road crosses the range near the source, but the river is only a modest stream flowing between the stones of a rocky valley. It comes down to Covilhã, at 2,000 feet and now a largish city. Apart from the shepherds and their dogs, several thousand people are engaged in making woollens, and the industry combines large factories with cottage looms in a way congenial to the Portuguese. The Pombaline Royal Factory has been turned into barracks, and the modern factories are strewn up and down the hillside. The *concelho* consists of twenty-seven parishes, but the main church was damaged by the Earthquake of 1755 and has been much restored. The Misericórdia dates from the seventeenth century. Pero da Covilhã was one of the two travellers sent by John II to discover the land-route to India and Ethiopia, where he settled down and did not return. John III gave the town to the Infante Dom Luis, and it was here that the prince found Violante Gomes 'Pelicana', the mother of his son, Dom António, Prior of Crato, whose claim to the succession gave Philip II such trouble.

From Covilhã the road proceeds to Belmonte, a small town with a ruined castle on a hill. It was once the seat of the Cabral family, the marchers of the province of Beira, whose remote ancestor was Aires Pires Cabral, a follower of Afonso III. Another Cabral was the Giant of Beira who carried a Herculean club. According to legend, the loyalty of the Cabrais was so automatic that they were not required to take the oath to the crown. The most famous member of the ancient house was Pedro Álvares Cabral, chosen to command the thirteen ships that sailed to India to clinch Vasco da Gama's discovery: setting a course to the west, he found Brazil on the way. Gama had come from the minor nobility, but Cabral was chosen because of the traditional services to the crown of his family.

A mile or two away from Belmonte at Centum Celas, is one of the most problematic Roman remains in Portugal: a tower of granite blocks in three storeys, with the foundations of two flanking buildings. It stands near the Zêzere and the road from Idanha to Viseu. The upper floor was altered in medieval times, but had a balcony of which the supports are visible. The mountain district has numerous traces of Roman mining-operations.

The need for frontier defence arose with the reconquest and the emergence of separate states from the Empire of Leon. This accounts for the position of Guarda, the highest city in Portugal. It is more than thirty miles from the actual frontier at Vilar Formoso, and 750 feet above its railway-station four miles away. The place was a desert in the days of Afonso Henriques and was first fortified by Sancho I in 1199. In medieval terms the fortress, if well stocked, could cut off the supply-lines of an army advancing through the rocky waste; in the Spanish invasion of 1385, the invaders were aided by a party within the country. The cathedral was one of the new structures erected in 1504 to 1517, and is of granite on a scale intended to impress by its solidity and strength. It has two squat octagonal towers ornamented with battlements and pinnacles which overawe the modest doorway between twisted colonnettes. The interior has lofty arches also with some of the twisted columns dear to Boytac. The general effect, like the climate outside, is cold, if bracing. Of the circuit of walls, three of the five gates survive, and suggest a large citadel with room for a numerous garrison. At one end, the tower of the iron-workers, Torre dos Ferreiros, is a square work defending a double gate: it gives wide views over the frontier landscape. Half-way down the road from the city to the station is the small Romanesque hermitage of Mileu, which may be older than the city itself. The oldest private house in Guarda is the residence of the Alarcão family, which has a courtyard of granite in two floors.

The sector between Guarda and the Douro became famous during the Peninsular War. After Elvas, the most important fortress on the Portuguese frontier was Almeida, a small place on a hill commanding the frontier plain, four miles behind the border. It occupies the site of an ancient castle rebuilt for King Manuel. It had not performed well in 1762, in the Seven Years War, and was rebuilt on more modern lines under the supervision of the Jesuit colonel, Fr Cosmander, in the form of one irregular six-pointed star superposed on another. The ravelins reduce the vulnerable curtains to a minimum and the approaches are swept by cannon supplied from a central magazine. Almeida looks towards Ciudad Rodrigo on the Spanish side, considered much less formidable, 'a wretched place' in the words of William Warre, Wellington's aide. Early in 1810 Wellington's headquarters were at Celorico da Beira, a castle on a high hill which still preserves its walls. Beresford was at Fornos de Algodres, a few miles further down the valley of the Mondego, where he used the mansion of the Abreu-Castelo Branco family. Although the town stands at mid-height with views of the Estrela, the 'veranda of the Serra', Warre soon became bored with the place, for it rained continuously and the affectations of the local squirearchy, who aped their betters from afar, were irksome to the son of the wealthy British Consul, accustomed to the life of Oporto. Fornos he called a 'miserable little village on a very high mountain', but this was after a stay of three months in pouring rain.

He went to Trancoso, fifteen miles to the north, where there was a Portuguese brigade, with Wellington, and visited the convent: the troops were in good order, but the nuns, though at prayers, were in miserable poverty. It has now recovered, and still preserves its circuit of walls. It was chartered by Afonso Henriques. In 1543 it received a visitation from the Inquisition, causing the new Christians to flee, to the number of a hundred and seventy. Now the bus pulls up outside King Diniz's towered gate. Some of the houses have projecting eaves over arcades, one of them occupied by General Hill. It has a Romanesque church of Santa Luzia and an eighteenth-century chapel of St Bartholomew which replaces the chapel where King Diniz was married. The New Fountain is an imitation of a Greek templet. It is one of the more characterful places in the province. One of its sons was the arcane poet Bandarra, whose prophetic verses contributed to spread the myth of Sebastianism.

Pinhel, halfway between Trancoso and Almeida, is another former castle which retains two towers though it has lost its military significance. It was the seat of a bishop from 1770 to 1882, but its cathedral is now the church of São Luis. In it lies Luis de Figueiredo Falcão, secretary to Philip II, and founder of the Franciscan convent (1596). The town has several houses of prominent families, including the Casa Grande, occupied by Masséna. By 20 June 1810 Masséna was closely besieging Ciudad

Rodrigo, which bravely resisted even when the French heavy artillery was brought up. On 25 June Warre was near Pinhel when he reported hearing a 'most tremendous explosion' from the French line where a powder magazine blew up. It was seen or heard forty miles away and Brigadier Cox in Almeida reported that it shook the whole place. On 2 July Warre rode from Pinhel to Almeida, dined with Cox and viewed the French lines. On 24 July Crawford's light division was attacked and lost three hundred men. The French then entered Pinhel. On 26 August there was indeed a tremendous explosion, but it was in Almeida, where much of the fortress was suddenly demolished as the powder magazine went up. The catastrophe at Almeida made its surrender inevitable. Wellington was unable to relieve it, and retreat was the only course left open. The incident revealed some of Beresford's difficulties in integrating the British and Portuguese armies. Brigadier Cox had been given the 'step' all British officers received: he was a lieutenant-colonel. So too was Costa e Almeida, who was *tenente-rei* of Almeida, responsible to the Prince Regent. Costa e Almeida had given the signal for surrender, but Cox had hoped Wellington would perform some feat of magic. Costa e Almeida was shot on some military charge. His family mounted a wave of protest and published a long poem in his defence. Long after, when Beresford recommended Cox for promotion, the Prince Regent for the first time questioned his judgement. The case was referred to a mixed court; it unanimously exonerated Cox, but divided on national lines on the question of the conduct of Costa e Almeida.

16

Alentejo

Lisbon is a famous seaport, but it is not on the open ocean. A channel half a mile wide and twenty miles long leads into an inland sea several miles across and broad enough to hold all the world's navies. It is the Straw Sea, Mar de Palha. The name has nothing to do with straw, but suggests a false ocean, rather as the False Creeks explorers used to find, a 'man of straw', a dummy. The rim of this expanded river or miniature sea is the Outra Banda, or Other Side.

At the narrows ferries take about twenty minutes to cross, and ply constantly between the Terreiro do Paço or Cais de Sodré and Cacilhas. They are crowded at the rush-hours but otherwise provide a simple and inexpensive way to see Lisbon from the water. Formerly, travellers coming from the east would arrive at Aldeia Galega, the most distant part of the Mar de Palha, and wait for transport to Lisbon. The ferry from Lisbon to Montijo took an hour and a half and sitting on the deck in the sunshine afforded a pleasant way of passing an idle afternoon. The bay at Moita was rendered more attractive by the blue magpie or jay, found only in China and here. Who introduced this beautiful bird is not known; fifty years ago it was confined to Montijo or thereabouts, but now it is not uncommon over a large area.

The south bank seen from the height of the castle in Lisbon looks attractive in a faint veil of blue mist. It is a series of inlets now in part industrialised. Barreiro is the railhead for the southern railway, and passengers obtain tickets from the office near the Lisbon Terreiro and cross by ferry to the trains on the other side. The naval shipyard was traditionally at the Arsenal adjoining the Paço, but was transferred to Alfeite, a former royal estate. Barreiro has docks and yards for the repair of large oil-tankers and other vessels. The streams flowing into the Mar de Palha had water-mills, and one of these at Seixal has been rehabilitated as a tourist attraction.

Alentejo, 'Beyond the Tagus', is by far the largest province of Portugal and also the least populated. In contrast to the mountainous north, it is flat, though the land rises towards the Spanish frontier to form the serras of the Upper Alentejo. In modern times it has been deprived of the Outra Banda and of the coastal strip which are now regarded as a southward extension of Estremadura; and the Alentejo proper, rendered almost land-locked, is subdivided into two, Lower and Upper, either of which is bigger than Trás-os-Montes, the third largest province.

Much of the traffic to the south, human and freight, now uses one or other of the three bridges that give access to the Alentejo. The oldest is the Marshal Carmona bridge at Vila Franca de Xira, opened in 1951. Vila Franca is some twenty-five miles north of Lisbon and is the capital of the mounted cattlemen, *campinos*, who steer or navigate the cattle with long lances. The town, with its sporty reputation, was briefly famous in May 1823, when Prince Miguel at the head of an infantry regiment restored his father John VI to his traditional rights and overturned the first liberal government. The neighbouring cattle-ranges are open to visitors and the river is fished for *savel* or shad.

The second bridge was opened in 1966 at Alcântara on the west side of Lisbon. It soars over the narrows in a single span to the town of Almada. It was then the Salazar bridge, but has been renamed 25 April to commemorate the Revolution of 1974. Its opening has led to the erection of a forest of apartment-blocks at Almada. At the rush-hours, the dozen or more toll-booths have long lines, which the addition of a railway-line only partially alleviates. The cliff between Cacilhas and Almada is dominated by a lofty column with a statue of Christ the King erected in 1947. The great bridge was soon found to be insufficient to solve the growing traffic problems. In 1998 the voyage of Vasco da Gama to the Orient was commemorated by an exhibition on the eastern side of the capital. A new suburb named Oriente was formed and from it a graceful new bridge was built to cross the inland-sea. A single suspension section lifts the road above river-traffic and a long causeway skims the shallows for several miles to Montijo. It greatly facilitates access to the cities of Évora and Beja and joins the main highway to the Algarve.

Between Almada and the ocean the south bank consists of cliffs with breaks. They contain the former quarantine-house or lazaretto at Porto Brandão and the fishing-village of Trafaria, which Pombal burned down in 1777 for the crime of disobedience. Caparica has a long stretch of ocean sands and is the most popular holiday resort on the south bank: beyond it the sands sweep away to Cape Espichel. The best view of Lisbon is obtained from the hills of Palmela, reached by road from Cacilhas. Its castle, once the headquarters of the Knights of Santiago is now a *pousada*. It stands at 700 feet on a spur of the Serra da Arrábida which extends for twenty miles to Cape Espichel. The Serra abuts on a narrow strip of coast which ranks with Sintra as the most picturesque place in reach of Lisbon. The Knights of Santiago undertook the defence of the coastal zone. The grand-master was Dom Jorge, the illegitimate son of John II: he lies in the church, which dates from 1443. If the great king had had his way Dom Jorge would have been king, but instead the succession passed to the fortunate Dom Manuel, his wife's youngest brother.

The area was luxuriant in the times of the Muslims, who have left the place-names of Almada, Azeitão and Arrábida among others. The Serra de Arrábida was a *ribat* or retreat for those who led a monastic life in preparation for the religious war. It reaches 2,000 feet and plunges from a limestone ridge to sea-level. Its slopes are a refuge for shrubs and flowers of all kinds: the southern and drier side has cistus, lavenders, spurges and scented bushes; the northern slope is moister and carries beeches, oaks and tree-heaths. The *ribat* was replaced by a Christian hermitage where the poet Frei Agostinho da Cruz composed his melodious verses until his death in 1619. The 'old convent' was a group of tiny hostels to which the 'new convent' below was added by St Pedro de Alcântara in 1542. It can be reached from Palmela or by the direct road from Cacilhas to the fishing village of Sesimbra. Going due south, it passes a lagoon, the Lagoa da Albufeira, a haunt of wildfowl and game. Sesimbra begins with a castle of Muslim origin, restored recently; lower down is the village, fitted into a sheltered cove which fishermen share with pleasure-craft. The catch is auctioned and finds its way to the Lisbon market. It has a church dated 1536 and a Misericórdia. The Serra comes down to the sea at the Cabo, which has a shrine, the Senhora do Cabo, and shelter for those who come to its *romaria*.

To the west of Sesimbra is the cave of Santa Margarida, adorned with stalactites, and the tiny bay of Arrábida, the Portinho, and the Duke's Rock, an islet from which the nobleman used to fish, the setting for two eclogues by Camões:

> When shrouds of mist at early morning drape
> Arrábida whose slopes are hidden from the eye
> until the rising sun reveals their shape . . .
> Galatea alone disdains to heed,
> as with the weight of care my voice I blend
> and as my oar bends on the pliant sea
> by moonlight all my stock of cares I spend.
> Sweet-natured dolphins hearken to my plea,
> the waves grow still, the calm is set,
> but you alone disdain to hear and flee.
> Perhaps you scorn the fisher's simple net
> that sifts the sea, his barque borne on the wind,
> perhaps the youth himself who labours yet.
> Fortune may change and show herself more kind
> before the Sun himself has run his round,
> as those who toil upon the sea oft find.

The touchy duke may have liked these verses better than the longer eclogue that followed, where the shepherd with his pipe competes with the musical fisherman and his bagpipe. The poet notes the duke's illustrious descent without mentioning his royal pretensions. The duke was Dom João de Lencastre, the son of Dom Jorge and grandson of John II, Lencastre because of his descent from Philippa of Lancaster and John of Gaunt. He married and his son, who was quite legitimate, thought that the pious and colourless John III had offered him in marriage the heiress to the Counts of Redondo and Loulé, the richest prize in the land. But the king bestowed her on his own younger brother, and the disappointed suitor went to law, was arrested, and on his release refused to attend King John's court, devoting himself to hunting, fishing and literature; despite the reproaches of his friend the poet Sá de Miranda, himself an exile in the distant Minho, Dom João continued to nurse his grievance. His rival and the bride both died in 1534, but it was only in 1547 that he accepted the title of Duke of Aveiro (which then implied membership of the royal house) and married the young Dona Juliana Meneses, who was only just below him in rank. For the wedding he turned up at the royal chapel at Almeirim clad in black on a white horse. The press of spectators was so great that the black guard laid about them with their clubs; the king would not go in until he was assured that there had been no serious casualties.

Dom João had his country palace at Azeitão, the Vila Nogueira, which was sequestered when Pombal had the last Duke of Aveiro executed in 1760. The house was then converted into a textile-factory. Until 1855 Nogueira was the centre of the *concelho* then renamed Azeitão. It includes another famous Renaissance house, the Quinta da Bacalhoa at Vila Fresca. It was built for the mother of King Manuel, but acquired in 1528 by a son of Afonso de Albuquerque, who adorned it in the best style of the day, a plain house with corner turrets facing a square garden with clipped hedges, orange-trees in tubs and a tiled tank: the existing *azulejos* are of symbolic figures of rivers signed by Matos in 1565. The house was rescued from abandonment in about 1930 by an American lady. Also in Azeitão, the Quinta das Torres has a garden and tank with a cupola mounted on columns: it is used as a restaurant and guest-house.

The city of Setúbal was known to the English as St Ubes, a saint who appears not to exist. The name probably derives from the Roman Caetobriga when galleys put into the estuary of the river Sado, which is of no great size and has no populous hinterland. The port is one of the chief Portuguese fisheries and its first industry was probably the preservation and export of fish. It was also the centre of an orange-growing area and produced the muscatel wine which used to be sold everywhere in England. Its modern industrial experience has been less happy. The Renault motor company chose it for a plant which it abruptly closed, causing abiding problems. Its best-known monument is the church of Jesus, which was designed by the architect Boytac who used the twisted columns of stone ropes which are such a feature of his work at Belém. Setúbal was the birthplace of the eighteenth-century Bohemian poet Bocage, who followed the trail of Camões to the East: his square and monument are in the middle of the city.

Setúbal has no Roman remains of significance, but many sherds of pottery have appeared and in 1979 two amphoras were found containing a total of 18,000 coins of the fourth century. The estuary can be crossed to Troia, an ancient site on the long protruding tip of a sandy promontory. When first excavated it was more extensive than now, for the sands have encroached on the place. It has fish-preserving tanks, streets, ruined houses, one of them large and circular, and a cemetery, perhaps early Christian. The tanks for salting fish date back to Phoenician and Roman times, and the salt-pans are still in evidence in the Sado basin. The town on the south side is Alcácer do Sal, the Roman Salacia, once called 'imperial'. In the sixteenth century its salt was considered whiter and finer, perhaps owing to the stronger sun or better methods of panning. Dutch ships carried it to Germany and the Baltic until the Spanish occupation curbed the export-trade. The system of salt-pans has now been adapted into rice-paddies.

Alcácer do Sal retained its importance in Muslim times. The castle was rebuilt by the Knights of Santiago in the later thirteenth century. Muslim writers record its loss in 1217, when the defenders were vanquished by the knights after the foot soldiers had run away. It was then surrounded by pinewoods used for shipbuilding and exported wheat from the Alentejo. Within the walls, the church of Santa Maria 'of the castle' is a Romanesque building, unusual so far south. Half-way between Setúbal and Alcácer there is a great pine-wood at Pinheiro, once the property of the Knights, and then owned by Dom Jorge and his son, the first Duke of Aveiro, and confiscated when Pombal had the last Duke executed. There are those who believe that this coastal strip has people who are fairer and taller than those of the authentic Alentejo. It is perhaps no longer important. The area now adjudged to Estremadura extends to Santiago de Cacém, where there is a pleasant *pousada*, a converted private house with a shady garden. The castle is a rectangle with two towers and a solid barbican. Its church was built soon after the reconquest, and has a romano-Gothic side-door. The walk round the circuit of walls gives views over a wide area. The 'old castle' is the site of the Roman Mirobriga 'of the Celts'. Excavations have revealed a shrine from a fortified bronze-age settlement on which the Romans built a township with a temple probably dedicated to Venus, a forum, baths and shops, and half a mile away, vestiges of the only circus to be uncovered in Portugal.

Ten miles from Santiago is Sines, a sheltered port under its cape and the birthplace of Vasco da Gama. When he was born in 1460 or thereabouts, Prince Henry's discoveries comprised only the Atlantic Isles and the West African coast as far as Sierra Leone, and there was nothing to suggest that a son of this obscure port would bring together the two parts of the civilised world. Sines is now a major port for oil-tankers with installations for refining. South of Sines the coast slips away to the Algarve. From the village of Porto Covo the intrepid may visit the islet of Pessegueiro, which had a Roman fishing-station and curing-plant, with cottages, a store and baths of the fourth century AD.

The main body of the Alentejo is divided into Upper, with its capital at Évora, and Lower, which is administered from Beja. They are the only main centres of population, and are remote from the sea, therein differing from the country north of the Tagus. Both Évora and Beja are Roman cities and have been continuously occupied. Évora has its famous temple, and its Roman walls can easily be traced. Its leading citizens occupied large estates, which produced cattle and horses. Beja, once Pax Julia, was the centre of great wheatfields, *latifundia*, which have persisted until the present. The classical note is sustained by the olive and holm-oak or ilex. If the vine was neglected in Muslim times, it now flourishes. The Romans esteemed the white marble which is still quarried near Estremós. The rest of the Alentejo from the Tagus to the Algarve is level plain or rolling parkland. The main road south skirts the few towns, though it has fits of ribbon-development responding to the needs of travellers: cafés, restaurants and petrol-stations.

Parts of the Alentejo may be torrid in high summer. The topsoil is thin; it provides grazing for sheep rather than cattle. The Sado is a small river with a big mouth, and its affluents have nothing to say during the hot months. The trees are the olive and cork-oak: the chestnut and northern oak grow only in clumps on the higher ground of the north-east. There are patches of scrub on which nothing useful can be cultivated. These are the *charnecas*, a word loosely applied to waste sandy ground but used especially of these clearings often edged by straggling pines, but unfriendly even to the patient and adaptable vine. In much of the Alentejo there are few isolated houses. There are manors, the *montes*, occupied by landowners or large farmers, the distant heirs of the masters of Roman *latifundias*, but most of the population is congregated in small towns or large villages, which in the region of Beja may be as much as eight miles apart. Their houses are trim rows of attached white cottages with brown or red pantiles for roofing, and painted with a bright, low wainscot. The villagers do not share their tidy homes with the animals, but go out daily to the fields. When needed, the women go with them, tucking up their skirts in ample bloomers. Traction is by donkey or mule: there were more mules in the Alentejo than in all the rest of Portugal. The pigs are numerous and fend for themselves in the woods: they are usually black and lean, giving the well-flavoured ham called *serrano*.

The inequitable distribution of land poses a problem for political theorists who mull in cities and universities. After the overturn of 1974, urban zealots persuaded the country people to seize the farms for improvised collectives, which, having no knowledge of distribution, sold off cattle to meet immediate needs and felled cork-oaks for the simple object of finding something to do. Matters have been set to rights, but much of the Algarve is still a special agricultural zone. Its staple diet is wheat and oats, rather than maize or rye, mutton, especially *borrego*, spring lamb, often stewed, and broad beans. Its favourite herb is *coentros* or coriander. Its staple soup is *açorda*, a broth with coriander or garlic and pieces of wheaten loaf, with a poached egg floating on top. It may well have been the diet before the Christian reconquest. It is only in recent times that the Alentejo has come to compete with central and northern Portugal in the production of table-wines. Needless to say, Setúbal has long been known, and Azeitão is a name that appears on numerous bottles. This may be seen as an overspill, if that is the right word, from Lisbon. But as early as 1892 a Lisbon entrepreneur undertook at Rio Frio to plant millions of vines for the largest system of vineyards in the world, an experiment in production on a scale not then equalled.

Lisbon has always tended to encroach on the Alentejo, 'beyond the Tagus'. (If there was an indigenous name for it, it has been lost.) Évora was briefly the centre of a Muslim principality, which could not or would not come to the rescue when Afonso Henriques laid siege to Lisbon. The Templars looked south from the castle of Almourol, which they built in the middle of the river, and King John III and his court moved between Lisbon and Évora, where much of his nobility had houses or estates. (These royal migrations caused great inconvenience to everyone. A vast number of pack-animals was required and the medieval right of free billetting was much abused.) King John had his younger brothers educated at Évora and scholars of the Renaissance such as André de Resende and the Fleming Cleynarts or Clenardus stayed there. The former hoped that it would be the seat of the single university, but it was Coimbra that recovered the distinction in 1537. Évora was given a Jesuit college, which served as a second seat of learning from 1557 until the Society was suppressed. Évora's light as a beacon of the Renaissance was dimmed. Camões' contemporary and friend António de Resende, the nephew of the great scholar, was fired by the same ideals but ended his days as a disillusioned and grumpy scrivener.

The main road from Lisbon to Évora passes through *charnecas* to emerge at Vendas Novas at a building adorned with cannon. This is the artillery school, which replaces a palace erected in double-quick time in the middle of nowhere in 1728, when the opulent John V wanted a suitable location for the wedding of his son Joseph, later king, to Mariana Vitória, daughter of the King of Spain. This was coupled with the exchange of his own daughter Barbara of Braganza, an event of musical rather than architectural significance. The road goes on to Montemór o Novo, passing through fields dotted with the holm-oak and the cork-oak. The classical ilex was thought superior to the northern or Nelsonian oak by Portuguese ship-builders on account of its resistance to tropical worm: they were thinking of vessels in which a thousand tons seemed monstrous. The cork-oak is distinguished by its rounded and ragged-edged leaves and soft bark. When the tree reaches maturity, the bark is cut into rectangular sections and prised off. It is then stacked and carried away to stop bottles and serve a variety of purposes, leaving the reddish core of the tree to recover, as it does in about ten years. The sight of the red trunks peeled to shoulder-height is a feature of the landscape.

The castle of Montemór o Novo stands on a long ridge above the town and the modern road. It is called after its namesake near Coimbra and was built to defend access to Évora. It is now crumbling, but was a royal residence when King Manuel came to the throne. Here, having received the news that Vasco da Gama had reached India, he and his council took the momentous decision to proceed with the great adventure. The decision was doubly fateful, since the next command was given to Pedro Álvares Cabral, who discovered Brazil. Montemór was also the birthplace of St John of God, born in 1495, who devoted himself to the care of the insane: he died in 1550, and his house was turned into a monastery in 1625.

To the south of Montemór, the Serra de Monfurado reaches nearly 1,400 feet. It was not much visited until 1963, when its caves were found to be of archaeological interest. At the Sala estate in Santiago do Escoural there are some three dozen galleries with fourteen sketches of animals and (one or two) human beings datable to the Madgalenians of Altamira and Lascaux. The animals are the horse, cattle and goat, done in black and overlaid in places with stalactites: these sketches suffice to give a place to Portugal on page one of the family album of the first Europeans.

Before reaching Évora, a turning to the north leads to the small town of Arraiolos, now chiefly known for its rugs and carpets, though it also cures hams and sausages. Its ruined castle is placed on a hill ringed with white houses, mostly of one floor and roofed with pantiles. The fine rugs of wool and hemp come in light colours and geo-metrical patterns adorned with flowers and sprigs. The designs are related to rural embroidery, but are consciously organised in a well-considered tradition. Perhaps the women of Arraiolos excelled in needlework or had more time for it. The place was given by King Afonso II to the bishop of Évora in 1217, and they may have con-tributed to making the episcopal vestments. In the early fifteenth century the lordship belonged to Nun'Alvares Pereira, the Holy Constable. The present industry arose in the seventeenth century, and the legendary 'bride of Arraiolos' took a fortnight to deck herself.

Évora is the most Roman town in Portugal. Its name Eboracum suggests a Celtic origin, like Ebor or York. Its first sight is the temple, probably built in the second century AD for the cult of the emperors. The shrine was on a lofty rectangular platform surrounded by twenty-six Corinthian columns of which those on the north side are complete, though the frieze and roof have disappeared. It stands in a gardened space and enjoys extensive views over a vast area of fields and trees dotted with white houses, once part of *villae* owned by Julians and Calpurnians and other families who boasted of a Latin origin. The imperial cult was spread about under Vespasian but declined as the emperorship itself was devalued. The circuit of Roman walls is incomplete, but enough remains to show that the area enclosed in about 300 AD was quite small. The only sur-viving gate, named after Dona Isabel, was narrowed by a medieval addition.

Muslim Portugal continues Roman Portugal, but has left no single monument in the city though some of the street-scapes were formed before the Christian reconquest.

This is ascribed to Gerald the Fearless, Giraldo sem Pavor, who seized the city in 1166. His name is commemorated in the main square which lies just outside the Roman walled precinct. The cathedral of Évora follows the Romanesque plan of Coimbra and Oporto, but was begun later and its vaulting, cupola and cloister are Gothic. The dome over the crossing is capped by a conical structure surrounded by pinnacles, a feature much imitated in the Alentejo. The front with two unequal towers is asymmetrical, but the interior gains in grandeur from the cupola, which the historian Martin Hume thought repaid the journey from England. The main chapel was rebuilt for John V by Ludovice, the architect of Mafra.

The house of Avis takes its name from the Alentejan castle of which King John I was grand-master. His son King Duarte built the first royal palace which was rebuilt and extended by King Manuel. Much of the nobility traced its fortunes to the deeds of the Military Orders, and the over-generous Afonso V, 'the African', conceived Évora as his capital. His son John II began his struggles with the nobility with the *cortes* of Évora in 1481, and crushed the rival branch by executing his cousin the Duke of Braganza in the main square of Évora in 1482. It was largely through his influence that the Italian renewal entered Portugal. Three buildings in Évora illustrate the change. The convent or 'hermitage' of São Bras was built in about 1482 outside the walls: it has a row of cylindrical buttresses topped by small cones and joined by battlements, forming an original assemblage of conventional motives. The palace of King Manuel, later much disfigured, was a combination of an open arcade with the fashion for the Moorish, which King Manuel reintroduced. The small Augustinian church of the Graça, built in the early years of John III (1524–30), is a temple with an entry recessed behind columns, and an upper storey consisting of a classical portico between two rose-windows, surmounted at the corners by two globes upheld by giants in postures like idle Atlases. The giants – locally known as 'the lads' – caused Watson to consider it one of the most extraordinary buildings in the world. But the pagan revival did not spread far. It was replaced from 1542 onwards by the Jesuits, who liked simple lines but required ornamentation to have significance. The humanist Francisco de Holanda, sent to Italy to study with Michelangelo and other lights of the day, returned with plans for a Renaissance capital which King John III, the would-be Trajan, could no longer afford. André de Resende educated the younger brothers of the king, including Henry who became archbishop of Évora, cardinal and briefly king, the last of his line: he favoured the Jesuits, and founded their college, – later the university of Évora. The house of Garcia de Resende appears on the touristic menu, and his name is given to a modern theatre (where one might have expected to find Gil Vicente, who died at Évora in 1536). The Jesuit university is itself a handsome building. It was closed by Pombal in 1759, but restored two centuries later.

Évora has plenty of other monuments in the form of private houses, public fountains and convents. The former castle was replaced in 1666 by an episcopal house, which Archbishop Cenáculo (1802–14) made into a public library. The adjoining building is the regional Museum. The mansion of the Counts of Basto, built in about 1550, has twin windows in the Moorish style, and was resided in by King Sebastian and by Catherine of Braganza, the widowed Queen of England. The house of Cordovil and the Casa de Soure are typical examples of regional architecture. The Misericórdia occupies the house of Dom Luis, brother to King John III and father of the Prior of Crato: its marble baroque doorway was added in 1765. Évora's aqueduct was built in

1538 to bring water from Água de Prata six miles away. It served the fountain in the Praça de Giraldo, a handsome marble piece with a bronze crown dating from about 1570. Another civic fountain crowned with a globe stands in the Portas de Moura. Near this was the former convent of Paraíso, of which nothing is left but the taste. The nuns were famous for their sweetmeats, and Évora still relishes its cheesecakes, tipsy cake and nun's kisses, though these are now secularised.

The countryside of Évora is dotted with farmsteads. They replace the Roman *villae*, whose owners lived in style with underground heating, mosaics, shrines and out-houses for their dependants. In Muslim times Évora was regarded as rich, with a pros-perous trade, a castle and a cathedral-mosque. After the twelfth century, they made room for the Military Orders and adventurers from the north. They constituted the medieval nobility which in turn gave place to an oligarchy of professionals. It was not a place for small-holders. Isolated cottages were few: the rural practice was to dwell in villages by the road or on the outskirts of towns.

Outside the city is Cartuxa, known for its oranges. The Cartuxa or Charterhouse is one of only two Carthusian monasteries in Portugal, and has an impressive façade and a wide staircase of marble with three storeys. It was built in the Jesuit style of Terzi for Dom Teotónio de Bragança, nephew of the Cardinal-King Henry, and his successor as archbishop of Évora (1578–1602).

Seven miles south-west of Évora Cardinal Henry founded the Capuchin monastery of Mitra or Valverde: some of its cloister and other parts remain, but it has been con-verted into a school of agriculture. In the vicinity is the palace of Sempre Noiva, built for the royal bishop Dom Afonso de Portugal and transmitted to his nephew, the Count of Vimioso. The 'eternal bride' is said to have been Dona Isabel de Sousa Coutinho, who refused to marry the younger son of Pombal, was forced to comply, but took refuge in a convent until the marriage was annulled: she then married and (of course) lived happily ever after.

The upper Alentejo is the richest part of Portugal in prehistoric remains. The nearest megalithic site to Évora is the dolmen at Outeiro das Vinhas five miles to the east. It con-sists of a capstone poised on half a dozen inward-leaning supports. The best place from which to visit other sites is Reguengos de Monsaraz, south-east of the city. They include the menhirs at Abelhoa and Outeiro, and a cromlech of 95 stones at Almendres, five miles west of Évora, and others at Xaraz. The first was described only in 1965.

The closest range to Évora is the Serra da Ossa, near whose end at São Miguel da Mota, Terena, there was a pre-Roman and Roman shrine with numerous pieces of stat-uary. This is rare in Portugal, particularly after the Muslim phase in which religious puritanism forbade representational art. The shrine was for the god Endovelicus, whose cult was widespread, in contrast with the Celtic native deities which are always local. He wears a kindly expression and carries a stave. He may have been a healer, or some divinised Viriatus, whose people remembered his feats of old. Many pieces are broken but take us into the first or second century AD.

The international highway linking Lisbon with Seville runs north of Évora and skirts round the Serra da Ossa. It reaches nearly 2,000 feet and the summit is rounded and bare, though its slopes enclose the luxuriance of orange-groves at the Vila do Infante. The crest at São Gens overlooks the whole border area. The hermitage of São Paulo was the home of the Order of Jesus Christ of the Poor Life, sanctioned by Pope Gregory XII (1406–17): it was later privatised. It was probably here that Camões took temporary refuge with the Coutinho family after his scrape in Lisbon. It also provided the setting for his third play *Filodemo*, set on the border with Spain and intended for the wedding of Prince John and his Spanish bride, but performed only in India by the poet and his friends. At the western end of the Serra the village of Évora-Monte has a castle dating from the reign of King Diniz: it was damaged by the earthquake of 1531 and rebuilt for John III. A plaque in the town marks the house where the 'War of the Two Brothers' was ended in May 1834, when the liberal generals received the submission of Dom Miguel's commander, who undertook that the prince should drop the legitimist claim and leave the country; Dom Miguel departed in a British warship from Sines.

The highway passes below the town of Estremós, famous for its marble. It is again in demand as banks and vestibules everywhere seek to advertise their opulence. The quarrying operations are conducted with earth-shifting apparatus and the excavations roped off in wired compounds by the roadside. The marble is found in houses and cottages of the area and was used to face the royal palace of Vila Viçosa, the chief seat of the Braganzas, which stands at the eastern end of the Serra. The title of duke was obtained by the eldest (but illegitimate) son of John I, and the family acquired many possessions in all parts of Portugal, abandoning its palace at Guimarães in favour of a place closer to the royal residence at Évora. The eighth duke, John IV, the first of the rulers of his house after the Restoration of 1640, dwelled here with his Andalusian wife Leonor de Guzmán and, until called upon to rule, devoted himself to the composition of music and to the chase. A catalogue of his vast collection of music was made in 1649, but the works themselves disappeared in the great Earthquake. Of his other activity, the chase, there remains the Tapada or Deer-park, roughly the same size as Richmond Park, but abandoned since the fall of the monarchy.

The Palace itself was designed in 1504, but later much extended. Its marble façade is nearly 150 yards long with more than 70 apertures in three storeys and an additional floor in the centre. The modern equestrian statue is of John IV. The main reception hall, the Sala dos Duques, has a painted ceiling and portraits of the royal family. The Chapel of the Chagas was the pantheon for ladies of the royal house. The formal gardens are best seen from the Palace windows. The Braganza Foundation also owns the great collection of early Portuguese books formed by King Manuel II during his long exile at Twickenham, where he resided until his death. The spacious forecourt is flanked by the eighteenth-century Agostinhos, later used as barracks. Before the building of the Palace the royal residence in the town was the castle, built for King Diniz. Its chapel, the Conceição, dating from the sixteenth century with various reconstructions, is now the main church.

Between Vila Viçosa and the highroad lies the small town of Borba, now best known for its table-wines, but also for its traditional buildings, in which marble is in general use, and for the vast convent of the Servas, one of the greatest in the Alentejo before its abandonment. Mr Sitwell thought Borba 'a little place entirely glittering in whiteness, where what is not whitewash is marble'. Estremós too was 'built of that scintillating marble made more picturesque still by the fortifications which in the diurnal moonlight created by so much whiteness seem to echo with ghostly bugle-calls'. I cannot admit to having shared this experience, but the area recalls the campaigns of the prolonged wars of Independence, which were as important for Portugal as Aljubarrota or the Lines of Torres Vedras.

The Palace at Vila Viçosa is only about twenty miles from the frontier city of Elvas, and was therefore quite vulnerable. When the Braganzas chose to settle there they were on friendly terms with Spain. It would perhaps be wrong to read too much into this: King John IV's wife Leonor de Guzmán was much more concerned that her children should be royalty than for her Andalusian birth. An earlier Duke, Dom Jaime, had also married an Andalusian, also named Leonor de Guzmán, whom he assassinated on suspicion of adultery.

Elvas was the key to the defence of Lisbon and of the Alentejo. The city stands on a steep hill and has narrow precipitous streets. It was probably a Roman stage on the road from Mérida to Lisbon. It has no Roman monument, but the neighbourhood has many vestiges of villas. The frontier is the little river Caia some seven miles away and half-way to the Spanish city of Badajoz. Political negotiations were conducted between the two cities and royal brides exchanged at the frontier. After the conquest of Ceuta in the Magrib in 1415 the revenues of Elvas were assigned to its upkeep. One of its sons, the still unidentified 'fidalgo of Elvas', wrote the account of the conquest of Florida, and another, the botanist Garcia da Orta, composed the earliest work on the herbs and drugs of India, which was printed at Goa, with Camões' first poem to appear in print. Elvas became a city in 1513, but lost the distinction in 1880. Its cathedral was designed by Francisco de Arruda in c. 1517, making use of marble from Estremós, and elaborately decorated with gilded woodwork in the eighteenth century. At the time of the Restoration its bishop was accused of conspiring against John IV, arrested and died still a prisoner. Its importance thereafter lay in its fortifications. These were developed in the wars of the seventeenth century and consist of a series of star-shaped bastions in the style attributed to Marshal Vauban. In the previous century Italian engineers had perceived that curtain-walls are vulnerable to artillery and had devised multiple salients capable of deflecting cannon-balls. The theory had engaged Leonardo da Vinci and may have been applied in the castle at Vila Viçosa. At Elvas the system of short panels with projecting bastions and ravelins is carried as far as it will go. The forts of Santa Luzia to the south and Graça a mile to the north were added later. Apart from the fortifications and the cathedral, the other monuments of Elvas are the Dominican nunnery, built in 1543 to 1557 on an octagonal plan with corresponding dome on marble pillars, and the aqueduct, bringing water from Amoreira five miles away. It is largely of the sixteenth and seventeenth centuries and has several hundred arches, at one point five storeys high and strengthened with cylindrical buttresses.

The delicacy of Elvas is its sugared greengage plums which with other preserved fruits are sold in small wooden boxes. In a dry year there is a shortfall in the plum-harvest and demand may exceed supply. This I can well understand.

The marble belt of Estremós extends to Borba and to Montes Claros, the 'white hills', where there is a marble column surmounted by a crown, erected to commemorate a crucial victory in the Wars of Independence on 18 June 1665, when Schomberg and Marialva defeated Don John of Austria, the illegitimate son of Philip IV. In 1663 Don John was able to enter Évora, but was defeated in June in the battle of Ameixial. It is on the road from Estremós to Sousel and is marked by a similar marble monument near Santa Vitória. Don John then gathered a large force and was able to sack Vila Viçosa, only to be defeated at Montes Claros.

The defences of Elvas were not again seriously tested until the rise of Napoleon. Late in 1800, the French, having reduced the sorry Charles IV of Spain and his minister

Godoy to servitude, pressed them to invade Portugal. When Charles IV declared war on 27 February 1801, the Spaniards were repelled at Elvas and Campo Maior, but overran Portalegre, Castelo de Vide and other places in the 'War of the Oranges'. Peace was made at Badajoz in June, and the Spanish conquests were returned, with the exception of Olivença. In the treaties that ended the wars, the return of Olivença was not included and it remains a piece of Portuguese *terra irredenta* in Spain. It is now a largish town a little to the south of Badajoz, and has streets named after both Vasco da Gama and the Reyes Católicos. When I asked a young man if he spoke Portuguese, he said no but a few older people did. I then asked an older man, who told me that of course he did, but there were some younger people who did not: I felt inclined to believe that both were telling the truth.

The district of Portalegre is the area south of the Tagus and taking in the frontier zone from the gorge of Rodão, where the river makes a spectacular entrance into Portugal, as far south as Elvas. It includes the Serra de São Mamede which reaches over 3,000 feet and looks down on a vast area of the Spanish meseta as well as long stretches of sparsely inhabited parkland. The city of Portalegre lies well to the east in the foothills of the Serra. It can be reached from Lisbon by either bank of the Tagus or from Estremós. The railway from Lisbon follows the right bank to Santarém and the south for a little way to Abrantes, where an international line wanders across the countryside to Ponte de Sor and Torre das Vargens. There are no large towns to stop at and the array of azulejos at the station of Torre das Vargens was probably intended to impress upon the international traveller that he was indeed in Portugal. There was perhaps little local traffic, and an autorail from Abrantes suffices to get to the upper Alentejo. The northern fork leads to Castelo de Vide and the southern eventually to Elvas, leaving Portalegre without a station until a feeder was added. Coaches and cars, not being shackled to steel rails, are free to make any combination. One may cross the river at Abrantes and follow the left bank by Gavião and Alpalhão to Castelo de Vide, or cross the Tagus at Santarém and pass through Almeirim and Alpiarça, returning to the other side at Chamusca and Golegã, and so by Constância to Abrantes.

Chamusca grows melons, wheat, beans and maize and breeds cattle. Golegã on the opposite bank has a horse and cattle fair and prizes itself for its olives, wheat and its bucolic setting. Its church of the Conceição has a Manueline door which includes the twisted columns, botanical decorations and heraldry typical of grander churches. It dates from 1510 to 1520 and reflects the work of Boytac and the Arrudas. Ponte de Sor, already in the district of Portalegre, is the centre of the cork-growing area, which provides the city with its best-known industry.

The Roman road from Mérida to Lisbon, the Lusitanian highway, ran across this area. The two streams, the Sor and the Seda, have now been dammed and serve to water a wide tract which is hospitable to the eucalyptus. One of the best-preserved Roman bridges is that across the Seda at Vila Formosa. It has six spans of trimmed granite, and is broad enough for a main route. Fragments of milestones have been found and traces of rural estates. However, the largest and most continuous group of *villae* was round Estremós and Elvas.

Avis and Alter do Chão are connected with the medieval expansion of the Military Orders. Avis is indissolubly associated with the dynasty founded by King John I and Queen Philippa. Its castle stands on high ground. Of its six towers only three remain, including the fifteenth century keep. The church is of various periods, the sacristy being of the fifteenth century, and the woodwork of the high altar of the late seventeenth. Its treasures have been dispersed. A tablet in the church of São Roque commemorates the first Master of Avis Fernão de Anes and its foundation in 1214.

Crato was the headquarters of the Hospitallers, or St John of Jerusalem, established at Leça do Balio near Oporto, until 1350. The Prior then was the father of Nun'Alvares Pereira, King John's heroic general and saintly Constable. Dom Alvaro Gonçalves Pereira has his tomb at Flor de Rosa, now a *pousada*, two miles away. The Knights, with their white cross of Malta on a black ground, formed a grand priory, which owned a dozen villages. The famous Prior of Crato was Dom António, the illegitimate son of Dom Luis, brother of John III. He escaped from Philip II and sought help in France and from Queen Elizabeth, receiving for a time the backing of the Earl of Essex. In 1589, the year after the Armada, Drake and Norris failed to put him on the throne, and he died in Paris in poverty in 1596. The castle was razed in the Spanish invasion of 1662.

Alter do Chão has a castle built for King Pedro I near the stream called the Chão. It is ruined, but there is a fine *chafariz* dated 1556 with a canopy supported on Corinthian columns. There are two eighteenth-century mansions in the town. Alter gives its name to the typical Portuguese horse, bred at a stud founded by John V in 1748, the *coudelaria real*, which supplies the cavalry and the Republican Guard. It is a stocky, round-bodied animal, reaching a metre fifty-five or sixty. However, the beast of traction in the Alentejo is the mule or donkey, and the animal of commerce is the sheep. The Aletenjo has more sheep than any other province, and is noted for its spring lamb and sheep's cheese.

The woollen industry probably accounts for the growth of the city of Portalegre. The Serra de São Mamede, the highest in the Alentejo, affords ample grazing between it and the Spanish frontier. Despite the number of vestiges of Roman settlement between Alter do Chão and Elvas, none has been discovered at Portalegre, which is scarcely noticed before the fifteenth century. It was one of the three new dioceses created in 1545, and the imposing tomb of Bishop Jorge de Melo is its most notable monument. The houses include a number of wealthy mansions of the seventeenth and eighteenth centuries, and the place is invested with the cheerful atmosphere of having resources beyond simple agriculture. The industry arises partly from the efforts of Pombal to ensure that the wool of the Serras was used to clothe the Portuguese army, which also boosted the economy of Fundão and Covilhã in the Serra da Estrêla. But Portalegre became in the nineteenth century the place where cork was turned to use, as bottles replaced barrels for the shipment of wine. One of the oldest and most thriving factories is that founded by Mr George Robinson in the only Rua Robinson in Portugal. It is highly advanced in its methods and readily accessible to visitors.

The heights of Alentejo are at Marvão and Castelo de Vide. The autorail stops at the station of Beirã. Outside, a group forms to wait for the *carreira*. It is a bus which, duly loaded, climbs up towards the awe-inspiring serra ahead, or almost overhead. It stops at the village of São António das Areias 'in the skirts of Marvão'. Somewhere near is the resort of Fadagosa where the Caldas have a Hotel das Termas, with waters to treat rheumatism and ailments of the skin. The waters at the Fonte da Pipa are described as 'extremely frigid', *frigidíssimas*. The *carreira* winds its way up to the town gate of Marvão, too narrow for it to enter, and takes its rest at a clearing by the abyss. The granite gate will take a car and the town is arranged in a loop on a ridge which widens enough to hold the castle, church, town-hall, *pousada* and a thousand inhabitants. By taking the left road one can enter the *pousada* from the kitchen. The rooms are as folksy as one could wish, and the restaurant commands tremendous views over the Spanish meseta. At night in winter, a gale may blow around the heights of Marvão, shrieking in frustrated rage, and perhaps causing a blackout. Two men play at a board in the flickering light of a candle: it is not light enough for chess, but they use chessmen to play draughts.

Marvão is virtually inexpugnable and played its part in the Peninsular War. It is said to derive from the Arabic Marwãn, a ninth-century warlord who held out against the central authority in Cordova, as did other independent spirits: he was possibly the ibn Marwãn, governor of Mérida until he was murdered in 828: his son 'Abdu'r-Rahman, called 'the Galician', rebelled on various occasions between 868 and his death in 889, holding Badajoz and the 'castle of the Serpent' (Hisn al-hanash) or Serpa. The existing castle dates in part from King Diniz and in part from more recent times. When Dickson, then major of artillery, visited it in February 1810, he found it in good order and hard to take unless by surprise; the governor, a major of engineers, had to refer to his book when asked about the number of men in service, but his wife, a lively lady, could give the information at once. His description is accurate, except that the church of Santa Maria is now an interesting small museum, and there is the *pousada*, a *pensão* and a souvenir-shop. The views are as extraordinary as in Dickson's day. The standard phrase is that from aloft you see the backs of the kites wheeling below.

Below the craggy and rock-strewn waste that prehistoric men also saw, there are trees of all kinds, for there is no lack of water. On the road to Castelo de Vide, the Sintra of the Alentejo (or one of the suitors to the title), there are *quintas* and groves of oaks, chestnuts and walnuts. The convent of the Estrela is a Franciscan house founded in 1448, and later Manuelinised, with a wayside cross and an eighteenth-century chapel. Castelo de Vide is fresh, well-watered and picturesque, standing halfway up the Serra de São Mamede and facing the peak of Senhora da Pena which is crowned by a small and glistening sanctuary. There is an old quarter around a castle attributed to King Diniz, though older, which preserves its keep and arches. The town seems scarcely altered since the sixteenth century, each house preserving a lack of symmetry under attractive pink pantiles and white-washed walls, and ogival doorways garnished with geraniums, daisies and herbs. The newer town is more obedient to the rules of geometry. The town fountain, enclosed in four columns with an Alentejan cone, has its own little precinct. Castelo de Vide was the birthplace of the great statesman and reformer Mousinho da Silveira (1780–1849) who, almost alone of his generation, perceived that the liberal revolution of 1820 was not to satisfy greed for power and wealth, but to adjust an order of society that had become unjust and inefficient: he died in Paris in relative obscurity. His birthplace is now the hospital; his residence is marked with a plaque.

North of Portalegre is Nisa, on a stream flowing from the Serra de São Mamede to the Tagus. The title of Marquis of Nisa was given to the family of Vasco da Gama. Old Nisa was destroyed in the wars of the thirteenth century, and the present castle was built by King Diniz. It has a tradition of pottery, adorning its reddish clay with themes borrowed from embroidery. From Nisa the new highway to the north crosses the Tagus into Beira at the dam of Belver, once belonging to the priors of Crato. It stands on a lofty spur, was built in about 1194 and rebuilt by the Holy Constable in 1390. This bypasses the gorges of the Tagus where it enters Portugal from Spain. The old road from Nisa led to Vila Velha de Rodão, in Beira, which has a *pelourinho*. The river pours down a deep cleft in the quartzite under the Gates of Rodão.

The capital of the Lower Alentejo is Beja. The main road south from Évora, a matter of fifty miles, goes by Portel and Vidigueira, both of which are by-passed. Portel is one of the pleasant small towns of the Alentejo, a former seat of the Braganzas: its castle was rebuilt by Francisco de Arruda in c. 1510. It enjoys extensive views over the woods and wheatfields. Vidigueira was the seat of the countship conferred on Vasco da Gama in 1519, twenty years after his great feat: he died in India in 1524, but his remains were at the Quinta do Carmo until 1898, when he was reburied in the Jerónimos at Belém.

A secondary road from Évora to Beja takes in the towns of Viana do Alentejo, Alvito and Cuba. Viana has a castle built for King Diniz and later rebuilt. Its chief monument is its church, which dates from the late fifteenth and early sixteenth centuries, with a row of flying buttresses adorned with cones and pinnacles, symbols of the Order of Christ and of King Manuel, and *azulejos* of the same period. Four miles from Viana is Agua de Peixes, one of the most typical of Alentejan noble houses with an inner courtyard and open first-floor galleries in the *mudéjar* style. It belonged to the marqueses of Ferreira and passed to the Cadaval family. Some five miles away, Alvito belonged to the treasurer of John III. It was begun in 1494, and completed by the second baron of Alvito, Diogo Lobo, who left a well-preserved banker's fortress, a rectangle with round corner-towers. The church of Alvito has a panelling of azulejos dated 1675.

Mr Sitwell, writing in 1954, thought that the South began somewhere between Évora and Beja; he did not say where, but he was looking for something like the break of the Sierra Morena that separates the Spanish meseta from Andalusia. In Portugal, there is no need for anything so dramatic. South of the Tagus the long straight roads begin. The Roman engineers found few problems. Now, the roads are lined with eucalyptus trees, without which there is little shade. The streams are dry in summer, but the water is collected in reservoirs. The fields are brown in winter, light green in spring and yellow in summer, but the white of far-off clusters of cottages is always dazzling. Storks fly straight home with the frogs they have caught to their untidy nests in church-towers or electricity-poles, or wherever human beings have provided for them. Their young stand aloft clappering, at an age when other birds would have learned to look after themselves. The parents, like the Romans, take the shortest way. The birds of prey move high aloft in circles, hoping to spot something of interest and too high to be distinguished. The horizons are wide and the air full of light like a fine summer day in Lincolnshire.

Beja itself is Latin: Pax Julia pronounced by an Arabic-speaker. Its newspaper is *Bejense* but its people are still referred to in municipal style as *pacenses*, a word that

reflects the Colonia Pacensis founded by Caesar or Augustus. Only one of its Roman
gates still stands, the Porta de Évora. Its senatorial class owned large *villae* of which the
biggest and most visible is at Pisões, Santiago Maior, four miles to the west. Another
such is São Cucufate, Vila de Frades, Vidigueira, where the original villa was replaced
in the third century AD and used as a monastery until the sixteenth century. In the
sixth century, Beja was stimulated by the Byzantine revival: its bishop Apringius, who
wrote a commentary on the Apocalypse, was probably a Greek. The last ruler of the
Suevi was confined to its monastery when overthrown by the Goths.

There is no single monument to Beja's importance in the Muslim period. It has a
Rua dos Mouros, which consists of one-storeyed attached cottages, not much different
from streets in other Alentejan towns. The Muslims and the Christians of Beja were
simply Pacenses under different names.

In Beja, the castle stands on the site of a Roman predecessor. It is chiefly of the age
of King Diniz, and rises to 120 feet, with a spiral staircase. Beja was reconquered in 1162,
after having changed owners several times. It owes its revival to King Afonso V, who created the dukedom for his younger brother Dom Fernando, after whom it passed to King
Manuel and thereafter to the eldest son of the king, who until the nineteenth century
was duke of Beja. The palace, now destroyed, stood next to the convent of Conceição,
or Clares, founded in 1459, the wealthiest in the Alentejo. The nuns acquired the palace
in 1703. What survives is the body of the church and the cloisters with sixteenth-century
azulejos comparable with those at Sintra. The convent was the setting of the *Lettres
portugaises* attributed to the nun Sor Mariana and published by, or for, one Chamilly at
Paris in 1669. The letters may be authentic or pastiches: whether they make any contribution to French literature is for the French to decide. The book had some fifty reprint-
ings and was eventually in 1819 translated into Portuguese with seven authentically
apocryphal letters. It was the custom for women to be entrusted to nunneries, and a
Mariana Alcoforado existed and died at the convent in 1723.

The church of Santo Amaro has Romanesque or Byzantine origins and was a parish
church until the seventeenth century. The hermitage of Santo André resembles São
Brás in Évora, a rectangular basilica with six cylindrical lateral buttresses capped with
cones and merlons. Although Beja has in the past demolished many memorials of its
history, the regional museum initiated by Bishop Cenáculo, later Archbishop of
Évora, has brought together a varied collection of paintings and objects of all periods.

A more circuitous and interesting route from Évora to Beja goes through the part
of Portugal lying to the east of the Guadiana. From Reguengos it leads through
Mourão to Moura and Serpa, or from Portel to Moura. Mourão has a castle rebuilt in
the fourteenth and sixteenth centuries, and roads still awaiting attention. The route
by Portel is better, though subject to diversion until the international question of possession of the waters of the Guadiana is resolved. Moura is a large bright white town
reconquered with Serpa in 1166 but for a time an independent bailiwick under the
unruly sway of the 'Infante of Serpa', younger brother of King Sancho II. Its crumbling castle stands like a crotchety but dignified old lady between the antique and the
medieval. The Câmara has an arcade and a wall on which the elders of the place watch
the bus arrive; it boasts an inscription making it the *civitas* of the Aruccitani. Outside
is a small spa with a public garden under the shadow of the keep and a balustrade
with views across the valley and a bandstand. The road down to the river, the Rua da
Olaria or Pottery Row, runs between ancient one-storeyed cottages each with its

chimney built flush with the street, and an enclosed well, the 'Moorish Well'. An elderly lady goes down to the river to fill a plastic bag with tiny white-shelled snails, to me an untried gastronomic pleasure. She says the snails are scarce because it has not rained. In the square, the church of St John has a Manueline door and a tower with its cone or *corucheu* with merlons. The road down the hill leads to the Convent of the Carmo, the first of the Order in Portugal, now used as a hospital. It was several times extended, and has a tomb (which I failed to find) declaring: 'Here lies João de Abril, who died of laughing'. The upper part of the town is modern, with a fine municipal garden, and a Grand Hotel, which is a delight. Its breakfast-room has a ceiling adorned with green plaster relief. The patio is apt to be filled with international geologists from everywhere who learn their science in English from a Dutch school in Delft. When I doubted if the geology of Moura had anything special to offer, I was told: 'That is what they find out.'

Between Moura and Serpa, according to the song, 'There goes Serpa, there goes Moura, with Pias in between': Pias is a village amidst the fields of wheat. On the road there is little but wheat and olives, with the occasional car or delivery van. Serpa has not changed a letter of its name since Roman times. It stands on a hill and preserves its keep and two of its five gates, that on the Beja road a narrow exit between two full-bottomed round towers, with a long stretch of battlemented wall of reddish brown rough-cast. A flight of stairs leads up to the ruined keep which has the best views, and the white parish church of Santa Maria, which has round buttresses with conical caps redolent of the days of King Manuel, and adorned inside with his symbols and with later *azulejos*. The largest house is the sixteenth-century home of the Count of Ficalho, who wrote stories about life in Serpa in the late nineteenth century and continued the botanical tradition of the Abade Correa da Serra, Portugal's first minister to the United States. The new part of the town combines the straightness and whiteness of the old, with its russet pantiles. The *pousada*, outside the town, has wide views and a spacious swimming-pool, much visited by swallows and swifts, as well as other passing tourists.

The road from Serpa to Beja is uneventful. The river Guadiana follows the Iberian practice of dwindling in the summer. It was never navigable, owing to the waterfall at the Pulo do Lobo, the Wolf's Leap, a semi-circular gorge with a drop of three hundred feet. In ancient times the highest port up the river was Mértola, once Myrtilis, whose Greek name may reveal its origins. It was used by the Romans and Byzantines, and has the most complete mosque to have survived. It stands on a platform overlooking the city, which clustered about wharves on the river-front. When the Order of Christ took over the defence, it preferred to build its castle nearer the estuary at Castro Marim. The church or mosque is now the best point from which to see the town. The castle, rebuilt by the Templars, has recently been excavated, and there is more to be revealed, though the narrowness of the space between it and the river suffices to explain why most of the ancient buildings have disappeared. Archaeologists have divided it into zones, Roman, 'Visigothic' (probably Byzantine), and Islamic, but for practical purposes they overlap.

Until recently, Mértola served to convey passengers by river down the Guadiana or to ferry them over to the tapering piece of Portugal beyond the river. The mines of São Domingos produced copper for a century until 1965, when they were exhausted, and the population has dwindled away.

17

Algarve

Algarve is Portugal's 'other kingdom' which is in many ways different from the rest of the country. Its name recalls that it was once the Far West, as seen from Egypt or Syria. In late Muslim times, its capital was Silves, but it was only a kingdom dependent on the Abbadid rulers of Seville. In 1471, Afonso V 'the African' assumed the title of 'King of Portugal and of the two Algarves, on this side and on that', thus stressing its ancient connection with Morocco, the Magrib. His son, the great John II, came to take the waters of Monchique, where he died in 1495. His chronicler noted that he died 'at a small place outside of Portugal'. Under the Philips, its governor was referred to as a viceroy, but the designation has now no political implication. Since the tourist boom which began in about 1960, Faro has become the second busiest airport in Portugal, and it is possible to visit the Algarve without seeing the rest of the country, regrettable though this may be. It is marked off from the neighbouring Alentejo by a line of hills, which rise to nearly 3,000 feet in the Serra de Monchique and only half as high in the Malhão further east. They form a sort of amphitheatre, containing the undulating coastal plain which stretches for a hundred miles behind a succession of sandy beaches that catch the sun. It is in sharp contrast with the long levels of the adjoining Alentejo, which is bare grazing country with a relatively small population. The Algarve is only a fifth of the size of the Alentejo, but carries a higher population than either part of its neighbour.

The territory is too narrow to have any great river or estuary to attract a large population. As in the north, the coast is more populous than the interior, and has a string of small ports administered from Faro, which before the tourist boom had a population of only 13,000 and was chiefly engaged in the export of fish or fruit from its fertile hinterland. The Algarve is an orchard of almonds, which blossom in January, oranges, lemons and figs, as well as apples, pears, cherries and other fruit, and a market-garden for tomatoes, onions, cauliflowers, melons, aubergines, pimentos and so forth. If the Alentejo is Roman in its expanse of wheat and olives, the Algarve is Near Eastern in its profusion of fruits and greenstuff.

The profusion of vegetation is sufficient to set the Algarve apart. Its people are often thought to be cheerful and garrulous. A nineteenth-century writer from the north thought them rather surly and inhospitable. Such judgements are perhaps of little value. They are now as polite and attentive as other Portuguese, and if not quite bilingual, accustomed to the eccentricities and whims of foreigners. Most of them are the descendants of those who have always lived there. At the time of the Christian

Reconquest in the thirteenth century, many left, and the rest were ruled by the
Military Orders, a small alien minority. It was only later that there was a strong
influx of peoples from the north, mainly the over-populated Minho, who were drawn
mostly to the townships of the coast. Until the nineteenth century, the Algarve was
relatively isolated except by sea. The road across the Alentejo was long and at times
dangerous. It was followed by the railway, which reached Faro in the 1880s.
Passenger trains have become infrequent, and the great bulk of transport is by road.
The main highway starts from the great bridge across the Tagus. Since 1998 it has
been supplemented by that from the Vasco da Gama bridge on the east side of
Lisbon. The roads meet and skirt the towns of Setúbal and Alcácer do Sal. The drive
across this part of the Alentejo is not the most interesting in Portugal. There are alter-
nating stretches of single and dual carriage-way, as well as sections of ribbon development that have grown up round service-stations and way-side restaurants and
cafés. The coaches of the main company cross the hills and pull up at the Vale do
Paraiso, where the passengers are divided, one coach taking in Faro and the eastern
points and the other the resorts to the west. There is a different direct service to and
from Silves.

For those arriving by car, the direct N2 road reaches São Bras de Alportel, where
there is one of the first of the *pousadas*, a country-house only a short way north of Faro
with splendid views over the coastal countryside. The coastal road across the Algarve
passes through the main towns and is liable to be overcrowded in summer. This is
averted by the IP (*Itinerário Principal*), a dual carriage-way running from the level of
Albufeira to the Guadiana and the Spanish frontier at Vila Real de Santo António,
connected to each of the towns by feeders. West of Portimão there is only the coast
road, which is liable to congestion. Other entries are by the coast road from Sines or
by the Guadiana river from Mértola. This is little frequented and less well surfaced: it
is far from the world of large hotels, apartment-blocks and bathing-beaches
with which the word Algarve is now associated. It has no special monuments, though
the villages on the Guadiana facing Spain are very attractive. It is of interest to bird-
watchers: the Great Bustard, long extinct in Britain, is found on a stretch of grassy
scrub between the Alentejo and the Algarve. I first passed this way before the tourist
boom occurred, and it had not much changed when I followed it two years ago. Hence
these nostalgic lines.

> Southward from Mértola the road unwinds
> its wandering thread amid the hills in bloom.
> The fading sun with heavy fingers binds
> in scented garlands rosemary and broom,
> and as the way unfolds a sorrowing bird
> brings back her laughter on that far-off day,
> a distant memory like hope deferred
> of when we first came by this chartless way.
> We left no record on the place we passed,
> held to the twisted skein that was our doom.
> That day has vanished, as all others must.
> But now the scent of rosemary and broom
> embalms a reminiscence of that past,
> a bitter-sweet recall of timeless dust.

The western entry to the Algarve by the coastal road is also relatively unfre-
quented, though there are beaches at Odeceixe on the border with the Alentejo,
Aljezur and Carrapeteira. Here the road runs between the sea and the Espinhaço do
Cão, the Dog's Back, which runs in line with the Serra de Monchique, and is also rich
in wild flowers and bird-life.

The Algarve is not rich in historical monuments. Its architectural heritage lies
rather in a tradition of craftsmanship than in palaces and castles. The Romans are best
represented at the ruins of Milreu, at Estoi, not far from Faro. The one great monument of the Islamic years is the fortified city of Silves. Both it and the Christian cathedral are of the local red sandstone, in complete contrast with the granite prevalent in
the cathedrals, walls and cottages of the north. There are some castles of stone in the
Algarve, the most complex being at Castro Marim, the headquarters of the Templars
after the conquest. The castle at Alvor, where John II was first buried, was once an
important stronghold. Another was at Tavira, where the former Muslim castle was
taken over by the Templars. Its mosque was replaced by the church of Santa Maria, in
which Paio Peres Correia, the Master of the Templars, is buried. Its fortifications were
extended in the sixteenth century, and have now been meticulously repaired.

But the place that most recaptures the past is the wonderful natural setting of the
twin promontories of Sagres and St Vincent that mark the western limit of Europe as
known to the ancients. St Vincent, with its towering cliffs and low vegetation cowering
from the Atlantic winds, owes its name to the saint of Saragossa whose remains were
carried by sea to Lisbon in a little ship, attended, according to legend, by two ravens
who sat fore and aft. In medieval times the monks looked after passing seamen with
hospitality open to all. The ships continued to pass, more freely than before, after 1250
when Mediterranean shipping was able to reach the Atlantic Ocean. In 1797 Jervis,
with the aid of Horatio Nelson, defeated the French off the Cape and became Earl
St Vincent. In the nineteenth century, the great age of steam navigation, a large part of
the world's shipping passed by. But now the seas are, if not empty, much less used.
There is a hotel at Belixe, and the cliffs are inhabited by ravens and choughs and the
rocks below by fish-eating shags; some of the ground-loving plants are unique.

Its companion Sagres, the Sacred Promontory of the ancients, is rather lower and
not quite so grand, though it is the best place to admire St Vincent. It is closely associated with the memory of Prince Henry, whose dedication made modern seafaring,
if not possible, at least necessary. The fort at the end of the long treeless promontory
is dedicated to his memory. An enormous wind-rose of stone is said to date from his
time. Along the road there are hotels and restaurants. It is a place for fishing and boating rather than for the beach, but has a timeless quality of its own quite different from
the relaxation restless people seek. There is now no trace of the Prince's estate, the
Vila do Infante, except the remains of his modest chapel. The road to the Algarve
passes Rapouseira, where he is supposed to have dwelt, and abandons the austerity of
the Cape as it comes to more sheltered settings on the great bay of Lagos where
Hannibal wintered part of his army, probably because plenty of fish was available.

In the fifteenth century Lagos was the port from which the Prince and his successors conducted the voyages of exploration down the African coast. From Lagos Gil
Eanes was the first to round Cape Bojador and open up the sea-way to West Africa in
1434. However, the centre of ship-building was already Lisbon, where King Diniz had
his navy: the house of Avis favoured its guilds and by the end of the century both

shipbuilding and commerce were firmly anchored in the capital. By 1449, the ship-wrights of the Algarve were at the 'new town' of Portimão on the eastern side of the great bay. It is sometimes said that King Sebastian sailed from Lagos in 1578 on the fatal expedition to North Africa in which he perished and many of his nobles were captured. Sebastian had an obsession to lead a crusade in North Africa. In 1573 he arrived at Lagos but desisted on hearing of the death of his Spanish mother. In the fol-lowing year he returned and sent boyish letters to his nobles to meet him at Tavira: he crossed the Straits, but returned, partly for lack of horses. He then spent some days in the monastery at St Vincent. When he returned in 1578 he gathered his army at Lisbon and put in for only a night at Lagos before crossing from Cadiz to Tangier: the disastrous Battle of the Three Kings was at al-Qaṣr al-kabir on 4 August 1578. After that, the Algarve did not play a conspicuous part in Portuguese history. At the Restoration of 1640 Ceuta remained with Spain, and the function of supplying the African outposts was no longer needed. The ports of the Algarve devoted themselves to the export of fruit and fish, and the import of a variety of goods. There were few foreigners: only one or two English merchants were resident. Things did not change much until Pombal set up the town of Vila Real de Santo António at the mouth of the Guadiana to form a new fishing-port.

Lagos now combines fishing with pleasure craft. It has an attractive and well-gardened water-front with palms and orange-trees, hotels and restaurants. Portimão remained a fishery and took up the preservation of fish and canning. It was promoted to the status of a city in 1924 and has become a large town with its own crafts and delicacies. The whole bay of Lagos is remarkable for its rock formations, single pillars, clusters, arches and caverns. A couple of miles from Portimão is the Praia da Rocha, one of the most spacious and best-known of the beaches of the Algarve; it is now overshadowed by hotels and apartment-blocks, is crowded with cars and has a wealth of keepsakes and souvenirs.

There are only two small streams that find their way to the great bay. One is the Alvor, which gives its name to the castle and a pretty fishing-village with a church dec-orated in Manueline style. The place is said to have been heavily damaged by the Earthquake of 1755 and is now a quiet resort. Ten miles inland, in the Serra, is the spa of Monchique. The Caldas, or hot springs, are famous for their medicinal waters. Though they did not cure King John II, they remained popular, and the spa, with the faded grandeur of such places, has a park, the Mata, with a variety of exotic trees: there are walks to the two heights of the Serra, the Picota and Foia. Like Castelo de Vide and other places, it is compared with Sintra, but unlike Sintra it can boast that in February the almond and mimosa are in blossom. At the height of 2,700 feet, the climate and the vegetation change, and the views extend to cover almost the whole of the Algarve, rimmed always by the ocean. The large village of Monchique is some distance beyond the Caldas and stands between the Picota and Foia at about 1,400 feet. It has a church with a Manueline door and a ruined Franciscan monastery. In King John's day it produced earthenware for much of the Algarve, and still has its own crafts and *estalagem* (small hotel).

The other river which reaches the sea near Portimão is the Arade. In the middle ages it was navigable as far as Silves. The entry to the river at Ferragudo was once guarded by a castle, but is now a picturesque harbour for small fishing-boats. Silves itself is out of sight of the sea, some ten miles inland, set in the most fruitful part of the Algarve. It was almost depopulated in 1577 when Faro became the capital of the province. It had no hotel until the Colina dos Mouros was opened in 1999 on a hill facing its rose-red walls which rise above groves of oranges and almonds and market-gardens. There are *pensões* in the town and several restaurants, one of which supplies roast beef, Yorkshire pudding and apple-pie to satisfy the nostalgia of English visitors: another, by the river-side, does Welsh mutton. Just over the 'Roman bridge' (which in fact is medieval) is the Roman Restaurant, much frequented by wedding parties and tourists alike: its owner has an eye for 'collectables' and has let himself go with an array of antique sewing-machines. He has a few commodious rooms.

Apart from these curiosities, the great monument of Silves is the walls and the entrance gate, all of the local red sandstone. The place was sacked by crusaders in 1189, and the fortifications were perhaps strengthened after that. The Palace of the Varandas, the Sharajib, which the poet king al-Mu'tamid recalled with such *saudade* a century earlier, is no longer there. There is no mention of the festivities and luxury described by the poets. When King Sancho I took Silves in 1189 (a feat which has earned him a modern statue), the main mosque was demolished to make way for the cathedral. The present building, of the fourteenth century, is in the same red stone, perhaps a simplified but still large version of Alcobaça. It was begun with some pre-tensions, but either not completed or not improved by later generations owing to the decline of the city. A modern museum in the town houses the remaining vestiges of Islamic Silves. A plaque marks the birthplace of J G Domingues, whose modest work laid the foundation for studies of Muslim Portugal.

The villages round Silves include Estômbar, the birthplace of the famous Sousa Reis, the Remexido, the legitimist partisan who took to the hills and kept the old cause alive in the Algarve and Alentejo after the defeat of Dom Miguel; he was captured and shot as a bandit at Messines in 1838. Four years later, the distant Minho erupted against the tyranny of the liberals imposed on it by politicians and foreigners. The Algarve did not respond. Perhaps its people were less devout, but it seems more probable that they had no big city to rebel against. Faro was not Oporto or Lisbon. The village of Alcantarilha, a cluster of white houses adorned with flowers and set on a slope amidst orchards, is now considered a model of the Algarvian garden city. The landscape is still dominated by the fruits and foliage of Muslim times. Water is distributed by the water-wheel, here known as the *cegonha* or stork. But the lyricism of the Arabic language disappeared between the time of al-Mu'tamid and the senti-mental romantic, João de Deus, who was born at Messines in 1830. Lagôa has nothing special to single out: it is a market town with shops and restaurants, but only a stop for birds of passage.

Between Portimão and Faro there is a string of fishing-villages converted into resorts of various kinds: in most of them the tourists share the beach with brightly-painted boats and retired fishermen mending their nets at leisure. The boats are drawn up above tide-level. The chief quarry in these seas was the tunny, which passes in its annual migration between the Mediterranean and the Atlantic. It is a relation to the 'tuna-fish' of the Pacific, in my opinion the nearest thing to edible wood. Suitably conserved, it pleased the Phoenicians and the Romans. It is a large and courageous crea-ture, and catching it has been compared to a Spanish bull-fight. The hunters in their boats encircle their victim and harpoon him. When he ceases to dive and lash the water, they haul him aboard. The skilled manipulator of the harpoon requires as much strength as a picador and matador combined. Not surprisingly, the old fishermen enjoy mending the nets and idling by the shore: unlike bull-fighters, they do not bask in the adulation of *aficionados* or retire in opulence.

The chief beaches are Carvoeiro, Armação da Pera, Albufeira, Vilamoura and Quarteira. Carvoeiro is a place for seaside villas and cottages: its former taverns have become restaurants. Armação was once a shipyard, as the name implies, and is now a resort with rocky cliffs and caves, a large hotel on the cliffs and apartment blocks. Further east is Albufeira which is delightfully placed and preserves its Algarvio atmosphere with white walls, straight chimneys, narrow alleys and a tunnel leading down to the beach. It is highly anglicised and satisfies the needs of sufferers from anglo-nostalgia. Quarteira is now dwarfed by the development of Vilamoura, with hotels, apartment blocks and an airstrip as well as several golf-courses, horse riding, tennis, fishing, shooting and what have you. There is plenty of room for yachts and powerboats. It is a far cry from the sugar-canes of the *Quinta* of Quarteira, which John I gave to a Genoese merchant in 1404, when sugar was prized as an exotic spice.

Inland is Loulé, 'up-hill' in Arabic, a market-town set among groves of fruit-trees. Its church dates from the time of King Denis and once belonged to the Franciscans. The town was much modernised in the early twentieth century, and has an active market and industry in local copper-ware. It still has *chaminés*, the decorated chimney-pots standing on straight smoke-stacks typical of the Algarve, and a Misericórdia with a Renaissance doorway. Outside the town, the village of Cadouço has a hermitage of c. 1500, and a small and ancient bridge over a rivulet, which in summer is only a bed of stones. North of Loulé is the central weald of the Algarve and the Serra do Caldeiro, an eastward extension of Monchique running as far as the river Guadiana. It reaches 1,700 feet at the northern point of Mu. Alte, on a steep slope above the stream of the same name, is a pretty village with an old church, a cascade and restaurant.

The long line of sandy beaches and rocks is interrupted at Faro, the centre and capital of the Algarve. It was the pre-Roman Ossonoba which produced its own coins showing a sailing-ship and a pair of tunnies. It went by this name in the tenth century, but by the twelfth had become Santa Maria. Faro is supposed to derive from Harun, but might equally denote a *pharos* or lighthouse. It is still grouped around a dock, but is some way from the open sea, being approached by a channel through salt-marshes and sand-banks which extend off the shore for some forty miles. The islets are covered with sea-sedge, which is harvested to fertilise the fields. They open into a broad lagoon rich in shellfish and clams. The town replaced Silves as the capital in 1577, when it became the seat of the bishop. It was sacked by the Earl of Essex in the Cadiz expedition. The bishop was the learned Jerónimo Osório who had composed a tract urging Queen Elizabeth to mend the error of her ways. His books were carried off and some rest in the Bodleian at Oxford. It was not for this feat that Essex was executed; he gained an unmerited reputation as a commander which went to his head and lost both in his rebellion of 1600.

Faro was only gradually restored. It owes much to Bishop Avelar, who saw to its improvement by building the Misericórdia, the Seminary, the city Arch and other buildings: he died in 1816 and is commemorated by a public garden near the dock, a statue, street and the meteorological station. His Arco da Vila was designed by an Italian and is a classical structure in marble intended to give the place self-respect. The cathedral is of no special note apart from its tower and entrance, but the seminary is an attractive eighteenth-century building graced with orange-trees. On the opposite side of the dock, part of the harbour-master's quarters is a Maritime Museum with models of caravels, *naus* and other ships and exhibits of the history of fishing. The town itself was compact, but its airport and administrative functions have brought it hotels and restaurants. There are numerous Algarvian fish-dishes and sweets made with figs. There are two brandies, one of figs and the other distilled from the fruit of the *madronho*, or arbutus.

A little to the north of Faro is the village of Estoi and in a by-road the Roman remains of Milreu, once the headquarters of a governor or magnate who could survey from it his domains from the sea to the inland hills. The site is well-known, but pleasantly informal. Most of the ancient *villa* is reduced to ground-level, though part of the mosaic showing a maritime theme survives. It underwent several modifications, but the walls of a Christian basilica remain: it probably dates from the Byzantine revival of the sixth century. The village of Estoi itself has the mansion, gardens and collection of the Count of Carvalhal and later Viscount of Estoi, which has passed to the municipality of Faro as a museum. The taste was varied, and the house is not always open, but the gardens are attractive.

The towns to the east of Faro are Olhão, Tavira and Vila Real de Santo António. To the northeast the streams flow eastwards into the Guadiana, in part through woods and in part grassland. The climate more resembles that of the Alentejo, with hot dry summers and cold winters. There are small fields of wheat, and the fig and carob grow, but the villages are small and isolated. As in other parts of Portugal, most of the population is concentrated near the sea. Olhão, like Faro, stands back from the open sea and uses the same channel through the salt-marshes. In appearance it is the most North-African looking place in Portugal with its white-washed, box-like houses. Tradition says that it was founded by independent-minded fishermen who settled there to enjoy their autonomy and that Gil Eanes, the first of the navigators to sail beyond Cape Bojador in 1434, was born at Olhão. The people of Olhão did not lose their adventurous spirit: when Napoleon and the French were expelled from Portugal, a small shipmaster and his crew set out from Olhão for Rio de Janeiro to be the first to inform the Prince-Regent without any of the resources now available to single navigators. The Prince rewarded them by granting Olhão the title 'Olhão of the Restoration': the epithet has been forgotten, but the feat has not. Olhão is still a fishing-centre, where the catch is auctioned: the flavour lingers in the air. It has several restaurants in the town and on the foreshore. The white boxes have given Olhão the fame of a cubist city. Formerly the women wore the *bioco*, a long cowled cape, suggestive of the Islamic past; its disappearance was due less to the fulminations of the clergy than to the circulation of fashion-magazines.

Beyond Olhão, the marshes turn into a long string of sandy islets that follow the coast as far as Tavira and beyond. They widen to embrace a broad lagoon rich in shellfish, and are themselves the home of water-fowl, some of exceptional rarity such as the purple gallinule and avocet. The danger of pollution is great since the rapid growth of human population, and the whole area of marsh and sand-spits is protected as the Nature Park of Ria Formosa. The area round Castro Marim further east forms the Nature Reserve of Sapal. There are several specific places for the protection of birds, and the Ria Formosa has an office at Quelfes between Faro and Olhão. Some of the off-shore islands are inhabited and can be reached by ferry from Olhão or Tavira. An old fishing-village with access to the islets is Fuzeta, known for its mussels. Fishermen are rarely town-planners, and their clusters of cabins are gradually replaced by houses, to which those who have emigrated, the *americanos*, either add their own contribution or initiate new place-names. The next place of consequence is Tavira. It has an inscription suggesting that it, or Senhora da Luz near by, was the Roman Balsa. Its bay served very well as an anchorage for ancient shipping and was used to supply the Portuguese outposts in North Africa. But it was too shallow for large ships. Arab writers mention it as a dependency of Faro or of Silves, and it still has a street called the Mouraria. Its mosque was replaced by the church of Santa Maria adjoining the castle, in which the Master of the Templars and his companions are buried. It became Christian in 1242, but kept its community of 'free Moors' who retained the same privileges as those in Lisbon. The Misericórdia dates from 1541 and its doorway is considered the finest in the Algarve. The town suffered from several earthquakes in the middle ages and from the great catastrophe of 1755. Pombal attempted to revive its fortunes with a tapestry-factory, which did not last. However, the water-front is lined by handsome white mansions. Its broad bay is the estuary of a small river, the Gilão or Asseca, and is crossed by an ancient bridge.

The nature-reserve and the sand-spits continue to Cacela and the beach of Manta Rota. Cacela stands between the sea and the main road, and was populated in Roman times. The light-house stands on the site of an eighteenth-century fort, and it was here that Charles Napier landed Terceira and Palmela with the liberal army in June 1833 in the War of the Two Brothers. The last of the resorts of the Algarve is Monte Gordo where the pinewoods come down to the shore. It was already a summer resort favoured by Portuguese families before the development of the beaches further west began. It is only a short way from Vila Real de Santo António, the last town in Portugal, with a ferry across the Guadiana to Ayamonte in Spain. It was laid out for Pombal as a fishing-capital for the Algarve. It is built on straight lines with a large square paved with black and white stones that radiate from the centre, like the streets of Lisbon. Its centre is an obelisk dedicated to the Marquis, and it has acquired some of the industry he desired to establish. It was something of a feat to have created a new town on reclaimed land in the space of five months. As a specimen of town-planning Vila Real stands comparison with the Baixa of Lisbon, yet the orderly style that fits a great city seems out of place, to the tourist at least, in the relaxed and undragooned atmosphere of the Algarve.

Afterword

The first reader of this script remarked that I might have said more about contemporary Portugal. The thought had occurred to me, but it was not my intention to be involved in the complexities of today's world scene, of which future historians will take care. Nor can I pretend to be an expert on the night-life of cities, of which any hotel porter knows more than I. The entry of Portugal into the Euro-zone has been smoothly done, but its economic consequences can hardly be measured. It is no more difficult to travel in Portugal than in any other part of Europe, and less expensive, safer and pleasanter than most. The face of Lisbon is changing, but less offensively than that of London: its traffic jams may be noisier but they last less. There has been no wholesale abandonment of the countryside, and the flooding of water-courses for hydroelectric and agricultural ends makes an agreeable addition to a varied landscape.

Contemporary Portugal is not a great power and no longer the seat of a far-flung empire. Lisbon and especially the Algarve are more cosmopolitan. Those returning from Goa have been fully absorbed, but there are no whole sectors of activity in Indian hands, as has happened in London. The restaurants remain predominantly European, though Chinese are sufficiently represented. Even in the national game of *futebol*, Portugal prevails. Lisbon has more Africans than before. They come to study and work. It is the centre of the Portuguese communities of autonomous Africa, to which Portugal can offer a salutary friendship and an alternative to petty tyrants and predatory capitalism.

The Portuguese past is built into the present. The splendid new bridge across the Tagus to link Lisbon with the Alentejo and the Algarve was built to commemorate Vasco da Gama's opening of the sea-way to India in 1498, the climax of the epic Discoveries, with Pedro Álvares Cabral's discovery of Brazil in 1500. As well as the handsome modern station of Oriente, the event has produced the new oceanic aquarium, said to be the finest in the world, which replaces the more modest affair at Dafundo, the fruit of King Carlos's oceanic excursions. The pioneer of the Portuguese voyages of discovery, Prince Henry, was commemorated by the imposing collective monument at Belém, erected at the quincentenary of his death in 1940. At Oporto, his birth-place, the whole water-front has been marked for conservation because of its European, and perhaps especially English, significance. Meanwhile, the subsoil of the city has been explored to make channels for the long overdue underground system. Sagres in the Algarve, his residence, is also marked for permanent conservation. He has at last been given a statue facing the Portuguese embassy in London. His mother, Queen Philippa, daughter of 'time-honour'd Lancaster', is commemorated in Oporto and Madeira, but patiently awaits recognition in the land of her birth. The other royal symbol of the Portuguese Alliance, Queen Catherine of Braganza, was in 2002 recognised by the unveiling of a bust outside her Lisbon home, the former palace of Bemposta: it is by an English artist. Ambitious plans to honour her in the New York borough of Queen's, named after her, remain in gestation.

Portugal's place in Europe must necessarily be beside her only land neighbour, Spain, and the frontier is now everywhere open, thanks to the simultaneous entry of both into the European Union. The way is open for a more balanced and fruitful era of collaboration instead of the ancient legacy of mistrust and indifference. If only because of the exposed nature of the Portuguese economy, there is room for equilibrium and mediation, and the European Union does not abrogate the Ancient Alliance. The use of the Portuguese language has become an essential key to Portugal's place in the world. The name of Camões who bestowed on it its permanent form is properly venerated. Present-day Portuguese is still closer to him than our English is to that of Shakespeare, forty years his junior, although it is now tinged with Brazilian usage in the press and television. The headlines of newspapers may be more direct, but journalists are expected to write in good and acceptable style. The spoken language is endowed with as rich a variety of sounds as English, though local and dialectical differences are small. If there is no parallel in Brazil to the strong United States interest in the British past, there are perhaps compensations. Although Castilian Spanish is widely understood, it is seldom spoken and best avoided. Educated Portuguese used to speak first French and then English. Now the order is reversed. My friend's great-grandson of nine, at his bilingual school, is fluent in English and knows French; he is taught some Chinese and can show on the globe the places in Europe he has visited and those in Mozambique his mother remembers.

In the nineteenth century, the primacy of the written language passed from the narrative in verse to prose and the novel. Camilo Castelo Branco, who died in 1890, exploited the tormented history of his youthful days, when the newspaper ruled and the public for national fiction was limited. But the great Eça de Queirós, who survived him by a decade, was a much more international figure. Portugal has an active publishing industry, which promotes translations from many languages. Perhaps because of this, its own writers face something of a conflict of taste between those so inoculated and those with traditional and local preferences. José Saramago has been awarded a Nobel Prize for literature. Born in a village on the Tagus and resident in the Spanish Canaries, he has an abundant imagination. Portuguese painters and composers face similar problems. The ministrations of the Gulbenkian Foundation have done much to break down Portuguese isolation by providing facilities unknown since the palmy days of King John V. Others are trained and make their mark abroad. Soloists seek an international reputation outside Portugal: such are Artur Pizarro, trained in North America and resident in London, and Maria João Pires, who travels from Portugal to find her audiences. The artist Helena Vieira became well known by making her home in Paris, and Paula Rego has won esteem in London. Many others await discovery in Portugal. There has always been a preference for local artisanship over the articles made for the mass market. Many Portuguese villagers believe that their wine is the best in Portugal. Perhaps it is, when you are on the spot. It is seldom made in such quantities as to satisfy the demands of mass markets, though concessions must be made in the interest of the balance of trade. The array of pottery and other mementoes displayed everywhere for the visitor is perhaps fair proof of the fidelity of the Portuguese, and is a gentle protest against the encroachment of heart-less standardization.

CAMÕES

The poet whose great mind I most admire
proclaims his passion in eternal verse,
fed by a fancied potion of desire
sucked from the bosom of a savage nurse.
The eyes that lit his fire are long since dulled.
Those parted lips are far departed too.
The oaths they once exchanged Time has annulled:
only his Rimes kindle their power anew.
He did not see the land of Santa Cruz,
but in the foreword to its history, still brief,
promised new *Lusiads*, awaited still.
He gave the words and measures that we use
that shape our lives and loves and our belief
with songs that haunt the speech of our Brazil.

Index